刘月华，毕业于北京大学中文系。原为北京语言学院教授，1989年赴美，先后在卫斯理学院、麻省理工学院、哈佛大学教授中文。主要从事现代汉语语法，特别是对外汉语教学语法研究。主要著作有《实用现代汉语语法》《趋向补语通释》《汉语语法论集》等，对外汉语教材有《中文听说读写》《走进中国百姓生活》等。

刘月华

魏久安，美国加州大学伯克利分校语言学博士，曾在康奈尔大学（1987—1997年）和麻省理工学院（1997—2006年）主持中文教学项目，近来在新加坡和中国（香港）两地走访教学。其著作包括《汉语基础教材》（两册）（耶鲁大学出版社出版）、《汉语动词和语法要点》（麦格劳·希尔公司出版），以及与他人合著的数本教科书。

魏久安

刘宪民，1994年毕业于美国明尼苏达大学，获汉语语言学博士学位。毕业后一直从事汉语教学，曾任教于美国俄勒冈大学、俄亥俄大学、哈佛大学等。自1999年起，转聘至美国范德堡大学，主持其汉语教学项目至今。研究方向：汉语句法、语用学及汉语教学语法。发表过多篇学术论文，参与了刘月华教授所主编的《走进中国百姓生活》《中国百姓身边的故事》课本的编写工作。

刘宪民

Yuehua Liu

Yuehua Liu, a graduate of Department of Chinese Language and Literature of Peking University. Yuehua Liu was Professor in Chinese at Beijing Language and Culture University. In 1989, she continued her professional career in the United States and had taught Chinese at Wellesley College, Massachusetts Institute of Technology and Harvard University for many years. Her research concentrated on modern Chinese grammar, especially grammar for teaching Chinese as a foreign language. Her major publications include *A Practical Grammar of Modern Chinese*, *A Complete Explanation of Directional Complements*, and *Writings on Chinese Grammar* as well as the Chinese textbook series *Integrated Chinese* and *Reality Chinese*.

Julian K. Wheatley

Julian Wheatley obtained a Ph.D. in Linguistics from the University of California at Berkeley. He has managed Chinese language programs at Cornell University (1987-1997) and at Massachusetts Institute of Technology (1997-2006). More recently, he has held visiting teaching positions in Singapore and China (Hong Kong). Relevant publications include the two-volume textbook, *Learning Chinese* (Yale University Press), and *Chinese Verbs and Essentials of Grammar* (McGraw Hill) as well as several co-authored textbooks.

Xianmin Liu

Xianmin Liu, graduated from the University of Minnesota in 1994 with a doctorate degree in Chinese linguistics. She has been in the field of Chinese instruction since graduation, teaching at universities that included University of Oregon, Ohio University and Harvard University. Since 1999, she has been teaching at Vanderbilt University, and in charge of the Chinese language program. Her research interests are primarily Chinese syntax, pragmatics, and Chinese pedagogical grammar. She has published numerous academic papers and co-authored the textbooks *Reality Chinese* and *Scenario Chinese*, led by Professor Yuehua Liu.

博雅 对外汉语教学名家指导丛书

补语释析

UNDERSTANDING COMPLEMENTS

[美] 刘月华（Yuehua Liu）
[美] 魏久安（Julian K. Wheatley）
[美] 刘宪民（Xianmin Liu）——编著

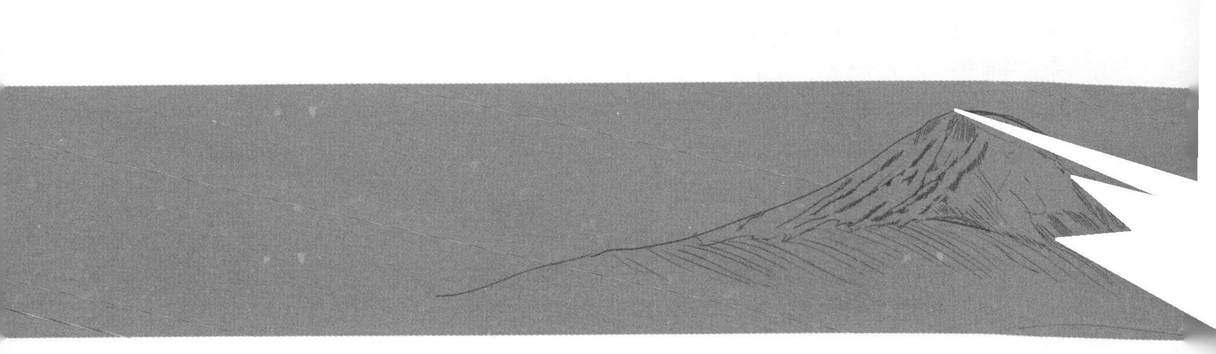

北京大学出版社
PEKING UNIVERSITY PRESS

图书在版编目（CIP）数据

补语释析 / (美) 刘月华, (美) 魏久安, (美) 刘宪民编著. — 北京 : 北京大学出版社, 2022.11

（对外汉语教学名家指导丛书）

ISBN 978-7-301-32569-8

Ⅰ. ①补… Ⅱ. ①刘… ②魏… ③刘… Ⅲ. ①汉语－补语－对外汉语教学－教学参考资料 Ⅳ. ①H195.4

中国版本图书馆CIP数据核字（2021）第208333号

书　　名 补语释析
BUYU SHIXI

著作责任者 [美] 刘月华（Yuehua Liu） [美] 魏久安（Julian K. Wheatley）
[美] 刘宪民（Xianmin Liu） 编著

责任编辑 路冬月

标准书号 ISBN 978-7-301-32569-8

出版发行 北京大学出版社

地　　址 北京市海淀区成府路205号 100871

网　　址 http://www.pup.cn 新浪微博：@北京大学出版社

电子信箱 zpup@pup.cn

电　　话 邮购部 010-62752015 发行部 010-62750672
编辑部 010-62753334

印 刷 者 北京宏伟双华印刷有限公司

经 销 者 新华书店

720毫米×1020毫米 16开本 22.25印张 453千字

2022年11月第1版 2022年11月第1次印刷

定　　价 78.00元

前言
Preface

补语长期以来一直是对外汉语教学中的一个难点。原因有三：一是一般外国学生的母语中没有类似汉语的补语这种语言现象可以借鉴；二是补语结构类型多样，成分复杂，且种类最多的趋向补语类，多具引申意义，与其实在意义相去甚远，容易混淆；三是常用的一些对外汉语教材往往专注于补语结构形式的单一介绍，缺少不同类型补语之间的比较和分析。

The topic of complements has long posed difficulties for the teaching of Chinese as a foreign language. There are three reasons for this. The first is that, for the most part, the native languages of our foreign students do not possess comparable linguistic structures to draw on for guidance. The second is that in Chinese there are many different types of complements with a complicated array of components; moreover, directional complements have the greatest variety, and most of those also have the broadest range of senses, some of which stray so far from the basic senses as to be easily confused. The third reason is that many of the more popular textbooks for foreign students introduce complement structures without attempting to compare the various types or offer any analysis.

有鉴于此，我们编写了《补语释析》这本书，希望能为从事对外汉语教学的教师以及学习中文的外国学生，尤其是母语为英语的学生，提供一本系统的补语学习工具书。

With these issues in mind, *Understanding Complements* has been written in the hope of providing a systematic reference tool for teachers involved in the teaching of

Chinese to foreign students and for foreign students studying Chinese—particularly those whose native language is English.

基于长期的对外汉语教学实践，我们根据补语结构的特点以及以英语为母语的外国学生的需要，将在本书中重点讨论动词补语中最常用也是最重要的四大类型：结果补语（第二章），趋向补语（第三章），可能补语（第四章），以及描写性补语（第五章）。

Based on the authors' extensive experience teaching Chinese to foreigners, and taking into account the special features of Chinese complement structures and the needs of English language speakers, *Understanding Complements* focuses on the four most common and most important types of complements: resultative complements (chapter 2); directional complements (chapter 3); potential complements (chapter 4); and descriptive complements (chapter 5).

本书通过大量的例句、浅显易懂的讲解、一目了然的图示，详细地解析了各类补语的语义区别，并在趋向补语部分提供了大量带例句的对照表格，来帮助学生理解同类补语之间的细微差异以及异类组之间的语义联系。针对教师和学生在教学与练习中可能遇到的难点和问题，本书还提供了一些教学建议。书后附录了大量基于教学实践及实际生活场景的形式多样的练习以及练习答案，以便学生正确掌握补语的应用。

Understanding Complements is replete with example sentences; it provides easy to understand explanations, clear illustrations, detailed explanations of the various senses of the complements; and for the chapter on directional complements, it provides a large number of comparative tables with example sentences to help students understand the subtle differences between similar complements and the semantic connections between heterogeneous groups. To allay the difficulties and problems that teachers and students may face in teaching and practicing complement structures, the book offers some advice and suggestions. The appendix at the end of the book contains a large number of diverse exercises complete with answer keys. These exercises are derived from teaching practices, incorporate real-life scenarios, and are designed to help students master the use of the wide array of complements introduced in the book.

为方便学生阅读，本书采取了中英文对照的格式，在所有的中文解说与例句之下，都附加了英文译文，供学生参考。此外，所有的例句也都加注了汉语拼音，以方便初学者阅读。

In order to allow learners to use the book effectively, a Chinese-English dual language format has been adopted, with the Chinese text and all example sentences followed by English translations. In addition, all examples include a Pinyin Romanized transcription so that the Chinese can be read out even by beginning students.

本书第一作者刘月华教授，一生从事汉语教学，成就斐然，著作等身，其中《实用汉语语法》《趋向补语通释》《汉语语法论集》等作，均已成为对外汉语教学领域的经典，影响深远。由刘教授主导编著的《中文听说读写》《走进百姓生活》等汉语教材和“汉语风”系列分级读物，至今仍然深受欢迎。她也因此荣获了全美中文教师学会颁发的终身成就奖。这本《补语解析》，集刘教授一生对汉语补语研究之精华，应用于对外汉语教学。

The primary author of this book is Professor Yuehua Liu, a scholar of wide reputation, whose publications include *A Practical Grammar of Modern Chinese, A Complete Explanation of Directional Complements*, and *Writings on Chinese Grammar*. These have become classics in the field of Chinese language teaching, with far-reaching influence. And Chinese textbooks such as *Integrated Chinese* and *Reality Chinese,* graded readers *Chinese Breeze*, for those of which Professor Liu is the lead author, remain popular to this day. Professor Liu has been honored with the Lifetime Achievement Award from the Chinese Language Teachers Association (USA). *Understanding Complements* contains the essence of her life-long research on Chinese complements and applies it to the teaching of Chinese as a foreign language.

本书第二作者魏久安博士，语言学者，主要在美国康奈尔大学和麻省理工学院任教，有多年汉语教学经验，也是多本汉语教材的作者。负责本书的翻译工作。

The second author, Dr. Julian K. Wheatley, is a linguist with many years experience in teaching Chinese, primarily at Cornell University and at the Massachusetts Institute of Technology. He is the author or co-author of a number of textbooks and materials for the study of Chinese. He is responsible for the English translation of this book.

本书第三作者刘宪民，汉语语言学专业博士，语言学者，资深汉语教师，曾任教于美国俄勒冈大学、俄亥俄大学、哈佛大学等，教龄三十余年，目前在范德堡大学任教。负责本书练习与答案的编写以及中英文意的核对。

The third author is Xianmin Liu, a linguist with a doctorate in Chinese linguistics. She is an experienced teacher who has been teaching Chinese for over thirty years at University of Oregon, Ohio University and Harvard University. Currently, she holds a teaching position at Vanderbilt University. She is responsible for the exercises and the answer keys, as well as for verifying the Chinese and English texts.

在这里我们诚挚感谢北京大学出版社责任编辑在本书出版过程中所做的大量校正与协调工作。

Finally, we would like to give heartfelt thanks to the editors at Peking University Press who have been responsible for the careful checking and coordination involved in the publication of this book.

目录
Contents

第一章　导言 /1
Introduction

第二章　结果补语 /19
Resultative complements

第一节　结果补语与句中其他成分的意义关系 /22
Semantic relationships between resultative complements and other sentence elements

第二节　包含结果补语的句子的结构特点 /29
Special constraints on sentences with resultative complements

第三节　充任结果补语的词：形容词和动词 /34
Words that can serve as resultative complements: adjectives and verbs

第四节　动词作补语时意义虚化 /39
Verbs that lack semantic content when they serve as resultative complements

第五节　结果补语教学建议 /52
Suggestions for teaching resultative complements

第三章　趋向补语 /55

Directional complements

第一节　趋向补语简述 /56

Directional complements in brief

第二节　趋向补语分述 /72

Directional complements in detail

一　来 /73

Lái

二　去 /77

Qù

三　“上”组 /83

“Shàng” group

四　“下”组 /108

“Xià” group

五　“进”组 /135

“Jìn” group

六　“出”组 /141

“Chū” group

七　“回”组 /152

“Huí” group

八　“过”组 /157

“Guò” group

九　“起”组 /186

“Qǐ” group

十　“开”组 /208

“Kāi” group

十一　“到”组 /221

“Dào” group

第三节　趋向补语教学建议 /228

Suggestions for teaching directional complements

第四章　可能补语 /231

Potential complements

第一节　A类可能补语 /233

A-type potential complements

第二节　B类可能补语 /243

B-type potential complements

第三节　C类可能补语 /246

C-type potential complements

第四节　可能补语教学建议 /248

Suggestions for teaching potential complements

第五章　描写性补语 /251

Descriptive complements

第一节　描写性补语与句中其他成分之间的意义关系 /253

Semantic relationships between descriptive complements and other sentence elements

第二节 描写性补语的功能 /260
The function of descriptive complements

第三节 包含描写性补语的句子的结构特点 /262
Special constraints on sentences with descriptive complements

第四节 描写性补语教学建议 /265
Suggestions for teaching descriptive complements

第六章 动词后其他非名词成分 /267
Other non-nominal post-verbal elements

综合练习 /290
Exercises

综合练习答案 /318
Answer keys to exercises

第一章 Chapter 1

成年人学习一种外语，通常要学习那种语言的发音规则、词汇、语法规则等。学习汉语语法，主要要学习汉语的词怎样构成句子以及比句子更大的单位——段落、篇章。

When adults study a foreign language, they generally study the rules of pronunciation, the lexicon, the rules of grammar, and so on. When studying Chinese grammar, the important thing is to learn how words in Chinese are composed into sentences and larger units of discourse—paragraph and text.

1. 汉语句子的结构
The construction of Chinese sentences

为了掌握汉语用词造句的规则，首先要了解句子的结构。我们知道汉语的句子可以先分析成主语、谓语两部分；如果谓语中心语是动词，它又可包括宾语、补语和状语。宾语是动词后的名词性成分；补语主要是动词后的非名词性成分；状语是动词前的修饰成分。主语和宾语可以有修饰语，叫定语。定语和其他成分不在一个层次上，我们用括号括起来：

In order to master the rules for composing sentences out of words in Chinese, one first has to understand the structure of sentences. We know that sentences in Chinese can be decomposed first into a subject and a predicate. If the head of the predicate is a verb, then the predicate can include objects, complements and adverbials. Objects are noun phrases that follow a verb; complements are generally post-verbal elements other than noun phrases; and adverbials are modifying elements that precede verbs. Subjects and objects can have modifying elements called attributives. Attributives are not at the same level of constituency as other elements and for this reason, we enclose them in parentheses:

（定语）主语	‖	谓语			
(attributive) subject	‖	predicate			
		状语	动词	补语	（定语）宾语
		adverbial	verb	complement	(attributive) object

① 我弟弟	‖	晚上十点 才	写	完了	作业。
Wǒ dìdi	‖	wǎnshang cái shí diǎn	xiě	wánle	zuòyè.

My younger brother didn't finish his homework until ten in the evening.

② 你	‖	把墙上的照片	拿	下来。
Nǐ	‖	bǎ qiángshang de zhàopiàn	ná	xialai.

Take the photos off the wall.

③ 妹妹	‖		走	得很快。
Mèimei	‖		zǒu	de hěn kuài .

Younger sister walks quite fast.

④ 我	‖		跑	不动了。
Wǒ	‖		pǎo	bu dòng le.

I can't run a step more.

形容词作谓语时，后边也可以有补语：

When the predicate consists of an adjective, it can also be followed by a complement:

⑤ 小王	‖		高兴	得跳了起来。
Xiǎo Wáng	‖		gāoxìng	de tiàole qilai.

Xiao Wang jumped for joy.

⑥ 灯光	‖	渐渐	暗	下去了。
Dēngguāng	‖	jiànjiàn	àn	xiaqu le.

The lamp light slowly faded.

2. 补语在汉语中是非常重要的语法现象

Complements are a particularly important grammatical feature of Chinese

结果补语和趋向补语是汉语中十分常见、十分重要的一种语法现象，也是汉语语法教学的难点之一。我们曾经做过一个简单的统计。从陆文夫的小说《美食家》中选取了第一、第二及第四节，共600多个句子，其中有200多个句子包含不能用补语的动词，如“是、在、成、会、能、可以、使、叫、让、觉得、懂、承认、憎恨、认为、好像、进行、加以”等。在其余的句子中，就有200多个有补语，这个比例不能算小。当然，这与我们用小说作语料有关系。《趋向补语前动词之研究》①一文中提到，趋向补语出现最多的语体是叙述语体，结果补语与趋向补语不完全相同，但在叙述性文字中出现的频率也明显高于议论性文字。我们可以说补语是汉语叙述性文字中非常重要的语法现象。

Resultative complements and directional complements are an extremely common and important grammatical feature of Chinese. They are also one of the more difficult issues in the teaching of Chinese grammar. Using data from Lu Wenfu's novel *The Epicurean*, we have done a simple statistical analysis. We chose over 600 sentences from the first, second and fourth sections of the book and found that over 200 of them included verbs that could not take a complement. These included “shì, zài, chéng, huì, néng, kěyǐ, shǐ, jiào, ràng, juéde, dǒng, chéngrèn, zēnghèn, rènwéi, hǎoxiàng, jìnxíng, jiāyǐ”, etc. In the other sentences, there were over 200 which contained complements — quite a significant proportion. Of course, the choice of a novel may have had some influence on our data. The article “A study of verbs that take directional complements”, indicated that in narrative writing, directional complements were the

① 刘月华（1997）趋向补语前动词之研究，《第五届国际汉语教学讨论会论文选》编辑委员会编《第五届国际汉语教学讨论会论文选》，北京：北京大学出版社。

Liu Yuehua. 1997. A study of verbs that take directional complements. In *Selected Papers from the 5th International Conference on Chinese Language Teaching*, edited by the editorial board of *Selected Papers from the 5th International Conference on Chinese Language Teaching*. Beijing: Peking University Press.

most common complement type. Although resultative complements and directional complements are not completely identical in that respect, their frequency in narrative writing is certainly higher than in argumentative writing. We can say that complements are a particularly salient grammatical feature of Chinese narrative writing.

我们所以说补语是十分重要的语法现象，还因为当叙述一个有结果的动作时，说汉语的人就要用补语把这个结果说出来。补语可以表示各种各样的结果状态。我们先以动词“切”为例：

The reason we say that complements are an important feature of Chinese grammar is because when, in a narrative, there is an action leading to a result, Chinese speakers will use a complement to express that result. Complements can express all kinds of situations involving result. Let us first examine the verb “qiē (cut)” as an example:

① 他切开西瓜一看，是生的。

Tā qiēkāi xīguā yí kàn, shì shēng de.

He cut open the watermelon and took a look—it wasn’t ripe.

② 她把西瓜切下来一块，递给了我。

Tā bǎ xīguā qiē xialai yí kuài, dìgěile wǒ.

She cut off a slice of watermelon and gave it to me.

③ 他一刀切下去，西瓜“咔嚓”一声裂开了。

Tā yì dāo qiē xiaqu, xīguā “kāchā” yì shēng lièkāi le.

When he cut it, the watermelon split open with a loud “crack”.

④ 这个西瓜他切进去一寸多就切不动了。

Zhège xīguā tā qiē jinqu yí cùn duō jiù qiē bu dòng le.

He cut into the watermelon a little more than an inch, then the knife stuck.

⑤ 她从东边一个一个切过来，切了十几个西瓜。

Tā cóng dōngbian yí ge yí ge qiē guolai, qiēle shíjǐ ge xīguā.

She sliced the watermelons one at a time, starting from the east, slicing over ten of them.

⑥ 她切西瓜切上瘾来了。

Tā qiē xīguā qiēshàng yǐn lai le.

She sliced watermelons to the point of addiction.

⑦ 你再切下去，西瓜都没有了，明天的客人吃什么？

Nǐ zài qiē xiaqu, xīguā dōu méiyǒu le, míngtiān de kèren chī shénme?

If you go on slicing the watermelons, you won't have any more and then what will the guests eat tomorrow?

⑧ 你怎么切起来没完了？

Nǐ zěnme qiē qilai méi wán le?

How come you're still slicing after all the time?

⑨ 她切西瓜切到了天亮。

Tā qiē xīguā qiēdàole tiānliàng.

She sliced watermelons until dawn.

⑩ 她切西瓜不小心，一刀切在了手上。

Tā qiē xīguā bù xiǎoxīn, yì dāo qiēzàile shǒu shang.

She wasn't careful slicing the watermelon and cut herself on the hand.

⑪ 你先把西瓜的把儿切掉吧。

Nǐ xiān bǎ xīguā de bàr qiēdiào ba.

Why don't you cut the watermelon stem off first?

⑫ 她把西瓜切成了很多块，让大家吃。

Tā bǎ xīguā qiēchéngle hěn duō kuài, ràng dàjiā chī.

She cut the watermelon up into a lot of slices, then let everyone eat.

⑬ 你切错了，切了人家的西瓜。

Nǐ qiēcuò le, qiēle rénjia de xīguā.

You've made a mistake and sliced someone else's watermelon.

⑭ 她切西瓜把手都切疼了。

Tā qiē xīguā bǎ shǒu dōu qiēténg le.

Her hands ache from slicing watermelons.

⑮ 他切完西瓜就吃了起来。

Tā qiēwán xīguā jiù chīle qilai.

He finished slicing the watermelon and started to eat it.

⑯ 她给大家切西瓜，切得很高兴。

Tā gěi dàjiā qiē xīguā, qiē de hěn gāoxìng.

She merrily sliced the watermelon for everyone.

⑰ 她切西瓜切得满头大汗。

Tā qiē xīguā qiē de mǎntóu dàhàn.

She sliced the watermelon until she was covered in sweat.

……

不同的补语表示不同的结果状态，非常富于表现力。这些句子的意思如果用英语表达，可能在动词后用介词，或者用两个句子表示汉语一个句子的意思，或者要花费点儿心思才能把相应的汉语句子的意思准确细致地表达出来。如果把句子中的补语都去掉，那就很难让说汉语的人接受了。比较：

Different complements express different resultative situations. It is an extremely productive means of expression. If you try to express the same meanings in English, you may have to use prepositions after the verbs, use two sentences to express what is a single sentence in Chinese or, in many cases, spend a long time trying to figure out some way to express precisely the same meaning. If in Chinese, you omit the complements in such sentences, it is unlikely that Chinese speakers will accept them. Compare:

⑱ 他从冰箱里拿出来一个西瓜，放在桌子上，然后拿出刀来，先一刀把西瓜切开，再切成一块一块的，请大家吃。

Tā cóng bīngxiāng li ná chulai yí ge xīguā, fàngzài zhuōzi shang, ránhòu náchū dāo lai, xiān yì dāo bǎ xīguā qiēkāi, zài qiēchéng yí kuài yí kuài de, qǐng dàjiā chī.

He took a watermelon out of the refrigerator and put it on the table; then he took a knife, cut it open, sliced it up and invited everyone to have some.

? 他从冰箱里拿了一个西瓜，放桌子上，然后拿了刀，先一刀把西瓜切了，再切一块一块的，请大家吃。

? Tā cóng bīngxiāng li nále yí ge xīguā, fàng zhuōzi shang, ránhòu nále dāo, xiān yì dāo bǎ xīguā qiē le, zài qiē yí kuài yí kuài de, qǐng dàjiā chī.

从上面的句子中可以看出来，说汉语时，补语不是可有可无的。汉语表示动作的动词大多本身不同时表示结果。比如“看”必须加上“见、到、完、懂、会”等才表示“看”的结果。正因为如此，当动作有结果时，除非句子中有“了、过、着、是……的”等，否则如果不用补语，句子的意义与结构就不符合汉语的要求。再看下面的句子（选自《美食家》）：

The above example shows you that when you speak Chinese, complements are not optional. Verbs that express actions in Chinese do not, for the most part, imply the result. So with “kàn (look) ”, you need add “jiàn, dào, wán, dǒng, huì” and so on to express the result of the “looking”. It is precisely for this reason that, when the action implies a result, the sentence has to have either a “le，guò，zhe” or “shì……de” (construction) or a complement, otherwise it will not accord with the semantic or grammatical requirements of Chinese. Observe the following sentences (taken from Lu Wenfu's novel *The Epicurean*):

⑲ 我睡得迷迷糊糊的时候，才听见他的黄包车到了门前。
Wǒ shuì de mími-hūhū de shíhou, cái tīngjiàn tā de huángbāochē dàole ménqián.
I was already half asleep by the time I heard his rickshaw pull up to the door.

⑳ 阿二替朱自治掀掉膝盖上的毡毯。
Ā Èr tì Zhū Zìyě xiāndiào xīgài shang de zhāntǎn.
Ah Er lifted the blanket that was covering Zhu Ziye's knees.

㉑ 这一觉起码三个钟头，让那胃中的食物消化干净，为下一顿腾出地方。
Zhè yí jiào qǐmǎ sān ge zhōngtóu, ràng nà wèizhōng de shíwù xiāohuà gānjìng, wèi xià yí dùn téngchu dìfang.
He napped for at least three hours so that the food in his stomach could be completely digested to make room for the next meal.

㉒ 朱自冶登上茶楼之后，他的吃友们便陆续到齐。

Zhū Zìyě dēngshang chálóu zhīhòu, tā de chīyǒumen biàn lùxù dàoqí.

After Zhu Ziye climbed up to the teahouse, all his meal-mates showed up, one after the other.

㉓ 一长串油光锃亮的黄包车……在酒店门口徐徐地停下。

Yì cháng chuàn yóuguāng zèngliàng de huángbāochē …… zài jiǔdiàn ménkǒu xúxú de tíngxia.

A procession of polished rickshaws … slowly pulled up to the entrance of the restaurant.

㉔ 他老远便掏出三炮台香烟递过来，我连忙摸出双斧牌香烟把它挡回去。

Tā lǎo yuǎn biàn tāochu Sānpàotái xiāngyān dì guolai, wǒ liánmáng mōchu Shuāngfǔ pái xiāngyān bǎ tā dǎng huiqu.

While he was still quite far off, he pulled out some "Three Castles" cigarets and offered me one; I followed right away with my "Marshal" brand and fended it off.

㉕ 戏台上的小姐饮酒总是用水袖遮起来。

Xìtái shang de xiǎojiě yǐn jiǔ zǒngshì yòng shuǐxiù zhē qilai.

When the girl on the stage drank wine, she always hid it with her long sleeves.

㉖ 我滔滔不绝地讲起苏联来了，就和现在的某些人讲美国似的。

Wǒ tāotāo bùjué de jiǎngqǐ Sūlián lai le, jiù hé xiànzài de mǒuxiē rén jiǎng Měiguó shìde.

I talked endlessly about the Soviet Union, just as some people now chat about America.

㉗ 他们一个个洗得干干净净，浑身散发着香皂味。

Tāmen yí gege xǐ de gāngān-jìngjìng, húnshēn sànfāzhe xiāngzào wèi.

They each scrubbed themselves clean so that they reeked of soap from head to toe.

㉘ 弄得朱经理出入不便，早晚都要到街上去叫车，有时候淋得像个落汤鸡。
Nòng de Zhū jīnglǐ chūrù búbiàn, zǎowǎn dōu yào dào jiē shang qù jiào chē, yǒu shíhou lín de xiàng ge luòtāngjī.
It made coming and going inconvenient for Manager Zhu; there'd be times he'd have to go out on the street to call a rickshaw and sometimes he got completely drenched in the rain.

有些动词表示的动作一旦发生，自然会有某种结果，但是后面也往往有一个表示结果的补语。比如“腾”：

For some verbs, the action they express takes place over a very short period, so there will inevitably be certain results; but even so, there will usually be a complement to express those results. Take “téng” for example:

㉙ 这一觉起码三个钟头，让那胃中的食物消化干净，为下一顿腾出地方。（同第8页例㉑）
Zhè yí jiào qǐmǎ sān ge zhōngtóu, ràng nà wèizhōng de shíwù xiāohuà gānjìng, wèi xià yí dùn téngchu dìfang. (same as example ㉑, p.8)
He napped for at least three hours so that the food in his stomach could be completely digested to make room for the next meal.

一般来说，“腾（地方）”的动作发生了，地方就“出”（由无到有）了，按说不必用补语“出”。

Generally speaking, when the action of “making space for” (téng) occurs, the idea of the space being carved “out” (chū) is understood; but even so, one still expresses the complement “chū”.

㉚ 朱自冶进澡堂只有举手之劳，即伸出手来撩开窗帘。
Zhū Zìyě jìn zǎotáng zhǐyǒu jǔshǒuzhīláo, jí shēnchū shǒu lai liāokāi chuānglián.
Zhu Ziye entered the bathroom, and it only took the slightest effort for him to extend his arm to lift up the curtains.

“伸”的结果自然是“（手）出来”，不用“出来”意思也清楚，但是这里还用了补语。

The sense of "extending" (shēn) naturally implies that the arms [extend] "outwards" (chūlai), and if "chūlai" is not said, the sense will still be clear. But even so, the complement tends to be expressed.

补语还是汉语语法最为复杂的现象之一，因此也成为把汉语作为外语的学习者的语法难点。本书试图通过较多的用例，简明地解释和分析，达到老师好教、学生好学的目的。

Complements are one of the most complicated features of Chinese grammar, and for this reason, they are a particularly difficult grammatical problem for foreign students studying Chinese. In this book, we set out to provide clear and simple explanations and analysis for a large number of examples in order to help teachers to teach, and students to learn.

3. 补语的范围

The range of complements

如前所述，补语是动词后的非名词性成分。汉语句子的动词后可以出现的非名词性词语很多，是不是都应该归入补语？有些从事汉语教学的非中国学者认为汉语的补语是一个大杂烩，应该缩小补语的范围，这个意见从汉语作为外语教学来说，我们觉得很有道理。

As we said earlier, complements are non-nominal sentence components that follow the verb. There are quite a lot of such elements in Chinese. Should they all be termed complements? Some foreign scholars who deal with Chinese language pedagogy feel that complements in Chinese are a hodgepodge and that the scope of what constitutes a complement should be reduced. From the point of view of teaching Chinese as a foreign language, this makes a lot of sense.

我们这里所说的"补语"的范围，主要指在对外汉语教材中把哪些语法现象归入补语。教材决定课堂教学。

For us, the scope of the term "complement" is based mostly on what are categorized as complements in pedagogical materials used for teaching Chinese as a foreign language. For us, the teaching materials determine the classroom pedagogy.

不同的汉语语法著作中，补语的范围是不同的。《实用现代汉语语法》（增订本）[1]的补语范围较广，将补语分以下几种：

Different authors writing on Chinese grammar treat the scope of the term "complement" differently. In *A Practical Grammar of Modern Chinese (revised edition)*, the scope is relatively broad, with the following types distinguished:

（一）结果补语 resultative complements

（二）趋向补语 directional complements

（三）可能补语 potential complements

（四）情态补语 modal complements

（五）程度补语 degree complements

（六）数量补语 quantitative complements

（七）介词短语补语 prepositional phrase complements

上述（一）（二）（四）类都属于动词后的非名词成分，而且下面将要谈到，它们表示近似的意思，所以我们归入补语；可能补语虽然与上述三类在意义上不同，但在结构上与（一）（二）有关，我们认为也归入补语为宜。

Types 1, 2 and 4 above all involve non-nominal elements following verbs and, as we will show later, they express similar meanings, so we will categorize them as complements. Although potential complements differ in sense from these three types, they are related structurally to types 1 and 2, so we feel that it is appropriate to regard them as complements as well.

吕文华在《对外汉语教学语法讲义》[2]中介绍了一些学者对补语的处理意见：

Lü Wenhua in her article, *Lectures on the Teaching of Chinese Grammar to Foreigners,* presents the views of some scholars on dealing with complements:

---

① 刘月华、潘文娱、故铧（2001）《实用现代汉语语法》（增订本），北京：商务印书馆，第533–628页。

Liu Yuehua, Pan Wenyu & Gu Wei. 2001. *A Practical Grammar of Modern Chinese(revised edition)*. Beijing: The Commercial Press. pp.533-628.

② 吕文华（2014）《对外汉语教学语法讲义》，北京：北京大学出版社，第152—153页。

Lü Wenhua. 2014. *Lectures on the Teaching of Chinese Grammar to Foreigners*. Beijing: Peking University Press. pp.152-153.

（1）柯彼德（1990）：

Peter Kupfer (1990) :

1）传统语法体系中的结果补语、趋向补语、可能补语归入动词结构，作为复合动词的附类，名称可采取美国汉学家的提法，叫结果动词，它们有可能式。

Traditional grammars categorize resultative, directional and potential complements as verbal elements that form various types of verb compounds. We can use the terms adopted by American scholars of Chinese and call them all "resultative verbs". All have potential forms.

2）原来的介宾结构作补语，如"住在""开往""借给"等，是另一种复合动词，可以看作关系动词。

What were formerly considered complements introducing objects, as in "zhùzài (live at)" "kāiwǎng (travel to)" or "jiègěi (lend to)" form another kind of verb compound, which can be called "relational verb".

3）传统语法体系中的时量补语、动量补语、数量补语应归入宾语。

The complements of duration, frequenry and quantity in traditional grammars should be categorized as objects.

4）汉语中的补语只有用"得"作标志的具有独特句法性质的一类，才叫补语。

Only those cases which have the syntactic property of allowing the insertion of "de" will be called "complements".

（2）马庆株、王红旗（1998）：

Ma Qingzhu and Wang Hongqi (1998):

以是否能构成可能式把补语分为两类。能构成可能式的，又分为：

Two kinds of resultative complements can be distinguished, according to whether or not they have potential forms. Those that do have potential forms can be further divided into:

- 趋向补语 Directional complements
- 非趋向补语 Non-directional complements

不能构成可能式的，又分为：

Those complements that do not have potential forms can be further divided into:

- 状态补语（前面有“得”，意义实在）
  Predicative complements (preceded by “de”; actual sense)
- 程度补语（前面有“得”或无“得”，意义虚空）
  Degree complements (with or without “de”; null sense)
- 时地补语（含有介词）
  Complements of time or location (containing prepositions)

（3）张旺熹（1999）：

Zhang Wangxi (1999):

把补语分为以下三种形式：基本式、扩展式1、扩展式2。

Distinguishes the following three types of complements: Basic Style, Expanded Style 1, Expanded Style 2.

基本式（VC结构） Basic Style (VC Construction)	VC_1(动+动) VC_1 (V+V)	跑来 pǎolái (run here) 气死 qìsǐ (furious)
	VC_2（动+形） VC_2 (V+Adj.)	洗净 xǐjìng (to clean up) 画好 huàhǎo (complete the painting)
	VC_3（动+数量短语） VC_3 (V+quantifier)	关三天 guān sān tiān (close for three days) 吃三顿 chī sān dùn (eat three meals)
	VC_4（动+介宾短语） VC_4 (V+preposition-object phrase)	卖给她 màigěi tā (sell to her) 跑到教室 pǎodào jiàoshì (run to class)

扩展式1（可能式） Expanded Style 1 (potential)	V+不/得+C V + bu/de + C	
扩展式2（现实式） Expanded Style 2 (actual)	V+得（很）+C V + de (hěn) + C	

吕文华的意见是“对外汉语教学中的补语系统可如此简化，其中的结果补语、趋向补语、介宾补语作为短语词，从补语系统中分离出去，而可能补语可以看作动结式和动趋式短语词的可能式。对外汉语教学中的8类补语可简化为带“得”的程度补语，以及带数量词的时量补语和动量补语”。①

Lü Wenhua expressed the following view: “In teaching Chinese to foreigners, the complement system can be simplified by distinguishing phrases composed of resultative, directional and preposition-object complements from the rest of the complement system, and treating potential complements as the potential forms of resultative and directional verb phrases. The eight kinds of complements distinguished in the teaching Chinese as a foreign language can be simplified to complements of degree that take ‘de’, duration complements and frequency complements composed of number plus measure phrases”.

如前所述，我们认为结果补语、趋向补语在汉语中非常重要，甚至是表达上不可或缺的，加上其意义、结构十分复杂，如果像离合词那样归入短语词，那么结果补语、趋向补语、可能补语的意义和结构在哪里处理？把汉语语法的这一大块拿掉，很简单、很干净，但是学生到哪里去学呢？毕竟结果补语、趋向补语、可能补语比离合词复杂多了。

As we said earlier, we feel resultative and directional complements play a particularly important role in Chinese. In fact, they are indispensible, and their senses and structures are extremely complicated. So if we treat them as phrases like verb-

---

① 吕文华（2014）《对外汉语教学语法讲义》，北京：北京大学出版社，第156页。
Lü Wenhua. 2014. *Lectures on the Teaching of Chinese Grammar to Foreigners*. Beijing: Peking University Press. p.156.

object compounds, where would we deal with the sense and structure of the various resultative, directional and potential complements? Grouping them in the same category as verb-object compounds would make the grammar simple and clear-cut, but how would students learn [to use] them? Resultative, directional and potential complements are, after all, much more complicated than verb-object compounds.

语法书要给每一种语法现象一个位置，《实用现代汉语语法》（增订本）在确定补语的范围时，征求过几位语法学大家的意见，也反反复复讨论，最后确定那7类，好像在我们接触的语料中没有遗漏。但是对外汉语教学不同，我们也主张简化语法体系，但要突出汉语语法重点，不能舍弃学生学习的语法难点。

A grammar book should cover every major grammatical feature of the language. To determine the range of complement structures, *A Practical Grammar of Modern Chinese (revised edition)* sought the opinions of a number of experts and considered the options over and over again before settling on seven types. Judging from the corpus that we have examined, they covered all of them. But teaching Chinese to foreigners is different. We also advocate keeping the grammatical presentation simple. But we also want the important features of Chinese grammar to stand out. We cannot ignore those parts of the grammar that students find particularly difficult.

《实用现代汉语语法》（增订本）中的（五）（六）（七）三类补语在结构上和前几种补语虽然有某些相似之处，但意义不太相同，而且从减轻学生的负担、方便教学出发，我们主张在教材中不作补语处理。如何处理这些语法现象，我们将在后面具体说明。

Although in *A Practical Grammar of Modern Chinese (revised edition)*, the 5th, 6th and 7th complement types have some features in common with the others, their sense are rather different, and for the purpose of lightening the burden on students and making teaching more convenient, we recommend that, for teaching purposes, certain items not be treated as complements. How they are to be treated is something that will be discussed later in the book.

对补语的分类也是一个比较复杂的问题。一般有两种方法，一是根据意义，一是根据形式。但是实际操作起来，无论根据意义还是根据形式，都很难把补语分得清清楚楚。本书的四类补语分类主要根据结构和充任补语的词：

Determining complement types is also a rather complicated problem. In general there are two methods: one, based on sense; and the other, based on form. But in practice, whether by sense or by form, it is quite difficult to distinguish different types. The four complement types distinguished in this book are based primarily on structure but also on the type of words that can act as complements:

（1）结果补语 resultative complements

补语直接在动词后，充任补语的是形容词和动词。

The complement consists of an adjective or a verb and follows the verb directly.

（2）趋向补语 directional complements

补语直接在动词后，充任补语的是“来、去、上、下”等趋向动词。

The complement consists of directional verbs such as “lái, qù, shàng, xià”, etc. and follows the verb directly.

（3）可能补语 potential complements

从结构上来说，是由结果补语或趋向补语中间加上“得/不”构成的，虽然其历史来源并不如此。

In terms of structure, they are formed by the insertion of “de” or “bu” into a resultative or directional complement (though historically, that is not the way the construction arose).

（4）描写性补语 descriptive complements

是由“得”连接的补语。这类补语学术上经常称作情态补语，因为具有描写性，也许叫作描写性补语更好。

They are connected [to the verb] by “de”. These complements often referred to modal complements, but because they serve a descriptive function, we prefer to call them “descriptive complements”.

第二章 Chapter 2

结果补语主要指直接跟在动词后的形容词或动词。如：

Resultative complements primarily refer to adjectives or verbs that follow a verb directly. For example:

① 我昨天把刚买来的那本书看完了。

Wǒ zuótiān bǎ gāng mǎilái de nà běn shū kànwán le.

Yesterday, I finished reading that book I just bought.

② 这个字你写错了。

Zhège zì nǐ xiěcuò le.

You've written that character incorrectly.

③ 老师说的话我都听懂了。

Lǎoshī shuōde huà wǒ dōu tīngdǒng le.

I understood everything that the teacher said.

有的形容词后也可以有结果补语。如：

Some adjectives can also be followed by resultative complements. For example:

④ 她昨天干活累着了。

Tā zuótiān gàn huó lèizhao le.

She's exhausted from the work she had to do yesterday.

⑤ 这个地方乱出了名。

Zhège dìfang luàn chūle míng.

This place is well known for its turmoil.

例⑤的结果补语是一个动词短语"出了名"。

The resultative complement in example ⑤ is a verbal phrase, "chūle míng (be famous)".

形容词带结果补语远没有动词带结果补语常见。

Adjectives with resultative complements are not nearly as common as verbs with resultative complements.

结果补语一般都是一个形容词或者一个动词，如上面的“完”“错”“懂”。有时一个动宾短语也可以作结果补语，如上面例⑤的“出名”。再如：

Generally, resultative complements consist of a single adjective or a single verb, such as “wán” “cuò” and “dǒng” in the examples above. Sometimes a verb-object phrase can also be a resultative complement, as we saw in example ⑤ above, with “chū míng (be famous)”. Other examples are:

⑥ 他玩电子游戏玩上了瘾，不睡觉，也不吃饭。

Tā wán diànzǐ yóuxì wán shàngle yǐn, bú shuì jiào, yě bù chī fàn.

He was addicted to playing video games and didn’t sleep or eat.

⑦ 弟弟常常听歌听入了迷，忘了吃饭。

Dìdi chángcháng tīng gē tīng rùle mí, wàngle chī fàn.

Younger brother often gets into such a trance listening to songs that he forgets to eat.

这种结果补语比较少见。

This type of resultative complements is rather rare.

结果补语与句中其他成分的意义关系可以分为三类。

We can distinguish three types of semantic relationships between resultative complements and other sentence elements.

1. 与动词有关

Relating to the verb

结果补语对动词所表示的动作进行判断或说明。也就是说，这一类结果补语在意义上和动词有关系。

The resultative complement elaborates the action expressed by the verb. In other words, this type of resultative complement is semantically linked to the verb.

① 妈妈说做完了功课才能看电视。（做—完）

Māma shuō zuòwánle gōngkè cái néng kàn diànshì. (zuò — wán)

Mum says you can't watch TV until you finish your homework.

② 他上了床就睡着了。（睡—着）

Tā shàngle chuáng jiù shuìzháo le. (shuì — zháo)

He went to bed and fell asleep.

③ 我的钱包找到了，落在公共汽车上了。（找—到）

Wǒ de qiánbāo zhǎodào le, làzài gōnggòng qìchē shang le. (zhǎo — dào)

I found my wallet; I left it on the bus.

④ 明天的考试你真准备好了吗？（准备—好）

Míngtiān de kǎoshì nǐ zhēn zhǔnbèi hǎo le ma? (zhǔnbèi — hǎo)

Are you really prepared for tomorrow's exam?

有一种形容词作补语，也说明动作，但是表示不符合某一标准的意思。如：

There is also a type of adjective which, when used as a complement, elaborates the verbal action, but it expresses the notion that a certain standard has not been met. For example:

⑤ 这件衣服你买大了。

Zhè jiàn yīfu nǐ mǎidà le.

This item of clothing you bought is too big.

这个句子的意思是，这件衣服你买得不合适，比合适的尺寸大。

The meaning of the sentence is that an item of clothing bought does not fit; it is too big (i.e. bigger than the standard).

⑥ 老师让我们写20个字，你写了18个，写少了。

Lǎoshī ràng wǒmen xiě èrshí ge zì, nǐ xiěle shíbā ge, xiěshǎo le.

Teacher wanted us to write 20 characters; you've written 18 — too few.

⑦ 今天晚饭我吃多了，很不舒服。

Jīntiān wǎnfàn wǒ chīduō le, hěn bù shūfu.

I ate too much for dinner this evening; I don't feel well.

⑧ 对不起，我来晚了。

Duìbuqǐ, wǒ láiwǎn le.

Sorry, I'm late.

⑨ 我们来早了，晚会还没有开始。

Wǒmen láizǎo le, wǎnhuì hái méiyǒu kāishǐ.

We've arrived early; the party hasn't started yet.

⑩ 照片挂低了，应该再高一点儿。

Zhàopiàn guàdī le, yīnggāi zài gāo yìdiǎnr.

The photograph's hung too low; it should be a little higher.

“大、小；多、少；早、晚；深、浅；高、低”一类形容词作结果补语时，常常表示不合某一标准的意思。

When adjectives like “dà (big)” and “xiǎo (small)”; “duō (many)” and “shǎo (few)”; “zǎo (early)” and “wǎn (late)”; “shēn (deep)” and “qiǎn (shallow)”; “gāo (tall, high)” and “dī (low)” act as resultative complements, they often express the notion of not meeting a certain standard.

2. 与动词所涉及的事物有关

Relating to something involved in the verbal action

结果补语在意义上和动作所涉及的事物有关，表示事物的名词在句中作宾语或“把”字句中“把”的宾语。

The resultative complement has a semantic connection to something involved in the verbal action. The noun that expresses the thing is an object, or an object introduced by “bǎ”.

这类句子通常有致使意义，即通过某一动作，使动作所涉及的事物受到影响，发生变化。此类补语最常见。

Sentences with this type of complement generally have causative sense, i.e., the action of the verb involves something which is affected or changed in some way. This is a particularly common type of complement.

① 他划亮一根火柴，点着一根烟。（他—划—火柴，火柴—亮，他—点—烟，烟—着）

Tā huáliàng yì gēn huǒchái, diǎnzháo yì gēn yān. (tā — huá — huǒchái, huǒchái — liàng, tā — diǎn — yān, yān — zháo)

He struck a match and lit a cigarette.

这个句子的意思是：他划了一根火柴，使火柴亮了，他点了一根烟，使烟着了。

The meaning of this sentence is: “He struck a match and made the match light; he lit a cigarette and made the cigarette light.”

② 他不小心打破了一个杯子。（他—打—杯子，杯子—破了）

Tā bù xiǎoxīn dǎpòle yí ge bēizi. (tā — dǎ — bēizi, bēizi — pò le)

He accidentally broke a cup.

③ 你怎么把妹妹气哭了？（你—气—妹妹，妹妹—哭了）

Nǐ zěnme bǎ mèimei qìkū le? (nǐ — qì — mèimei, mèimei — kū le)

How come you upset your little sister so much that she cried?

④ 妹妹写错了三个字，没得100分。（妹妹—写—字，三个字—错了）
Mèimei xiěcuòle sān ge zì, méi dé yìbǎi fēn. (mèimei — xiě — zì, sān ge zì — cuò le)
Younger sister wrote three characters incorrectly so she didn't get 100 points.

⑤ 他说的故事特别好笑，我们把肚子都笑疼了。（我们—笑，肚子—疼）
Tā shuō de gùshi tèbié hǎoxiào, wǒmen bǎ dùzi dōu xiàoténg le. (wǒmen — xiào, dùzi — téng)
His story was very hilarious; we were doubled up with laughter.

⑥ 你已经弄坏了两个iPad了，我不给你买了。（你—弄— iPad，iPad —坏了）
Nǐ yǐjīng nònghuàile liǎng ge iPad le, wǒ bù gěi nǐ mǎi le. (nǐ — nòng — iPad, iPad — huài le)
You've already messed up two iPads; I'm not buying another for you.

⑦ 太阳太厉害了，花儿都晒死了。（太阳—晒—花儿，花儿—死了）
Tàiyáng tài lìhai le, huār dōu shàisǐ le. (tàiyáng — shài — huār, huār — sǐ le)
The sun's too strong; it's killed all the flowers.

⑧ 我洗干净衣服就去做晚饭。（我—洗—衣服，衣服—干净）
Wǒ xǐ gānjìng yīfu jiù qù zuò wǎnfàn. (wǒ — xǐ — yīfu, yīfu — gānjìng)
I'll make dinner after I wash the clothes.

⑨ 飞机票卖光了，你星期一走不了了。（航空公司—卖—飞机票，飞机票—光了）
Fēijīpiào màiguāng le, nǐ Xīngqīyī zǒubuliǎo le. (hángkōng gōngsī — mài — fēijīpiào, fēijīpiào — guāng le)
The plane tickets have been sold out; you won't be able to leave on Monday.

⑩ 独生子女很多都叫父母惯坏了。（父母—惯—独生子女，独生子女—坏了）
Dúshēng-zǐnǚ hěnduō dōu jiào fùmǔ guànhuài le. (fùmǔ — guàn — dúshēng-zǐnǚ, dúshēng-zǐnǚ — huài le)
A lot of only children get spoiled by their parents.

3. 与动作者有关

Relating to the "actor"

补语在意义上和动作者有关系，动作者由作主语的名词表示。

The complement relates semantically to the "actor", expressed as the subject.

这类句子有时也有致使意义，即通过动作，使动作者受到影响，发生变化。

This type of sentence can also be causative, that is, carrying out the action affects or changes the agent.

① 他喝酒喝醉了。（他—喝酒，酒使他—醉了）

Tā hē jiǔ hēzuì le. (tā — hē jiǔ, jiǔ shǐ tā — zuì le)

He drank himself tipsy.

② 我听懂了中文老师说的话，非常高兴。（我—听—老师的话，我—懂了）

Wǒ tīngdǒngle Zhōngwén lǎoshī shuō de huà, fēicháng gāoxìng. (wǒ — tīng — lǎoshī de huà, wǒ — dǒng le)

When I understood what the Chinese teacher said, I was ecstatic.

③ 你说的意思，我听明白了。（我—听—你说的意思，我—明白了）

Nǐ shuō de yìsi, wǒ tīng míngbai le. (wǒ — tīng — nǐ shuō de yìsi, wǒ — míngbai le)

I'm clear about what you're saying.

④ 秋天了，树叶开始变红了。（树叶—变，树叶—红了）

Qiūtiān le, shùyè kāishǐ biànhóng le. (shùyè — biàn, shùyè — hóng le)

It's autumn and the leaves are beginning to redden.

⑤ 听了我的话，她的脸都气白了。（她—气，使她的脸—白了）

Tīngle wǒ de huà, tā de liǎn dōu qìbái le. (tā — qì, shǐ tā de liǎn — bái le)

Her face blanched with anger when she heard what I said.

⑥ 我学会了打高尔夫球。（我—学打高尔夫球，我—会了）

Wǒ xuéhuìle dǎ gāo'ěrfūqiú. (wǒ — xué dǎ gāo'ěrfūqiú, wǒ — huì le)

I've learned to play golf.

⑦ 你坐在椅子上。（你—坐，你—在椅子上）

Nǐ zuòzài yǐzi shang. (nǐ — zuò, nǐ — zài yǐzi shang)

You sit on the chair.

⑧ 我弟弟忘了女朋友的生日，把女朋友气跑了。（我弟弟—气女朋友，使女朋友—跑了）

Wǒ dìdi wàngle nǚpéngyou de shēngrì, bǎ nǚpéngyou qìpǎo le. (wǒ dìdi — qì nǚpéngyou, shǐ nǚpéngyou — pǎo le)

My younger brother forgot about his girlfriend's birthday, making her so angry that she ran off.

⑨ 我吃饱了，不吃了。（我—吃，我—饱了）

Wǒ chībǎo le, bù chī le. (wǒ — chī, wǒ — bǎo le)

I'm full; I won't have anymore.

1. 结果补语的否定形式

The negation of resultative complements

由于结果补语表示动作或变化的结果，所以其否定形式一般用“没”。否定结果补语时，要把“没”放在动词或形容词的前边，表示动作没取得某种结果。例如：

Since resultative complements express the consequences of actions or changes that have taken place, negation usually involves “méi”. When you negate a resultative complement, you should put “méi” in front of the verb or adjective phrase to indicate that the action did not achieve a particular result. For example:

① 这个故事我没听懂。

Zhège gùshi wǒ méi tīngdǒng.

I didn’t understand the story.

上面这个句子的意思是，“我”听了这个故事，“我”没懂。“没”主要否定的是结果补语“懂”。

This sentence indicates that “I” listened to the story, but “I” didn’t understand it. It is mainly the complement, i.e.,“dǒng (understand)”, that is negated.

② 有一次口语考试，我没听清楚老师的话，回答错了。

Yǒu yí cì kǒuyǔ kǎoshì, wǒ méi tīng qīngchu lǎoshī de huà, huídá cuò le.

Once on an oral exam, I didn’t hear clearly what the teacher said, so I responded incorrectly.

③ 昨天的功课你没做完，现在快做吧。

Zuótiān de gōngkè nǐ méi zuòwán, xiànzài kuài zuò ba.

You didn’t finish yesterday’s homework; quick, do it now.

④ 妈妈，我没吃饱，再给我盛一碗饭吧。

Māma, wǒ méi chībǎo, zài gěi wǒ chéng yì wǎn fàn ba.

Mum, I didn’t get enough to eat; let me have another bowl of rice.

⑤ 我连着划了三根火柴，都没划着。

Wǒ liánzhe huále sān gēn huǒchái, dōu méi huázháo.

I struck three matches in succession, but none of them lit.

只有在条件句中，结果补语才用“不”否定。如：

It is only in conditional sentences that resultative complements are negated with “bù”. For example:

⑥ 我不做完练习就不去游泳。

Wǒ bú zuòwán liànxí jiù bú qù yóu yǒng.

If I don’t finish my practice I don’t go swimming.

⑦ 你不说清楚不能走。

Nǐ bù shuō qīngchu jiù bù néng zǒu.

If you don’t say it clearly then you can’t leave.

2. 不能插入其他成分

No element can be inserted

结果补语与前面的谓语动词或形容词之间不能插入其他成分[1]。补语后可以用动态助词“了”“过”，但不能用“着”，在结果补语（以及“了”“过”）后还可以有宾语。

No element can be inserted between the main verb or adjective and the resultative complement. The aspect particles “le” and “guò” can appear after the complement, but not “zhe” . The complement (along with “le” “guò”) may also be followed by an object.

① 小燕做完了功课就睡觉了。

Xiǎoyàn zuòwánle gōngkè jiù shuì jiào le.

Xiaoyan finished her homework and went to sleep.

① 动词和结果补语之间可以插入“得/不”，但那将作为一个整体，成为可能补语了。

“De” or “bu” can be inserted between the verb and the resultative complement, but in such cases, the result is a potential complement which acts as a unitary element.

② 我很快就学会了游泳，可是妹妹怕水，到现在也没学会。

Wǒ hěn kuài jiù xuéhuìle yóu yǒng, kěshì mèimei pà shuǐ, dào xiànzài yě méi xuéhuì.

I learned how to swim quite quickly, but my younger sister is afraid of the water and even now, still hasn't learned.

③ 他从来没打断过别人说话。

Tā cónglái méi dǎduànguo biérén shuō huà.

He's never interrupted other people.

④ 我没听见过她唱歌，不知道她唱得好不好。

Wǒ méi tīngjiànguo tā chàng gē, bù zhīdào tā chàng de hǎo bu hǎo.

I've never heard her sing, so I don't know whether she sings well or not.

动词和结果补语后的宾语应看作动补短语的宾语，而不只是动词的宾语。如：

The object that comes after the verb and the resultative complement should be regarded as the object of the whole verb phrase rather than the object of just the verb. For example:

⑤ 看见了一个人。（看见——一个人。）

Kànjiànle yí ge rén. (Kànjiàn — yí ge rén)

I saw someone.

正因为如此，所以虽然有的不及物动词不能带事物宾语，但加上结果补语以后，便可以带事物宾语了。如：

This is the reason that, though intransitive verbs cannot take objects by themselves, they can take objects when followed by resultative complements. Examples:

⑥ 他跑丢了一只鞋。（跑丢——一只鞋）（*跑——一只鞋）

Tā pǎodiūle yì zhī xié. (pǎodiū — yì zhī xié) (*pǎo — yì zhī xié)

He lost a shoe while running.

⑦ 这件事听了叫人笑破了肚皮。（笑破—肚皮）（*笑—肚皮）

Zhè jiàn shì tīngle jiào rén xiàopòle dùpí. (xiàopò — dùpí) (*xiào — dùpí)

People cracked up with laughter when they heard it.

⑧ 小姑娘哭红了眼睛。（哭红—眼睛）（*哭—眼睛）

Xiǎo gūniang kūhóngle yǎnjing. (kūhóng — yǎnjing) (*kū — yǎnjing)

The girl cried her eyes red.

只有形容词和少数的动词可以作结果补语。

Only adjectives and a small subset of verbs can be resultative complements.

口语中常用的单音节形容词一般都可以作结果补语，部分口语中常用的双音节形容词也能作结果补语。

In spoken language, common single-syllable adjectives can, in general, be resultative complements and so can a number of common disyllabic adjectives.

① 我不小心摔碎了一个花瓶。

Wǒ bù xiǎoxīn shuāisuìle yí ge huāpíng.

I carelessly smashed a vase.

② 我打开墙上的灯，灯光照亮了房间里的一切，什么都看得清清楚楚。

Wǒ dǎkāi qiáng shang de dēng, dēngguāng zhàoliàngle fángjiān li de yíqiè, shénme dōu kàn de qīngqīngchǔchǔ.

I turned the light on the wall on and it lit up the whole room so I could see everything clearly.

③ 我不喜欢黄色，就把衣服染蓝了。

Wǒ bù xǐhuan huángsè, jiù bǎ yīfu rǎnlán le.

I don't like yellow so I dyed the clothes blue.

④ 这次考试，十道题我做对了八道，做错了两道。

Zhè cì kǎoshì, shí dào tí wǒ zuòduìle bā dào, zuòcuòle liǎng dào.

On this test, I answered eight of the ten questions correctly, and two incorrectly.

⑤ 这条裤子你买短了，换一条长的吧。

Zhè tiáo kùzi nǐ mǎiduǎn le, huàn yì tiáo cháng de ba.

The trousers you bought are small, why don't you exchange them for a longer pair?

⑥ 衣服洗了几次，颜色变浅了。

Yīfu xǐle jǐ cì, yánsè biànqiǎn le.

These clothes have been washed a few times and the color has faded.

⑦ 你听清楚了，同意以后就不能变了。

Nǐ tīng qīngchu le, tóngyì yǐhòu jiù bù néng biàn le.

Now listen clearly; once you've agreed, you can't change.

⑧ 第一次考试，题很难，我们做错了很多，后来老师把题改简单了，我们都做对了。

Dì-yī cì kǎoshì, tí hěn nán, wǒmen zuòcuòle hěn duō, hòulái lǎoshī bǎ tí gǎi jiǎndān le, wǒmen dōu zuòduì le.

On the first test, the questions were difficult and we got a lot of them wrong; afterwards, the teacher made them easier and we got them right.

⑨ 你把事情想复杂了，其实我要求你做的事很容易。

Nǐ bǎ shìqing xiǎng fùzá le, qíshí wǒ yāoqiú nǐ zuò de shì hěn róngyì.

You're making things too complicated; actually what I'm asking you to do is quite simple.

学习汉语的人，平时学习、阅读或者听中国人说话时，要留心哪个动词后边用哪个动词作结果补语。初学者，要把动词和后边的结果补语当作一个整体来学来记。

Usually, when students study, read or listen to Chinese speech, they need to pay attention to which verb has which verb after it as a resultative complement. Beginners should treat the verb and the following complement as a combination to be learned.

动词可以作结果补语的比较少，常见的有“见、成、懂、走、跑、哭、笑、住、掉、着、倒、翻、作、为、死、透、丢、在、给”等。

Relatively few verbs can act as resultative complements; the most frequent include the following:“jiàn, chéng, dǒng, zǒu, pǎo, kū, xiào, zhù, diào, zháo, dǎo, fān, zuò, wéi, sǐ, tòu, diū, zài, gěi”.

⑩ 你听见有人敲门吗?

Nǐ tīngjiàn yǒu rén qiāo mén ma?

Do you hear someone knocking at the door?

⑪ 他累哭了。

Tā lèikū le.

He's crying from exhaustion.

⑫ 他讲的故事很有意思，把我们都逗笑了。

Tā jiǎng de gùshì hěn yǒu yìsi, bǎ wǒmen dōu dòuxiào le.

The story he told was very interesting; it made us all laugh.

⑬ 请你把这本书交给小张。

Qǐng nǐ bǎ zhè běn shū jiāogěi Xiǎo Zhāng.

Please give this book to Xiao Zhang.

动词作结果补语不表示动作者或者动作所涉及的人的主动的动作，而是表示由前面的动作引起的一个被动的动作。如：

Verbs that act as resultative complements do not express the intentional actions of agents or of people involved with the action; rather, they express the results of some action expressed by the initial verb. For example:

⑭ 他的话把妹妹说哭了。

Tā de huà bǎ mèimei shuōkū le.

What he said made his younger sister cry.

妹妹不是自己想哭、主动哭，而是“被他说”哭了。

It is not that the younger sister is responsible for the crying; she is crying because of what someone else did.

⑮ 你说话不注意，把客人都气走了。

Nǐ shuō huà bú zhùyì, bǎ kèren dōu qìzǒu le.

You spoke carelessly and upset the guest so much [he/she] left.

不是客人想走，而是因为“你说的话”使“客人气”，结果“客人都走了”。再如：

It is not that the guest wanted to leave; it was what you said that made the guest leave. Other examples:

⑯ 我把桌子上的东西碰掉了。

Wǒ bǎ zhuōzi shang de dōngxi pèngdiào le.

I knocked the things off the table.

⑰ 我不小心把钥匙弄丢了。

Wǒ bù xiǎoxīn bǎ yàoshi nòngdiū le.

I carelessly misplaced the keys.

⑱ 你怎么把他推倒了？

Nǐ zěnme bǎ tā tuīdǎo le?

How come you pushed him over?

⑲ 他非常善良，连蚂蚁都不忍心踩死。

Tā fēicháng shànliáng, lián mǎyǐ dōu bù rěnxīn cǎisǐ.

He's very kind; he's so soft-hearted that he won't even step on an ant.

有些动词作结果补语时，词汇意义有所改变。现将常用的列举如下：

Some verbs change their senses when they are used as resultative complements. The more common ones are listed below:

4.1 “见”
“Jiàn”

“见”的基本意义是“看见”，即“看”有结果。作结果补语时，不限于表示“看”有结果，还可以表示听觉器官“听”、嗅觉器官“闻”有结果。如：

The basic sense of “jiàn” is the outcome of “looking”, that is “perceiving”, as in “kànjiàn (see)”. As a complement, it is not limited to vision; it can also express the outcome of “hearing” or “smelling”. For example:

① 孩子们看见我来了，都非常高兴。

Háizimen kànjiàn wǒ lái le, dōu fēicháng gāoxìng.

When the children saw me coming, they were all very happy.

② 这种物体发出的声音太小，我听了半天也没听见。

Zhè zhǒng wùtǐ fāchu de shēngyīn tài xiǎo, wǒ tīngle bàntiān yě méi tīngjiàn.

The sound this object makes is too soft; I listened for a long time and still didn't hear it.

③ 一进门我就闻见一股香味。

Yí jìn mén wǒ jiù wénjiàn yì gǔ xiāngwèi.

As soon as I went through the door, I caught a whiff of perfume.

“见”还可以在“遇、碰、梦”等动词之后作结果补语。如：

“Jiàn” can also act as a resultative complement after other verbs such as “yù (meet)” “pèng (bump into)” and “mèng (to dream)”. For example:

④ 你遇见老刘告诉他一声，今晚在家里等我。

Nǐ yùjiàn Lǎo Liú gàosu tā yì shēng, jīnwǎn zài jiā li děng wǒ.

When you see Lao Liu, tell him to wait for me at home this evening.

⑤ 昨天开会，碰见了几个小时候的朋友。

Zuótiān kāi huì, pèngjiànle jǐ ge xiǎo shíhou de péngyou.

At the meeting yesterday, I ran into some friends from my youth.

⑥ 我昨天梦见了我的一个老同学。

Wǒ zuótiān mèngjiànle wǒ de yí ge lǎo tóngxué.

Yesterday I dreamed of a former classmate of mine.

4.2 "住"

"Zhù"

"住"的基本意义是"居住"。作结果补语时，表示通过动作使人或事物的位置固定起来。

The basic sense of "zhù" is "to live". As a complement, it has the sense of someone or something ending up in a fixed or stationary position as the result of an action.

① 她听了我的话立刻站住了。

Tā tīngle wǒde huà lìkè zhànzhù le.

When she heard me, she immediately stood still.

② 汽车在我面前突然停住了，我吓了一跳。

Qìchē zài wǒ miànqián tūrán tíngzhù le, wǒ xiàle yí tiào.

The car in front suddenly came to a stop, which gave me such a fright.

③ 分别的时候，我紧紧握住老李的手，跟他说"再见"。

Fēnbié de shíhou, wǒ jǐnjǐn wòzhù Lǎo Lǐ de shǒu, gēn tā shuō "zàijiàn".

When we parted, I grasped Lao Li's hand tightly and said "goodbye" to him.

④ 窗户外有一棵大树，挡住了外面的阳光，屋子里很暗。

Chuānghu wài yǒu yì kē dàshù, dǎngzhùle wàimiàn de yángguāng, wūzi li hěn àn.

There was a large tree outside the window which blocked the sun so the room was quite dark.

⑤ 这些生词我记住了，明天考试没有问题。

Zhèxiē shēngcí wǒ jìzhù le, míngtiān kǎoshì méiyǒu wèntí.

I've learned this vocabulary; tomorrow's test won't be a problem.

⑥ 蜘蛛网上粘住了好几个小虫子。

Zhīzhūwǎng shang zhānzhùle hǎojǐ ge xiǎo chóngzi.

The spiderweb had lots of little insects stuck in it.

⑦ 你把犯人看住了，别让他跑了，我马上就回来。

Nǐ bǎ fànrén kānzhù le, bié ràng tā pǎo le, wǒ mǎshàng jiù huílai.

Keep an eye on the prisoner; don't let him run off; I'll be right back.

⑧ 张小姐让那个小伙子迷住了，虽然她根本不了解他，可还是跟他走了。

Zhāng xiǎojiě ràng nàge xiǎohuǒzi mízhù le, suīrán tā gēnběn bù liǎojiě tā, kě háishì gēn tā zǒu le.

Miss Zhang was infatuated by that young fellow; she left with him even though she didn't know much about him.

⑨ 这个世界的诱惑太多，如果我们没有一个清醒的头脑，就可能会被假象迷惑住。

Zhège shìjiè de yòuhuò tài duō, rúguǒ wǒmen méiyǒu yí ge qīngxǐng de tóunǎo, jiù kěnéng huì bèi jiǎxiàng míhuòzhù.

The world is too full of temptations; if we don't keep a clear head, we're likely to be seduced by appearances.

⑩ 咱们可别叫她给吓住啊，你该做什么就做什么。

Zánmen kě bié jiào tā gěi xiàzhù a, nǐ gāi zuò shénme jiù zuò shénme.

We really mustn't be frightened by her; do whatever should be done.

4.3 “着”

“Zháo”

（1）表示动作达到了目的。

Expressing achievement of the verbal action.

① 你说的那本书我借着了。

Nǐ shuō de nà běn shū wǒ jièzhao le.

I managed to borrow the book you were talking about.

② 这个谜语他没猜着。

Zhège míyǔ tā méi cāizháo.

He didn't guess the riddle.

③ 那本书我没找着。

Nà běn shū wǒ méi zhǎozháo.

I haven't found the book.

④ 孩子看着看着书睡着了。

Háizi kànzhe kànzhe shū shuìzháo le.

The child was reading the book and fell asleep.

这个意思的"着"用于否定情况（前面有"没"）时，要重读；用于肯定情况时，可以轻读，但是"睡着"的"着"要重读。

When used in the negative (with "méi" before the verb), "zháo" is fully stressed. When used affirmatively, it is unstressed, though in the case of "shuìzháo", it is stressed even in the positive.

（2）用在某些动词或形容词后，表示动作或某种情况对人或事物产生了不良后果。

Used after certain verbs or adjectives, "zháo" indicates that the action or the particular situation has negative consequences.

⑤ 这个孩子穿得太少，冻着了。（因"冻"而病）

Zhège háizi chuān de tài shǎo, dòngzhao le.

This child didn't wear enough clothes and got really cold.

⑥ 你们休息一会儿，小心别累着。（因"累"而对身体有不良影响）

Nǐmen xiūxi yíhuìr, xiǎoxīn bié lèizhao.

Take a short rest; be careful not to exhaust yourself.

⑦ 哎哟，磕着我了。

Āiyō, kēzhao wǒ le.

Ouch, I got bonked.

此类动词还有“凉、捂、碰、吓、硌、挤”等。“吓着了、硌着了、挤着了”等的“着（zháo）”，北京人有时读重音。

This type may include verbs such as the following: “liáng (cool), wǔ (muffle), pèng (hit), xià (frighten), gè (crush), jǐ (jostle)”. Of this set, Beijing speakers sometimes stress the complement “zháo” in the phrases “xiàzháole, gèzháole, kēzháole” and “jǐzháole”.

（3）表示“燃烧”。一般读重音。

When “zháo” means “to catch fire”, it is generally stressed.

⑧ 他划着了火柴，点上了灯。

Tā huázháole huǒchái, diǎnshangle dēng.

He struck a match and lit the lamp.

⑨ 他把邻居的房子用汽油点着了，犯了罪。

Tā bǎ línjū de fángzi yòng qìyóu diǎnzháo le, fànle zuì.

He set fire to the neighbor’s house with gasoline, committing a crime.

（4）表示“有资格、有责任”。要读重音，一般用可能补语的形式。

“Zháo” may also indicate qualification or responsibility. If so, it is stressed, and usually in the potential complement.

⑩ 你不是我的老师，你管不着！

Nǐ bú shì wǒ de lǎoshī, nǐ guǎn bu zháo!

You’re not my teacher; it’s none of your business!

⑪ 你也不是我的上级，批评不着我！

Nǐ yě bú shì wǒ de shàngjí, pīpíng bu zháo wǒ!

You’re not my supervisor; you shouldn’t be criticizing me!

（5）表示“有价值、值得”。要重读。

“Zháo” may also indicate that something is valuable, worthwhile; usually stressed.

⑫ 他这个朋友我可算交着了，对我的帮助太大了。

Tā zhège péngyou wǒ kě suàn jiāozháo le, duì wǒ de bāngzhù tài dà le.

I really feel I've made a friend; he's been a great help to me.

⑬ 这辆车你可买着了，真值。

Zhè liàng chē nǐ kě mǎizháo le, zhēn zhí.

This car's really a good buy for you — well worth it.

4.4 "好"
"Hǎo"

（1）"好"的基本意义是"使人满意"，与"坏"相对。

The basic sense of "hǎo (good)" as a complement is "to someone's satisfaction"; it is in contrast to "huài (bad)".

① 这个孩子以前偷东西，最近几年变好了。

Zhège háizi yǐqián tōu dōngxi, zuìjìn jǐ nián biànhǎo le.

This child used to steal, but in recent years, he's gone straight.

（2）作结果补语时，表示动作完成，而且常有为下一个动作做好了准备的意思。

When it's used as a resultative complement, it indicates that the action is completed; moreover, it often suggests preparations are completed for the next action.

② 饭做好了，开饭了。

Fàn zuòhǎo le, kāi fàn le.

The food's ready, so we can begin.

③ 爸爸把电脑修理好了，你可以用了。

Bàba bǎ diànnǎo xiūlǐ hǎo le, nǐ kěyǐ yòng le.

Dad's repaired the computer; go ahead and use it.

④ 参加舞会的衣服妈妈给你改好了，晚上可以穿了。

Cānjiā wǔhuì de yīfu māma gěi nǐ gǎihǎo le, wǎnshang kěyǐ chuān le.

Mum has altered your party clothes; you can wear them this evening.

⑤ 这篇文章写好了，交给你吧。

Zhè piān wénzhāng xiěhǎo le, jiāogěi nǐ ba.

I've finished the article; here's a copy for you.

⑥ 考试准备好了，可以睡觉了。

Kǎoshì zhǔnbèi hǎo le, kěyǐ shuì jiào le.

I've prepared for the test, so I can sleep.

⑦ 我跟小李约好了，明天一起看电影。

Wǒ gēn Xiǎo Lǐ yuēhǎo le, míngtiān yìqǐ kàn diànyǐng.

I made a date with Xiao Li for us to see a movie together tomorrow.

⑧ 咱们说好了，明年去中国学中文，你可不能改主意。

Zánmen shuōhǎo le, míngnián qù Zhōngguó xué Zhōngwén, nǐ kě bù néng gǎi zhǔyi.

We're all set; you mustn't change your mind about going to China to study Chinese next year.

4.5 "掉"
"Diào"

（1）表示"掉落"，这是"掉"的基本意义。

The basic sense of "diào" is "drop" or "fall".

① 小心点儿，别把她的博士帽碰掉了。

Xiǎoxīn diǎnr, bié bǎ tāde bóshìmào pèngdiào le.

Careful, don't knock her doctoral cap off.

② 忽然刮起一阵风，把树叶吹掉了很多。

Hūrán guāqi yí zhèn fēng, bǎ shùyè chuīdiàole hěn duō.

There was a sudden gust of wind which blew down a lot of leaves.

（2）表示"失去""消失"。

Signifies "dispersion" or "away".

③ 这件衣服太小了，扔掉吧。

Zhè jiàn yīfu tài xiǎo le, rēngdiào ba.

This piece of clothing is too small, let's throw it away.

④ 这一段话是多余的，删掉吧。

Zhè yí duàn huà shì duōyú de, shāndiào ba.

This paragraph is unnecessary; let's delete it.

⑤ 抓到他很不容易，你怎么让他跑掉了？

Zhuādào tā hěn bù róngyì, nǐ zěnme ràng tā pǎodiào le?

He's not easy to catch; how come you let him get away?

⑥ 很久没下雨了，坑里的水都蒸发掉了。

Hěn jiǔ méi xià yǔ le, kēng li de shuǐ dōu zhēngfā diào le.

It hasn't rained for ages; the water in the pit has completely evaporated.

⑦ 你要改掉这些坏习惯，身体才会好起来。

Nǐ yào gǎidiào zhèxiē huài xíguàn, shēntǐ cái huì hǎo qilai.

You won't get well until you get rid of these bad habits.

⑧ 这件衣服太长，去掉三寸正好。

Zhè jiàn yīfu tài cháng, qùdiào sān cùn zhènghǎo.

This item of clothing is too long; take off three inches and it'll be just right.

⑨ 小时候的事，我差不多都忘掉了，就是这件事还记得很清楚。

Xiǎo shíhou de shì, wǒ chàbuduō dōu wàngdiào le, jiùshì zhè jiàn shì hái jì de hěn qīngchu.

I've forgotten almost everything from when I was young, except for this, which I still remember quite clearly.

⑩ 老李不愿意听你们乱说，已经走掉了。

Lǎo Lǐ bú yuànyì tīng nǐmen luànshuō, yǐjīng zǒudiào le.

Lao Li didn't want to listen to your nonsense; he's already gone off.

⑪ 青菜买来几天没吃，都烂掉了。

Qīngcài mǎilai jǐ tiān méi chī, dōu làndiào le.

The vegetables haven't been eaten and it's been several days since they were bought; they've rotted.

⑫ 文章太长了，去掉这段吧。

Wénzhāng tài cháng le, qùdiào zhè duàn ba.

The article's too long; why don't you get rid of this part?

北方人常常在动词后用“了”表示“失去”“消失”的意思，上述例子中如果“掉”后面有“了”，“掉”一般都可以删去；南方人用“掉”较多。有些南方方言，“掉”可以用在很多动词、形容词后，比如“这个人疯掉了”“树叶黄掉了”等等。

Northern speakers often put “le” after the verb to express “dispersion” or “away”, so in the previous examples, if “diào” is followed by a “le”, then generally “diào” can be omitted. Southern speakers make greater use of “diào”. In some Southern dialects, “diào” can be used with lots of different verbs and adjectives. For example: “Zhège rén fēngdiào le (This person is insane)” “Shùyè huángdiào le (The leaves have turned yellow)”.

4.6 “在”
“Zài”

（1）表示通过动作使人或事物处于某个处所，后边一定要有处所宾语。

“Zài” introduces the location of something or someone following an action; it is always followed by a location or situation.

① 我坐在五排十一号。

Wǒ zuòzài wǔ pái shíyī hào.

I'm seated in the 11st seat in the 5th row.

② 你们把生词抄在本子上。

Nǐmen bǎ shēngcí chāozài běnzi shang.

Copy the vocabulary into your notebook.

③ 小王站在我面前。

Xiǎo Wáng zhànzài wǒ miànqián.

Xiao Wang is standing in front of me.

④ 问题出在计划性不强上。

Wèntí chūzài jìhuàxìng bù qiáng shang.

The problems stem from lack of good planning.

（2）表示事情发生的时间。

"Zài" can also indicate the time of an event.

⑤ 这个故事发生在古代。

Zhège gùshi fāshēng zài gǔdài.

This story took place in ancient times.

⑥ 时间定在明天上午八点。

Shíjiān dìngzài míngtiān shàngwǔ bā diǎn.

The time's fixed for 8 a.m. tomorrow.

有些语法书把"在、到、给"等归入介词短语作补语。这三个词本来也是动词。如：

Some grammar books treat "zài, dào, gěi" as prepositions that form complement phrases. All three derive from full verbs. For example:

⑦ 小黄在家吗？

Xiǎo Huáng zài jiā ma?

Is Xiao Huang at home?

⑧ 我今天早上刚到。

Wǒ jīntiān zǎoshang gāng dào.

I just arrived this morning.

⑨ 你把这本书给王朋。

Nǐ bǎ zhè běn shū gěi Wáng Péng.

Give this book to Wang Peng.

这三个动词放在动词后作补语，意思没有变。如：

When these verbs appear as complement phrases after other verbs, they keep their verbal senses. For example:

⑩ 你坐在椅子上。（你—坐，你—在椅子上）

Nǐ zuòzài yǐzi shang. (nǐ — zuò, nǐ — zài yǐzi shang)

⑪ 你把他送到机场。（你—送他，他—到机场）

Nǐ bǎ tā sòngdào jīchǎng. (nǐ — sòng tā, tā — dào jīchǎng)

⑫ 你把这本书交给王朋。（你交—这本书，这本书—给王朋）

Nǐ bǎ zhè běn shū jiāogěi Wáng Péng. (nǐ jiāo — zhè běn shū, zhè běn shū — gěi Wáng Péng)

我们把“在、到、给”归入结果补语，而不是像某些语法著作那样归入介词结构作补语，是因为在结构上，它们和其他结果补语一样，与前面的动词结合得很紧，如果有“了”，要放在“在、到、给”的后边。如：

Unlike other authors, we classify “zài, dào, gěi” as resultative complements rather than prepositional phrase complements. This is mainly because they are structurally like resultative complements in being tightly bound to the preceding verb; if “le” is present, it is placed after them. For example:

⑬ 她听了这句话，一屁股坐在了地上。

Tā tīngle zhè jù huà, yí pìgu zuòzàile dìshang.

When she heard the sentence, she sat on her bottom on the ground.

⑭ 他早就把小李接到了这里。

Tā zǎo jiù bǎ Xiǎo Lǐ jiēdàole zhèli.

He had long ago welcomed Xiao Li here.

⑮ 我已经把那本书交给了你哥哥。

Wǒ yǐjīng bǎ nà běn shū jiāogěile nǐ gēge.

I already gave the book to your older brother.

而介词后一般是不用“了”的。

Normally, “le” does not appear after prepositions.

从语音停顿上说，动词与“在、到、给”连在一起，停顿在“在、到、给”的后边，而不是“在、到、给”与后边的名词宾语连在一起，在动词后停顿。

Moreover, post-verbal “zài” “dào” and “gěi” may be followed by a pause, which indicates that they form a constituent with the preceding verb rather than the following noun phrase.

在学生学了四五个能带结果补语的动词（如“写、做、说、吃”）和可以作结果补语的形容词和动词（如“错、对、完”）后再教结果补语，否则学生很难练习，很难掌握。

Students should be taught about resultative complements after they have learned four or five suitable verbs [such as “xiě (write), zuò (do, make), shuō (say)” and “chī (eat)”] and a similar number of adjectives or verbs that can act as complements [such as “cuò (be mistaken), duì (be correct)” and “wán (finish)”] . Otherwise, it would be difficult to practice them and hard for students to master them.

一般先教补语说明动词的，因为在日常生活中最早需要。比如“做完、吃完、听懂、学会”等。而且这类补语，学生比较容易理解，也容易掌握。

It is generally best to begin with complements that refine the verbal sense, since these are common and needed from the start. For example: “zuòwán (finish doing), chīwán (finish eating), tīngdǒng (understand by hearing), xuéhuì (learn)” and so on. Complements such as these are easier for students to deal with and master.

在教补语描写动作的受事或动作者时，应该让学生弄清楚其间的语义关系，这对学生理解和掌握此类补语非常重要。

When teaching how a complement involves the patient (“recipient”) or agent of the action, it is very important that the sense of these semantic roles is made quite clear to students.

第三章 Chapter 3

虽然趋向补语只由十几个趋向动词构成，但其意义、结构和用法都十分复杂。在本章我们先概括地介绍一下趋向补语意义的分类、结构特点等等，然后再对所有的趋向补语逐一进行分析说明。

Although directional complements consist of a dozen verbs of direction, their senses, constructions, and usages present a great deal of complexity. In this chapter, we will start by summarizing the different senses and the special types of construction characteristic of directional complements. Afterwards, we will go on to offer a more detailed analysis of each of them.

1. 什么是趋向补语?

What are directional complements?

有一类动词表示动作的方向，叫趋向动词。趋向动词有“来、去、上、下、进、出、回、过、起、开、到”。趋向动词的趋向意义如下：“来”表示朝向说话人，“去”表示离开说话人向另一个处所；“上”表示由低向高，“下”表示由高向低；“进”表示由外面向处所里面移动；“出”表示由处所里面向外面移动；“回”由另一处到原处（出发地、家乡、祖国等）；“过”表示经过；“起”表示由低向高；“开”表示离开；“到”表示到达。

Directional verbs are those verbs that express direction, i.e., “lái, qù, shàng, xià, jìn, chū, huí, guò, qǐ, kāi, dào”. They have the following senses: lái “direction towards the speaker”; qù “direction away from the speaker”; shàng “direction upwards”; xià “direction downwards”; jìn “movement from outside to inside”, chū “movement from inside to outside”; huí “direction back to original place (to the point of origin, to one’s birthplace, to one’s country, etc.)”; guò “direction past”; qǐ “direction upwards”; kāi “away from”; and dào “arrive at, reach”.

趋向动词可以用在动词和形容词后作补语，叫趋向补语。

Directional verbs can follow verbs and adjectives as complements; in such cases, they are called “directional complements”.

趋向动词单独作补语时叫简单趋向补语；由“来、去”和“上、下、进、出、回、过、起、开、到”结合在一起构成的“上来、上去、下来、下去”等补语，叫复合趋向补语。 趋向补语列表如下：

Directional complements made up of single directional verbs are called "simple directional complements". Directional complements made up of combinations of the directional verbs "shàng, xià, jìn, chū, huí, guò, qǐ, kāi", and "dào" plus "lái" or "qù" are called "compound directional complements", such as "shànglai, shàngqu, xiàlai, xiàqu", etc. The following table shows the possibilities for both types:

简单趋向补语 simple directional complements	来	去	上	下	进	出	回	过	起	开	到
复合趋向补语 compound directional complements			上来	下来	进来	出来	回来	过来	起来	开来	到……来
			上去	下去	进去	出去	回去	过去	—	开去	到……去

为了称说方便，我们把“上、下、进、出、回、过、起、开、到”叫作“上”类字，把趋向补语中“上、上来、上去”叫“上”组，“出、出来、出去”叫“出”组等。在现代汉语中，“起”组只有“起”和“起来”，没有“*起去”；“到……来”“到……去”作补语时，中间一定要有处所词语。

For convenience, we label each group by the verbs on the top row: "shàng, xià, jìn, chū, huí, guò, qǐ, kāi, dào", which are collectively called the "shàng" etc. Then "shàng, shànglai, shàngqu" will be called the "shàng" group; "chū, chūlai, chūqu" will be called the "chū" group; and so on. In modern Mandarin, the "qǐ" group consists of "qǐ" and "qǐlai", but there is no "*qǐqu". The complements "dào……lai" or "dào……qu" require an intervening place word (a destination).

2. 趋向补语的意义分类

The senses of directional complements

趋向补语所表示的也是一种动作的结果，是方向的结果，但比一般的动词或形容词作结果补语，无论是在意义方面还是在结构方面都更为复杂。趋向补语表示的意义可以分为三大类：趋向意义、结果意义和状态意义。

Directional complements also express a type of result — one involving direction or orientation. But directional complements, both in terms of their senses and their structures, are more complicated than complements composed of ordinary verbs or adjectives. We can distinguish three types of sense for directional complements: directional, resultative and stative.

2.1 趋向意义 Directional sense

趋向补语的趋向意义指方向意义，也就是趋向动词本身的意义。如"上"表示"由低到高"，"下"表示"由高到低"等。这里所谓"趋向意义"，实际上也是一种结果，即表示通过某个动作，结果使动作者或者动作所涉及的事物在方向方面发生的变化。如"他走上楼"——通过"走"，结果使"他从楼下到楼上"，"我拿出来一本书"——通过"拿"，结果使"一本书出来"。

The directional sense of complements obviously involves direction, which is to say that the complements retain their basic verbal meanings of "up", "down" and so on. What we are calling "directional sense" is actually also a type of result, in the sense that the verbal action leads to a shift in the orientation of the actor or of the thing affected by the action. For example, in "Tā zǒushang lóu (He walks upstairs)", "zǒu (walking)" results in "tā cóng lóuxià dào lóushàng (he went from downstairs to upstairs)"; in "Wǒ ná chulai yì běn shū (I take out a book)", "ná (taking)" results in "yì běn shū chūlai (a book coming out)".

"来""去"无论作简单趋向补语，还是由它们构成复合趋向补语，都和参照点有关系。参照点主要指说话人（有时是正在叙述的事物或处所）所在的位置。"来"表示朝说话人的方向移动，"去"表示朝背离说话人的方向移动。这一点在后面第二节"趋向补语分述"中将会详细说明。

"Lái" and "qù" can appear as simple directional complements or as a part of compound directional complements. In both cases, they indicate the speaker's perspective: "lái", towards the speaker; "qù", away from the speaker. This point is discussed at further length in the second section "Directional cmplements in detail".

所有的趋向补语都有趋向意义，详见后面的分述。有的趋向补语有不止一个趋向意义，如“上”组（见第83—85页）和“下”组（见第108—110页）。

Directional complements all have directional senses, as will be illustrated in later section. Some directional complements, such as those in the “shàng” group (see pp. 83–85) and “xià” group (see pp. 108–110), have more than one sense.

表示趋向意义的补语，在意义上有的与主语（动作者）有关系，有的与宾语（动作的受事）有关系。如：

Complements that have directional senses may relate, semantically, to the subject (the actor) or to object (the patient). For example:

① 小明从外面跑进来。（小明—跑，小明—进来）
Xiǎomíng cóng wàimiàn pǎo jinlai. (Xiǎomíng — pǎo, Xiǎomíng — jìnlai)
Xiaoming runs in from outside.

② 小明从书包里拿出一本书来。（小明—拿，一本书—出来）
Xiǎomíng cóng shūbāo li náchū yì běn shū lai. (Xiǎomíng — ná, yì běn shū — chūlai)
Xiaoming takes a book out of his schoolbag.

2.2 结果意义 Resultative sense

趋向补语的结果意义表示动作的结果，与方向无关。如“闭上眼睛”的“上”表示“接触”的意思，“撕下一张纸”中的“下”表示“分离”的意思等等。

Directional complements with resultative senses express the result of action rather than direction. For example, the “shàng” of “bìshang yǎnjing (close the eyes)” indicates “coming together”; the “xià” of “sīxia yì zhāng zhǐ (tear out a sheet of paper)” indicates “separation”; and so on.

很多趋向补语有不止一个结果意义，如“上”组、“下”组、“起”组、“开”组等，详见后面的分述。

A lot of directional complements, in the “shàng” “xià” “qǐ” and “kāi” groups for example, have more than one resultative sense, as will be shown in later section.

趋向补语的结果意义又可分为基本结果意义和非基本结果意义。基本结果意义与其趋向意义联系紧密，非基本结果意义与其趋向意义的联系没有那么紧密。如“上”的趋向意义（二）表示“向前面的目标移动”：

Directional complements with resultative senses can also be divided into those with basic resultative senses and those with non-basic. The basic resultative senses are closely related to the directional senses; the non-basic resultative senses are not so closely related. For example, the 2nd directional sense of “shàng” indicates “movement forward towards a goal”:

[(X)] ←— ○ (X)[①]

其基本结果意义表示“接触、附着”：

While its basic resultative sense expresses contact or attachment:

[(X)] ←— ○ (X)

由上面两个图形可以看出，“上”的基本结果意义和趋向意义（二）之间关系密切。

These two diagrams show that the basic resultative sense of “shàng” has a close relationship to its 2nd directional sense.

“下”则相反，趋向意义（二）是“退离前面的目标”：

“Xià” is the opposite: the 2nd directional sense is “distance from a prior position reference”:

[(X)] ○ —→ (X)

基本结果意义是“分离”：

The sense of the basic resultatives is “separation”:

---

① “□”表示某一特定场所，“x”表示参照点，“（x）”表示可能的参照点，“○”表示移动的物体，“→”表示移动的方向。

“□” indicates a specific place, “x” indicates a point of reference, “(x)” indicates a possible point of reference, “○” indicates a moving object, and “→” indicates the direction of movement.

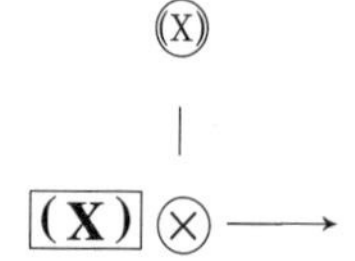

“上”还有其他几个结果意义，如：表示实现了预期目的或希望实现的目的（如：考上了大学、住上了新房）、表示成功地完成（如：这次考试，十道题我都答上了；学生太多，现在有的我还叫不上名儿），与趋向意义看不出有多少联系。

“Shàng” has other resultative senses. It can express the achievement of an anticipated or hoped for goal: “kǎoshangle dàxué (manage to pass the college entrance examination)” “zhùshangle xīnfáng (manage to move to a new house)”. It can express successful completion: “Zhè cì kǎoshì, shí dào tí wǒ dōu dáshang le (I managed to answer all ten questions on the exam)” “Xuésheng tài duō, xiànzài yǒude wǒ hái jiào bu shàng míngr (There are too many students; now I still can’t get some of the students’ names right)”. It is hard to perceive a close connection between these senses and the directional senses.

和结果补语一样，趋向补语的结果意义有的与动词有关系，有的和动作者或动作的受事有关系。比如“撕下一张纸来”，“下来”在意义上与动作的受事“纸”有关系；“他醒过来了”，“过来”与动作者“他”在意义上有关系；“十道题我都答上来了”，“上来”与动词“答”在意义上有关系（成功地完成“答”）。

Like resultative complements, the resultative sense of directional complements relates to the verb in some cases; but in other cases, it relates to the actor or patient. For instance, in “sīxià yì zhāng zhǐ lai (tear out a sheet of paper)”, the “xiàlai” relates semantically to the thing affected by the action “zhǐ” ; in “tā xǐng guolai le (He woke up)”, “guòlai” relates semantically to the actor “tā”; in “shí dào tí wǒ dōu dá shanglai le (I answered all ten questions correctly)”, “shànglai” relates semantically to the verb “dá” —“manage to answer successfully”.

2.3 状态意义[①]
Stative sense

趋向补语的状态意义也与动作的方向无关，主要表示状态的变化，如“唱起来”中的“起来”表示“由静态进入动态”或者“动作开始并继续”，“车停下来了”中的“下来”表示“由动态进入静态”等等。

The stative senses of directional complements are not connected to the directionality of the verb; instead, they express change of state. For example: in “chàng qilai (start to sing)”, “qǐlai” expresses “from rest to motion” or “verbal action beginning and continuing”; in “chē tíng xialai le (the car came to a stop)”, “xiàlai” indicates “from motion to rest”; and so on.

只有表示“由低到高”和“由高到低”的“上”组、“下”组、“起”组，以及“开”组有状态意义。

Only the “shàng” “xià” “qǐ” groups, which express “low to high” or “high to low”, and the “kāi” group, expressing “from rest to motion”, have stative senses.

2.4 特殊用法
Special usages

某些趋向补语表示的意义不属于以上三类，我们称为特殊用法。如“上”可以表示“达到”（你在北京住上半年，就能听懂中国人说话了）；用在表示伴随动作的动词后（你叫上小莉跟你一起去吧）等。

Those cases of directional complements other than the three just discussed are called special usages. “Shàng” for example, can express “arrival at”: “Nǐ zài Běijīng zhùshang bàn nián, jiù néng tīngdǒng Zhōngguórén shuō huà le (After you’ve lived in Beijing for a half year, you’ll be able to understand Chinese speech)”. It can also be

---

① 有的语法书将趋向补语的状态意义看作汉语的时体标志。关于汉语动词的时体问题，目前各语法著作的看法并不一致。而且，我们认为将“时体”引入教学只会增加学生的负担，而对他们学习汉语帮助不大。

Some grammars treat the stative senses of directional complements as tense-aspect markers. Current authors writing on grammatical issues disagree about the relevance of tense-aspect to Chinese. We feel that reference to tense and aspect would not help students in their study of Chinese and, in fact, would only add to their difficulties.

used after verbs that indicate “accompanying action”: “Nǐ jiàoshang Xiǎolì gēn nǐ yìqǐ qù ba (Get Xiaoli to go with you)”; and so on.

2.5 熟语 Idioms

如果“某个动词+某个趋向补语”已经凝结得很紧，像一个词一样，我们就作为“熟语”来处理。比如由“上”构成的熟语有“顾（得/不）上”“说得/不上”“谈得/不上”“犯得/不上”“豁上”等。用于熟语的趋向动词，可以结合的动词不多。熟语一般都可以在词典中查到。

In cases where a particular verb and a particular directional complement have congealed into a word-like unit, we treat the combination as idiomatic. Such idioms with “shàng” include “gù (de/bu) shàng (able to attend to or not)” “shuō de/bu shàng (able to talk about or not)” “tán de/bu shàng (can go so far as to say or not)” “fàn de/bu shàng (be worth it or not)” “huōshang (to risk or stake all)”. There are not a large number of idiomatic cases like these, and for the most part, they are listed in dictionaries.

看到上面这些分类，就可以知道趋向补语所表示的意义是非常复杂的。当你遇到某一个动趋短语（“动词+趋向补语”）时，一定要弄清楚这个趋向补语在这个短语中，表示的是哪一类和哪一个意义，才能正确地理解和运用它。

The various examples shown above make it clear that the semantics of directional complements are extremely complicated. When one encounters a directional verb phrase (that is, a verb plus a directional complement), it is crucial to identify the type and the sense of the complement before one can understand and use it properly.

3. 包含趋向补语的句子的结构 The composition of sentences containing directional complements

3.1 宾语的位置 The position of objects

我们用下面的公式说明在句子中趋向补语和宾语的位置。特别要注意处所词作宾语和一般名词作宾语位置的异同。

The following formulations show the relative position of directional complements and objects within a sentence. Note the similarities and differences of the position of place-word objects and common-noun objects.

（1）简单趋向补语和宾语的位置：

The relative position of simple directional complements and objects:

A. “来/去”作简单趋向补语：

“Lái /qù” as simple directional complements:

A1. （主语＋）动词＋处所词 / 一般名词＋来/去

(Subject +) verb + place word / common noun + lái/qù

① 上课了，同学们快进教室来。（趋向意义）

Shàng kè le, tóngxuémen kuài jìn jiàoshì lai.

It's time for class; quick, classmates, come on into the classroom. (directional sense)

② 妈妈慢慢上楼去了。（趋向意义）

Māma mànmàn shàng lóu qu le.

Mum slowly went upstairs. (directional sense)

③ 你别忘了，带一些钱来。（趋向意义）

Nǐ bié wàng le, dài yìxiē qián lai.

Don't forget, bring some money with you. (directional sense)

④ 你带一瓶水去。（趋向意义）

Nǐ dài yì píng shuǐ qu.

Take a bottle of water with you. (directional sense)

这一个句式既适用于处所词宾语，也适用于一般名词宾语，所以在教学中最好先教。

This pattern holds for both place-word objects and common-noun objects, so it is best to teach it first.

A2. （主语 +）动词 + 来/去+ 一般名词

(Subject +) verb + lái/qù + common noun

⑤ 他给我带来了一些钱。（趋向意义）

Tā gěi wǒ dàilaile yìxiē qián.

He brought some money for me. (directional sense)

⑥ 妈妈给女儿寄去了一些钱。（趋向意义）

Māma gěi nǚ' ér jìqule yìxiē qián.

Mum sent some money to her daughter. (directional sense)

⑦ 他爸爸吃不来南方菜。（结果意义）

Tā bàba chībulái nánfāngcài.

His dad isn't accustomed to southern food. (resultative sense)

⑧ 我买汽车花去了十万元，剩下的钱不多了。（结果意义）

Wǒ mǎi qìchē huāqule shíwàn yuán, shèngxia de qián bù duō le.

I spent 100,000 yuan buying a car; I don't have much money left over. (resultative sense)

宾语为处所词时，不能用于这个格式，如不能说：

When the object is a place word, it does not follow the same pattern. So the following are not acceptable:

⑨ * 上课了，同学们快进来教室。

* Shàng kè le, tóngxuémen kuài jìnlai jiàoshì.

⑩ * 你快回去家吧。

* Nǐ kuài huíqu jiā ba.

B. “上”类字作简单趋向补语：

The “shàng” etc. used as simple directional complements:

（主语 +）动词 + “上”类字 + 处所词/一般名词

(Subject +) verb + “shàng” etc. + place word / common noun

⑪ 他很快地走上楼。（趋向意义）

Tā hěn kuài de zǒushang lóu.

He walked upstairs in a hurry. (directional sense)

⑫ 上课了，学生很快地跑进教室。（趋向意义）

Shàng kè le, xuésheng hěn kuài de pǎojin jiàoshì.

It was time for class and the pupils quickly ran into the classroom. (directional sense)

⑬ 在黑板上写上你的名字。（结果意义）

Zài hēibǎn shang xiěshang nǐ de míngzi.

Write your name on the blackboard. (resultative sense)

⑭ 我从本子上撕下一张纸。（结果意义）

Wǒ cóng běnzi shang sīxia yì zhāng zhǐ.

I tore a sheet of paper out of the notebook. (resultative sense)

"上"类字作趋向补语，和结果补语一样，在句子中位置都是在宾语前，所以也有些语法著作或教材，把它们作为结果补语处理。但是我们认为趋向动词作补语时，所表示的结果意义和趋向意义有内在联系，所以都归入趋向补语是科学的。

Just as with resultative complements, the "shàng" etc. as directional complements appear before the objects, so some authors or teaching materials treat them as resultative complements. We feel that when the directional verbs as complements, there is a connection between the resultative and the directional senses, so it is reasonable that they be considered types of directional complements.

（2）复合趋向补语和宾语的位置：

The position of compound directional complements and objects:

C. （主语 +）动词+"上"类字+处所词/一般名词+来/去

(Subject +) verb + "shàng" etc. + place word / common noun + lái / qù

⑮ 上课了，我们走进教室去。（趋向意义）

Shàng kè le, wǒmen zǒujìn jiàoshì qu.

Time for class; let's go into the classroom. (directional sense)

⑯ 请给我搬上一把椅子来。（趋向意义）

Qǐng gěi wǒ bānshàng yì bǎ yǐzi lai.

Please bring a chair up here for me. (directional sense)

⑰ 你看出什么问题来了？（结果意义）

Nǐ kànchū shénme wèntí lai le?

What problems did you observe? (resultative sense)

⑱ 她从墙上摘下一张画儿来送给我。（结果意义）

Tā cóng qiáng shang zhāixià yì zhāng huàr lai sònggěi wǒ.

She plucked a picture off the wall and gave it to me. (resultative sense)

⑲ 这么紧张的时候，你怎么唱起歌来了？（状态意义）

Zhème jǐnzhāng de shíhou, nǐ zěnme chàngqǐ gē lai le?

How can you start singing at such a tense time? (stative sense)

这个句式既适用于宾语是处所词，也适用于宾语为一般名词，而且适用于趋向补语的各类意义，所以在教学中最好先教。

This pattern is used when the object is a place word as well as when it is an common noun. Since it is used with all meanings of directional complements, it is best to teach it early on.

D1. （主语 +）动词 + 复合趋向补语 + 一般名词

(Subject +) verb + compound directional complement + common noun

⑳ 老师从书包里拿出来一本书。（趋向意义）

Lǎoshī cóng shūbāo li ná chulai yì běn shū.

The teacher took a book out of the schoolbag. (directional sense)

㉑ 慢慢地，我也看出来问题了。（结果意义）

Mànmàn de, wǒ yě kàn chulai wèntí le.

Slowly does it — I've also detected a problem. (resultative sense)

D1不适用于宾语为处所词的句子。例如：

The D1 pattern is not used for sentences with place-word objects, such as the following:

㉒ ＊学生纷纷走出来教室。

＊ Xuésheng fēnfēn zǒu chulai jiàoshì.

D2. （主语＋）动词＋一般名词＋复合趋向补语

(Subject +) verb + common noun + compound directional complement

㉓ 他从书包里拿了一本书出来。（趋向意义）

Tā cóng shūbāo li nále yì běn shū chulai.

He took a book out of his schoolbag. (directional sense)

D2较少使用，可以不教。

The D2 pattern is rare and need not be taught.

3.2 构成可能补语的问题 About the formation of potential complements

多数动词和趋向补语之间加上“得/不”可以构成可能补语[①]。在后面的分述中，对于可以构成可能补语的，一般不特别说明。对于那些不能构成可能补语或只有可能补语用法的，会适当加以说明。如要详细了解某一个动词和某一个趋向补语是否可以构成可能补语，可以查看刘月华主编的《趋向补语通释》[②]。

Most verbs form potential complements by inserting “de” or “bu” between verbs and directional complements. In the following section, we will not generally go into detail about the formation of potential complements. Our remarks will be limited to those complements which never appear in the potential or which only appear in the

---

① 这里说的不是可能补语的历史。

This is not intended to be a history of the potential complement.

② 刘月华（1998）《趋向补语通释》，北京：北京语言文化大学出版社。

Liu Yuehua. 1998. *A Complete Explanation of Directional Complements.* Beijing: Beijing Language and Culture University Press.

potential. Readers who want a detailed explanation of whether a particular verb and complement can form a potential construction should consult *A Complete Explanation of Directional Complements* by Liu Yuehua.

3.3 关于相应的简单趋向补语和复合趋向补语的用法问题 Overlap between simple and compound directional complements

“上”类字可以作趋向补语，后面加上“来/去”也可以作趋向补语，而且一般意义相同。比如“撕下一张纸”和“撕下一张纸来”，意思一样。那么相应的简单趋向补语和复合趋向补语用法是否完全相同呢？回答不完全是肯定的。当“动词+趋向补语”位于句末时，一般用复合趋向补语（“上”的结果意义除外）；当趋向补语后边有宾语时，简单趋向补语和复合趋向补语都可以用。

Directional complements with just the “shàng” etc. also permit the addition of “lái” or “qù” with little change in meaning. For example: “sīxia yì zhāng zhǐ” and “sīxià yì zhāng zhǐ lai” have more or less the same meaning — tear off a sheet of paper. Are these two cases the simple and the compound identical in meaning? The answer is not necessarily. When the verb + directional complement comes at the foot of the sentence, the compound form tends to be used (and the resultative sense of “shàng” alone is exceptional); but when the directional complement is followed by an object, either the simple or the compound directional complement can be used.

① 你快上去吧，大家都在等你。
Nǐ kuài shàngqu ba, dàjiā dōu zài děng nǐ.
Hurry upstairs, everyone's waiting for you.

* 你快上吧，大家都在等你。
* Nǐ kuài shàng ba, dàjiā dōu zài děng nǐ.

她已经上楼去了。
Tā yǐjīng shàng lóu qu le.
She's already gone upstairs.

她很快跑上楼去。
Tā hěn kuài pǎoshàng lóu qu.
She ran upstairs very quickly.

把眼睛闭上！

Bǎ yǎnjing bìshang!

Close your eyes!

② 你把画儿摘下来吧。

Nǐ bǎ huàr zhāi xialai ba.

Take the picture down, okay?

* 你把画儿摘下吧。

* Nǐ bǎ huàr zhāixia ba.

他很快地摘下一张画儿来。

Tā hěn kuài de zhāixià yì zhāng huàr lai.

He quickly removed a picture.

他很快地摘下来一张画儿。

Tā hěn kuài de zhāi xialai yì zhāng huàr.

He quickly removed a picture.

③ 这本书你收起来吧。

Zhè běn shū nǐ shōu qilai ba.

Put the book away, please.

* 这本书你收起吧。

* Zhè běn shū nǐ shōuqi ba.

你收起书来走吧。

Nǐ shōuqǐ shū lai zǒu ba.

Put the book away and leave.

你收起书走吧。

Nǐ shōuqi shū zǒu ba.

Put the book away and leave.

来

Lái

1. 趋向意义

Directional sense

表示人或物通过动作向参照点移动。

Expressing action towards the speaker or some other point of reference.

① 姐姐看见我摔倒了，马上向我跑来。（参照点是"我"）

Jiějie kànjiàn wǒ shuāidǎo le, mǎshàng xiàng wǒ pǎolai.

When my older sister saw me fall down, she immediately ran towards me. (towards the speaker)

② 我看见很多人向图书馆走来。（参照点是"我"）

Wǒ kànjiàn hěn duō rén xiàng túshūguǎn zǒulai.

I saw a lot of people walking towards the library. (towards the speaker)

③ 我在楼上喊："你们快上楼来！"（参照点是"我"）

Wǒ zài lóushàng hǎn: "Nǐmen kuài shànglóu lai!"

I called out from upstairs: "Come up here quickly!" (towards the speaker, who is upstairs)

④ 老师说："上课了，请大家进教室来。"（参照点是"老师"）

Lǎoshī shuō: "Shàng kè le, qǐng dàjiā jìn jiàoshì lai."

The teacher said: "Time for class, everybody come into the classroom, please." (towards the teacher, who is in the classroom)

⑤ 我对妹妹说："给我拿一杯水来！"（参照点是"我"）

Wǒ duì mèimei shuō: "Gěi wǒ ná yì bēi shuǐ lai!"

I said to my younger sister: "Bring me a glass of water!" (towards the speaker)

⑥ 女儿，给妈妈拿几个苹果来。（参照点是“妈妈”）

Nǚ'ér, gěi māma ná jǐ ge píngguǒ lai.

Daughter, bring some apples to Mum. (towards the speaker — Mum)

2. 结果意义

Resultative sense

2.1 表示实现“醒”的状态，可用的动词只有“醒”

Only with "xǐng (wake up)", to express the realization of a state of waking

① 早上他醒来，已经10点多了。

Zǎoshang tā xǐnglai, yǐjīng shí diǎn duō le.

When he awoke this morning, it was already past 10.

② 我昨天晚上睡得不好，做了一个噩梦，醒来以后，再也睡不着了。

Wǒ zuótiān wǎnshang shuì de bù hǎo, zuòle yí ge èmèng, xǐnglai yǐhòu, zài yě shuì bu zháo le.

I didn't sleep well last night; I had a bad dream and after I woke up I couldn't get back to sleep again.

“醒”与“来”不能构成可能补语。

There is no potential form for "xǐng" with the "lái" complement.

2.2 表示“融洽”，可以一起用的动词只有“合、谈”等；动词前可以用程度副词；只有可能补语形式

Can be used with the verbs like "hé (accord with)" and "tán (chat with)" to express the notion of "being on good, friendly terms"; often preceded by an adverb of degree; only in the potential

① 他跟同屋合不来，常常吵架。

Tā gēn tóngwū hé bu lái, chángcháng chǎo jià.

He doesn't get along with his roommate; they're always fighting.

② 我跟小王还谈得来，每次见面都好像有说不完的话。

Wǒ gēn Xiǎo Wáng hái tán de lái, měi cì jiàn miàn dōu hǎoxiàng yǒu shuō bu wán de huà.

I get along quite well with Xiao Wang; every time we see each other we seem to talk endlessly.

③ 我跟他说不来，你还是找别人跟他谈吧。

Wǒ gēn tā shuō bu lái, nǐ háishi zhǎo biéren gēn tā tán ba.

We don't get along; you'd better find someone else to talk to him.

"合得来"表示相处得很好，"合不来"表示不能很好地相处；"说得来""谈得来"表示彼此思想、感情比较一致，有共同语言，"说不来""谈不来"表示相反的意思。

"Hé de lái" means "get along well"; "hé bu lái" means "not get along". "Shuō de lái" and "tán de lái' mean "understand each other" or "see eye to eye"; "shuō bu lái" and "tán bu lái" mean the opposite, "not understand each other".

2.3 表示"会"或"习惯"做某事，只有可能式，一般用否定式 Expressing "able to" or "accustomed to" doing something; only in the potential and generally in the negative

① 南方菜我吃不来，太甜。

Nánfāngcài wǒ chī bu lái, tài tián.

I'm not very fond of southern food; it's too sweet.

② 这种坏事他做不来。

Zhè zhǒng huàishì tā zuò bu lái.

He's not used to doing bad stuff like this.

③ 叫我演戏，我可演不来。

Jiào wǒ yǎn xì, wǒ kě yǎn bu lái.

You're asking me to pretend, but I'm just not good at pretending.

④ 这么难的事，我做不来。

Zhème nán de shì, wǒ zuò bu lái.

I'm not able to do something so difficult.

3. 特殊用法

Special usages

略去。（参见《趋向补语通释》第60—62页）

Omitted. (See *A Complete Explanation of Directional Complements*, pp. 60–62.)

4. 熟语

Idioms

“下不来台”

“Xià bu lái tái”

表示在别人面前受窘，不好意思。

It means “be embarrassed or uncomfortable in front of people”.

① 当着这么多人的面，她说出昨天晚上的事，让我有点儿下不来台。

Dāngzhe zhème duō rén de miàn, tā shuōchu zuótiān wǎnshang de shì, ràng wǒ yǒudiǎnr xià bu lái tái.

When she talked about what happened last night in front of so many people, I felt rather embarrassed.

② 你不听我的话，不赶快离开这里，我会叫你下不来台。

Nǐ bù tīng wǒ de huà, bù gǎnkuài líkāi zhèli, wǒ huì jiào nǐ xià bu lái tái.

If you don't listen to me and leave right away, I'm going to cause a scene.

去

Qù

1. 趋向意义

Directional sense

表示人或物体离开参照点移向另一处所。

Expressing movement away from the speaker, or other point of reference.

① 公共汽车来了，王文很快地上去了。

Gōnggòng qìchē lái le, Wáng Wén hěn kuài de shàngqu le.

When the bus arrived, Wang Wen quickly got on it.

② 上课了，快进教室去！

Shàng kè le, kuài jìn jiàoshì qu!

Time for class, so go right into the classroom!

③ 我要下山去，叔叔不让我走。

Wǒ yào xià shān qu, shūshu bú ràng wǒ zǒu.

I want to go down the mountain, but uncle won't let me.

④ 外面有人找你，你出去看看吧。

Wàimiàn yǒu rén zhǎo nǐ, nǐ chūqu kànkan ba.

There's someone outside looking for you; why don't you go and take a look?

⑤ 听见小王在楼上叫我，我就向楼上跑去。

Tīngjiàn Xiǎo Wáng zài lóu shang jiào wǒ, wǒ jiù xiàng lóu shang pǎoqu.

When I heard Xiao Wang calling me from upstairs, I ran upstairs.

⑥ 我看见女朋友来了，就很快地向她走去。

Wǒ kànjiàn nǚpéngyou lái le, jiù hěn kuài de xiàng tā zǒuqu.

When I saw my girlfriend had arrived, I quickly walked over to her.

⑦ 我这儿有一本小说，你拿去看吧。

Wǒ zhèr yǒu yì běn xiǎoshuō , nǐ náqu kàn ba.

Here's a novel, why don't you take it and have a look?

⑧ 你把这些书给哥哥送去吧。

Nǐ bǎ zhèxiē shū gěi gēge sòngqu ba.

Give these books to your older brother please.

2. 结果意义

Resultative sense

表示“去掉、失掉”。

Expresses “loss”.

① 小心一点儿，你的钱别叫他骗去。

Xiǎoxīn yìdiǎnr, nǐ de qián bié jiào tā piànqu.

Careful, don't let him cheat money off you.

② 请他吃一顿饭，用去了我一个月的零花钱。

Qǐng tā chī yí dùn fàn, yòngqule wǒ yí ge yuè de línghuāqián.

I used a month's pocket money taking him out for a meal.

③ 我买汽车花去了十万元，剩下的钱不多了。

Wǒ mǎi qìchē huāqule shíwàn yuán, shèngxia de qián bù duō le.

I spent 100,000 yuan buying a car; I don't have much money left over.

3. 特殊用法

Special usages

“看去”：表示从外表估计。

"Kànqu" suggests a rough appraisal or an estimate.

① 我们的老师看去只有四十多岁，实际上他已经快六十岁了。

Wǒmen de lǎoshī kànqu zhǐ yǒu sìshí duō suì, shíjìshang tā yǐjīng kuài liùshí suì le.

Our teacher only looks fortyish, but in fact he's already almost sixty.

② 远远看去那里，好像有一片水。

Yuǎnyuǎn kànqu nàli, hǎoxiàng yǒu yí piàn shuǐ.

From a distance it looks like there's a stretch of water there.

"看去"的这个用法与"看上去"（见"上去"，第103—104页）表示的意思与用法相同，但没有"看上去"常用。

"Kànqu" is identical in usage to "kàn shangqu" (see the section on "shàngqu", pp.103–104); however, it is not as common as "kàn shangqu".

4. 熟语
Idioms

4.1 "过得去"
"Guòdeqù"

意思是"不算差、还可以"。常用于生活状况，也可用于人的相貌、工作、学习以及人与人之间的关系等，没有否定形式。前面常有包含勉强语气的"还"。"过得去"一般位于句末。例如：

"Guòdeqù" has the sense of "more or less" or "roughly". It is often used in talking about living conditions, or appearances, work, study and interpersonal relations; it does not occur in the negative. It is often preceded by "hái" to give a sense of being reluctant, being tolerable. Generally, it is found at the foot of the sentence. Here are some examples:

① 他家两个人都工作，虽然收入不多，生活还过得去。

Tā jiā liǎng ge rén dōu gōngzuò, suīrán shōurù bù duō, shēnghuó hái guòdeqù.

Both people in his family work; although they don't have much income, they manage okay.

② 我看那姑娘长得还过得去，比你说的好看多了。

Wǒ kàn nà gūniang zhǎng de hái guòdequ, bǐ nǐ shuō de hǎokàn duō le.

The girl looks fine; she's much more attractive than you said.

③ 他和妻子的关系原来还是过得去的，只是最近一年不知道为什么，见面就吵。

Tā hé qīzi de guānxi yuánlái háishi guòdequ de, zhǐshì zuìjìn yì nián bù zhīdào wèi shénme, jiàn miàn jiù chǎo.

He and his wife used to get along fine; it's only in the last year, for some reason, they squabble whenever they meet.

④ 这个孩子学习还过得去，就是纪律差些。

Zhège háizi xuéxí hái guòdequ, jiùshì jìlǜ chà xiē.

This child studies well enough; he's just a little undisciplined.

这样用的“过得去”都可以用“说得过去”替换。

This usage of “guòdequ” can be replaced by “shuō de guoqu”.

4.2 “过不去”（一）
“Guòbuqù”(1)

用于人的感情方面，表示感情上不能接受，前面常用“感情上觉得”“心里觉得”等，一般用否定形式。例如：

Used in the sense of not being able to accept something, in which case it is often preceded by phrases such as “gǎnqíng shang juéde (to feel-emotionally)” or “xīn li juéde (to feel-in one's heart)”; generally used in the negative. For example:

① 他把自己的父母赶出家门，我看着感情上都觉得过不去。

Tā bǎ zìjǐ de fùmǔ gǎnchu jiāmén, wǒ kànzhe gǎnqíng shang dōu juéde guòbuqù.

He drove his own parents out of the home; seeing it, I felt quite troubled.

② 你给了我这么多帮助，我不能为你做点儿什么，心里觉得过不去呀！

Nǐ gěile wǒ zhème duō bāngzhù, wǒ bù néng wèi nǐ zuò diǎnr shénme, xīn li juéde guòbuqù ya!

You did so much for me; I feel so bad that I can't do anything for you.

"过意不去"也有这个意思。如：

The same sense is conveyed by "guòyì bu qù". For example:

③ 女朋友老给他洗衣服，他有点儿过意不去。

Nǚpéngyou lǎo gěi tā xǐ yīfu, tā yǒudiǎnr guòyì bu qù.

His girlfriend always washes his clothes, which makes him feel sort of uncomfortable.

④ 我们给你添了这么多麻烦，心里真觉得过意不去。

Wǒmen gěi nǐ tiānle zhème duō máfan, xīnli zhēn juéde guòyì bu qù.

We've caused you so much inconvenience; we really feel bad about it.

4.3 "过不去"（二）

"Guòbuqù" (2)

"过不去"还表示"难为人、和人作对"的意思，前边常有"跟/和+N（对象）"。如：

"Guòbuqù" also has the sense of "make it difficult for someone" or "be against someone"; often preceded by "gēn / hé + N (object)", as in the following:

① 刚才天气还很好，刚要去公园，突然下起雨来，他觉得天气好像成心跟他过不去。

Gāngcái tiānqì hái hěn hǎo, gāng yào qù gōngyuán, tūrán xiàqǐ yǔ lai, tā juéde tiānqì hǎoxiàng chéngxīn gēn tā guòbuqù.

A short while ago the weather was fine, but just as he was leaving for the park, it suddenly started to rain; he feels the weather's against him.

② 你干吗总跟老师过不去？你不怕成绩受影响吗？

Nǐ gànmá zǒng gēn lǎoshī guòbuqù? Nǐ bú pà chéngjì shòu yǐngxiǎng ma?

Why are you always clashing with the teacher? Don't you worry that your grades will be affected?

③ 我的同屋好像不喜欢我，总是跟我过不去。

Wǒ de tóngwū hǎoxiàng bù xǐhuan wǒ, zǒngshì gēn wǒ guòbuqù.

I don't think my roommate likes me; he's always clashing with me.

4.4 “下得/不去手”

“Xià de/bu qù shǒu”

表示“忍心/不忍心做某事”。如：

Has the sense of “be able to bear doing something or not”. For example:

① 干这种伤天害理的事，他怎么下得去手？

Gàn zhè zhǒng shāngtiān-hàilǐ de shì, tā zěnme xià de qù shǒu?

How can he bear doing such destructive, evil things?

② 用兔子做实验，我下不去手。

Yòng tùzi zuò shíyàn, wǒ xià bu qù shǒu.

I just can’t bear the idea of experimenting on rabbits.

“上”组

“Shàng” group

“上”组包括“上”“上来”“上去”，它们之间在语义上有密切的关系。表示趋向意义时，“上”没有固定的参照点，“上来”表示向参照点方向移动，“上去”表示离开参照点向另一个处所移动。如下图：

The “shàng” group includes “shàng” “shànglai” and “shàngqu”, all of which are closely related semantically. In expressing direction, “shàng” alone does not indicate the speaker’s perspective; “shànglai” indicates perspective towards the speaker, while “shàngqu” indicates movement away from the speaker or other point of reference, as shown in the chart below:

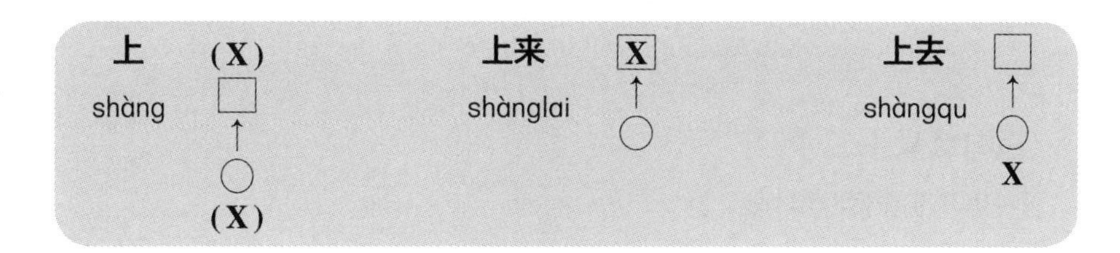

1. 趋向意义

Directional sense

1.1 趋向意义（一）

Directional sense (1)

表示由低处向高处移动，参照点可在高处，也可以在低处。“上”后常常有处所词。

Expresses movement from low to high, with the viewpoint either below or above. This "shàng" is often followed by a place word.

① 我们很快地走上楼。

Wǒmen hěn kuài de zǒushang lóu.

We quickly went upstairs.

② 气球飞上了天空。

Qìqiú fēishangle tiānkōng.

The balloons flew up into the sky.

③ 汽车慢慢开上了山顶。

Qìchē mànmàn kāishangle shāndǐng.

The car climbed slowly up to the peak.

④ 一位服务员把他送上二楼。

Yí wèi fúwùyuán bǎ tā sòngshang èrlóu.

A waiter took him up to the 2nd floor.

1.2 趋向意义（二）

Directional sense (2)

表示向前面的目标移动。

The 2nd directional senses indicates movement forwards towards a goal.

① 看见老师正在买书，我走上前跟他打了一声招呼。

Kànjiàn lǎoshī zhèngzài mǎi shū, wǒ zǒushang qián gēn tā dǎle yì shēng zhāohu.

When I caught sight of my teacher buying books, I went up to him and greeted him.

② 商店门口围着很多人，我挤上前想看看发生了什么事。

Shāngdiàn ménkǒu wéizhe hěn duō rén, wǒ jǐshang qián xiǎng kànkan fāshēngle shénme shì.

There was a crowd of people in the doorway of the shop, so I pushed to the front to see what was going on.

③ 我有急事找小李，看见她在前面跑，我跑了半天才追上她。

Wǒ yǒu jíshì zhǎo Xiǎo Lǐ, kànjiàn tā zài qiánmiàn pǎo, wǒ pǎole bàntiān cái zhuīshang tā.

I had an urgent message for Xiao Li; when I saw her running ahead of me, I ran for a considerable time to catch up with her.

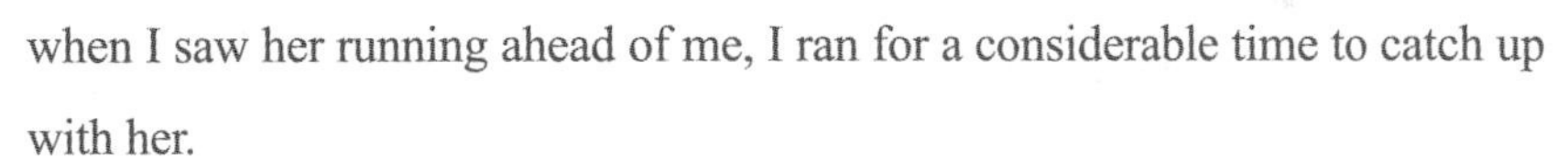

④ 妈妈已经把菜端上桌子，我们快吃饭吧。

Māma yǐjīng bǎ cài duānshang zhuōzi, wǒmen kuài chī fàn ba.

Mum's already served up the food; quick, let's eat.

⑤ 她看见多年未见的老朋友来了，就赶紧走上去跟他握手。

Tā kànjiàn duō nián wèi jiàn de lǎo péngyou lái le, jiù gǎnjǐn zǒu shangqu gēn tā wò shǒu.

She saw an old friend whom she hadn't seen for years and quickly walked up to him and shook hands.

2. 结果意义

Resultative sense

2.1 结果意义（一）——基本结果意义

Resultative sense (1) — basic resultative sense

表示“接触、附着以致固定”。例如：

In the sense of "touch or contact in order to fix". For example:

① 请大家合上书。

Qǐng dàjiā héshang shū.

Everyone close your books, please.

② 在这张纸上写上你的名字。

Zài zhè zhāng zhǐ shang xiěshang nǐ de míngzi.

Write your name on the sheet of paper.

"合上书"的"上"可以解释为"书中的纸和纸接触"，"写上"的"上"可以解释为"名字"附着在"纸上"。

The "shàng" of "héshang shū" can be glossed as "having the pages in the book all touch each other"; the "shàng" of "xiěshang" can be glossed as "having names come into contact with the paper".

③ 把门关上。（门和门框接触）

Bǎ mén guānshang.

Close the door. (door touches frame)

④ 你把这根绳子再接上一段。（绳子和绳子接触）

Nǐ bǎ zhè gēn shéngzi zài jiēshang yí duàn.

Add another length to this piece of string. (strings touch)

⑤ 这件衣服的扣子不好看，我买的新扣子配上以后好看多了。（扣子和衣服接触）

Zhè jiàn yīfu de kòuzi bù hǎokàn, wǒ mǎi de xīn kòuzi pèishang yǐhòu hǎokàn duō le.

The buttons on this item of clothing aren't very pretty; after I replace them with the bottons I bought, it looks much prettier. (buttons touch clothing)

⑥ 小心着凉，快把衣服穿上。（衣服和身体接触）

Xiǎoxīn zháo liáng, kuài bǎ yīfu chuānshang.

Be careful not to catch a cold; put on your clothes, quickly. (clothes touch body)

⑦ 昨天我在超市碰上了很多年没有见到的中学同学。（我和中学同学接触）

Zuótiān wǒ zài chāoshì pèngshangle hěn duō nián méiyǒu jiàndào de zhōngxué tóngxué.

At the supermarket yesterday, I bumped into a middle school classmate whom I hadn't seen for many years. (I and a classmate meet)

⑧ 我在院子里种上了一棵苹果树。（树和地接触）

Wǒ zài yuànzi li zhòngshangle yì kē píngguǒshù.

I planted an apple tree in the yard. (tree and ground meet)

⑨ A: 你要装一台电脑，我帮你吧。

Nǐ yào zhuāng yì tái diànnǎo, wǒ bāng nǐ ba.

You want to set up a computer? I'll help you.

B: 我已经装上了，谢谢！（电脑零件之间接触）

Wǒ yǐjīng zhuāngshang le, xièxie!

I've already set it up, thanks. (contact among computer parts)

“上”的基本结果意义和它的趋向意义（二）意义上联系很密切（见第61页）。我们应该注意以下几个问题：

The basic resultative sense of “shàng” is closely related to the 2nd of its directional senses (see p.61). We need to pay attention to the following points:

（1）我们所以说“上”的结果意义是“接触、附着以致固定”，是因为“上”所涉及的两个事物，有时不仅仅是接触，而是接触后固定在一起了。比如“牛奶里加上糖”“机器新买的零件装上了”“在盆里种上花儿”等等。

The reason we say that the resultative sense of “shàng” is “to have contact with”, or “to attach in order to fix” is because at times, the two things indicated by “shàng” not only come together, but once they are together, they stay together. For example “niúnǎi li jiāshang táng (adding sugar to milk)” “jīqì xīn mǎi de língjiàn zhuāngshang le (the new parts have been installed in the machine)” “zài pén li zhòngshang huār (plant flowers in the pot)” and so on.

（2）有的动词后边用“上”后“接触、附着”的意思不那么明显，但是一定涉及两个或更多的人或物体。如：

After some verbs, it is not that clear that “shàng” indicates “contact” or “attachment”; but there is certainly involvement of two or more people or objects. For example:

⑩ 在学习方面我比不上哥哥。（我和哥哥）

Zài xuéxí fāngmiàn wǒ bǐ bu shàng gēge.

In terms of studying, I can't compete with my older brother. (speaker and older brother)

⑪ 小李爱上你了，你还不知道？（小李和你）

Xiǎo Lǐ àishang nǐ le, nǐ hái bù zhīdào?

You still don't realize that Xiao Li's in love with you? (Xiao Li and you)

由上边的例子可以看出，"上"前面可以用的动词范围很广，我们学习时最好把动词和"上"一起记，比如"关上""接上""碰上""穿上""（把电视）蒙上""加上""盖上（房子）""比不上""看上"等等。实际上学习很多语言，都有一些动词短语（如英文中动词+介词，get up）要记，汉语的"动词+结果补语/趋向补语"也是需要一起记的，并不是汉语特殊，更不是汉语没有语法，对学生讲清这一点是很重要的。

The previous examples show that the range of verbs that can be used before "shàng" varies a lot, so when learning them, it is best to remember particular combinations of verb plus "shàng". For example: "guānshang (close up), jiēshang (connect), pèngshang (bump into), chuānshang (put on), [bǎ diànshì] méngshang (cover up [the television]), jiāshang (add), gàishang [fángzi] (roof over [the house]), bǐ bu shàng (not be able to compete with), kànshang (take a fancy to, settle on, favor)", and so on. In fact, lots of languages have verb phrases that have to be learned as units; English, for example, has numerous phrasal verbs such as "get up". So learning the phrasal combinations of verbs plus directional or resultative complements is not unique to Chinese.

（3）补语"上"所连接的两个事物很多不是对等的。比如"信封贴上邮票""用锁把门锁上"当中，"邮票"和"锁"是次要物体，"信封""门"是主要物体。这一点和与"上"的基本结果意义接近的"起来"不同。（详见第200—201页）

The joining or meeting of things indicated by "shàng" is not always equally weighted. For example, in "xìnfēng tiēshang yóupiào (the envelope has a stamp stuck on it)" and "yòng suǒ bǎ mén suǒshang (lock the door with a lock)", the "stamp" and "the lock" are secondary items; "the envelope" and "the door" are primary. This is unlike the sense of "qǐlai", that is (in other respects) similar in meaning to the basic resultative sense of "shàng". (For details, see pp. 200–201)

2.2 结果意义（二）

Resultative sense (2)

表示实现了预期的目的或希望实现的目的，这个目的一般来说是不太容易实现的。是一种口语用法。

It has the sense of realizing some anticipated goal or some hoped for goal, generally, one that is not easily realized; colloquial usage.

① 我去年没考上大学，今年才考上。

Wǒ qùnián méi kǎoshang dàxué, jīnnián cái kǎoshang.

Last year I failed to pass the college entrance exam; I didn't pass it until this year.

② 他工作10年之后，终于买上了自己的房子。

Tā gōngzuò shí nián zhīhòu, zhōngyú mǎishangle zìjǐ de fángzi.

After he had worked for ten years, he managed, in the end, to buy his own house.

③ 小张好不容易当上了飞行员，非常高兴。

Xiǎo Zhāng hǎo bù róngyì dāngshangle fēixíngyuán, fēicháng gāoxìng.

It's not been easy for Xiao Zhang to become a pilot; he's very happy about it.

注 意 Notes:

1.因为"上"的这个用法属于口语，所以有些单音节动词可以用这个"上"，而意义相同的双音节动词不能用。如："观看"（"看"可以）、"学习"（"学"可以）、"购买"（"买"可以）。

Because this usage of "shàng" is colloquial, there are certain monosyllabic verbs that can appear with it, while disyllabic verbs of similar meaning can not: thus it occurs with "kàn" but not "guānkàn (watch)"; with "xué" but not "xuéxí (study and learn)"; with "mǎi" but not "gòumǎi (purchase)".

2.不能用于"把"字句。比较：

This usage of "shàng" does not appear with the bǎ-construction. Compare:

① 那本书我好不容易才买上。

Nà běn shū wǒ hǎo bù róngyì cái mǎishang.

It hasn't been at all easy for me to get a copy of this book.

* 我把那本书好不容易才买上。

* Wǒ bǎ nà běn shū hǎo bù róngyì cái mǎishang.

② 我考上研究生了，很高兴。

Wǒ kǎoshang yánjiūshēng le, hěn gāoxìng.

I passed the postgraduate entrance exam; I'm so happy.

* 我把研究生考上了，很高兴。

* Wǒ bǎ yánjiūshēng kǎoshang le, hěn gāoxìng.

3.用“上”的结果意义（二）的句子所涉及的事情应该是好的、正面的。

Sentences which contain “shàng” in the 2nd resultative sense should involve good things or positive things.

2.3 结果意义（三）

Resultative sense (3)

表示成功地完成，多用可能补语形式。

Signifies successful completion, used more in the potential form.

① 你别买这么多菜了，说不上哪天我们就离开这里了。

Nǐ bié mǎi zhème duō cài le, shuō bu shàng nǎ tiān wǒmen jiù líkāi zhèli le.

Don't buy so much food; there's no telling when we will be leaving this place.

② 老师：最后一道题是加分题，答不上没关系。

Lǎoshī: Zuìhòu yí dào tí shì jiāfēntí, dá bu shàng méi guānxi.

Teacher: The last problem is for extra-credit; don't worry if you can't answer it.

③ 这种花儿我见过，可是叫不上它的名儿。

Zhè zhǒng huār wǒ jiànguo, kěshì jiào bu shàng tā de míngr.

I've seen that type of flower before, but I can't recall its name.

3. 状态意义

Stative sense

表示进入新的状态，即表示动作或状态的开始。

Signifies entering a new situation, i.e., the beginning of an action or a state.

① 大家都忙，你怎么玩上电脑游戏了？

Dàjiā dōu máng, nǐ zěnme wánshang diànnǎo yóuxì le?

With everyone so busy, how come you're playing video games?

② 他每天都练太极拳，你看刚5点，他又练上了。

Tā měi tiān dōu liàn tàijíquán, nǐ kàn gāng wǔ diǎn, tā yòu liànshang le.

He practices Taichi every day; look, it's just 5 o'clock and he's doing it again.

③ 听了她的话，他吓得哆嗦上了。

Tīngle tā de huà, tā xià de duōsuo shang le.

When he heard what she said, he shook with fear.

④ 不知道从什么时候开始，他们俩好上了。

Bù zhīdào cóng shénme shíhou kāishǐ, tāmen liǎ hǎoshang le.

I don't know when it started, but the two of them have fallen in love.

"上"用作状态意义有以下特点：

"Shàng", used in its stative sense, has the following features:

（1）用于口语。

It is colloquial.

（2）有比较明显的感情色彩，表示说话人对该动作、状态不欢迎、不喜欢。

It clearly suggests that the speaker does not welcome or appreciate the action or state.

（3）"上"前多用动词，而且可以用的动词比表示状态意义的"起来"少。表示进入新的状态时，多用"起来"。

"Shàng" tends to be preceded by verbs (rather than adjectives); and fewer verbs appear with "shàng" than with "qǐlai" in its stative sense; to express a new state of affairs, "qǐlai" is more often used.

4. 特殊用法

Special usages

4.1 表示达到一定的数目，后边有数量词，也是一种口语用法

Expressing the realization of a particular amount; followed by a measure word; also colloquial in usage

① 这个技术你好好儿学，学上几个月就掌握了。

Zhège jìshù nǐ hǎohāor xué, xuéshang jǐ ge yuè jiù zhǎngwò le.

Study this technique carefully; after you've studied it for a few months you'll have mastered it.

② 你熬了好几天夜了，睡上一天一夜也不算多。

Nǐ áole hǎojǐ tiān yè le, shuìshang yì tiān-yí yè yě bú suàn duō.

You've been staying up for several days, so sleeping for a day and a night isn't a lot.

③ 一篇课文，他看上两遍就能背下来了。

Yì piān kèwén, tā kànshang liǎng biàn jiù néng bèi xialai le.

Any text, if he reads it through twice he can have it memorized.

4.2 用在表示伴随动作的动词后，后边还有表示主要动作的动词（短语）

Used after a verb expressing accompanying action, followed by a verb (or verb phrase) that expresses the main action

① 你赶快带上孩子离开这儿吧，这儿太危险了。

Nǐ gǎnkuài dàishang háizi líkāi zhèr ba, zhèr tài wēixiǎn le.

Take the child away from here as quickly as you can; it's too dangerous here.

② 听了这个消息，他骑上车赶紧走了。

Tīngle zhège xiāoxi, tā qíshang chē gǎnjǐn zǒu le.

After hearing the report, he mounted his bike and hurriedly rode off.

③ 你要带上笔记本电脑，不然没法儿工作。

Nǐ yào dàishang bǐjìběn diànnǎo, bùrán méifǎr gōngzuò.

Take your laptop with you, otherwise it won't be possible to do any work.

5. 熟语
Idioms

很多由趋向补语构成的熟语或特殊用法，常以可能补语的形式出现。我们都放在“趋向补语”中说明。

A lot of idioms or special usages involving directional complements often appear in the potential form. We illutrate them under the heading of "Directional complements".

5.1 “顾得/不上”
"Gù de/bu shàng"

表示照顾到/不到、注意到/不到。

It has the sense of "taking into account" or "paying attention to" something or not.

① 我这几天忙着写论文，顾不上给家里打电话。
Wǒ zhè jǐ tiān mángzhe xiě lùnwén, gùbushàng gěi jiā li dǎ diànhuà.
These past few days I've been busy writing my thesis and have neglected phoning home.

② 台风马上就来了，我顾不上你了，你快离开吧。
Táifēng mǎshàng jiù lái le, wǒ gùbushàng nǐ le, nǐ kuài líkāi ba.
There's a hurricane coming; I can't deal with you—you need to leave right away.

③ 等他找到工作，就顾得上找女朋友的事了。
Děng tā zhǎodào gōngzuò, jiù gùdeshàng zhǎo nǚpéngyou de shì le.
After he find work, he can deal with the business of finding a girlfriend.

5.2 “说得/不上、谈得/不上”
"Shuō de/bu shàng" "tán de/bu shàng"

表示“可以/不可以算作、可以/不可以说是”。

It has the sense of "can/cannot be regarded as" or "can/cannot be said to be".

① 这儿的风景不错，但是“风景优美”还说不上。

Zhèr de fēngjǐng búcuò, dànshì “fēngjǐng yōuměi ” hái shuōbushàng.

The view isn't bad, but I wouldn't say it's “an outstanding view”.

② 我们俩说不上是什么男女朋友，不过是比较好的同学。

Wǒmen liǎ shuōbushàng shì shénme nánnǚ péngyou, búguò shì bǐjiào hǎo de tóngxué.

It wouldn't be right to call us boy and girl friend, but we are pretty close classmates.

③ 他做了这件事谈不上是什么错误，只是不太合适。

Tā zuòle zhè jiàn shì tánbushàng shì shénme cuòwu, zhǐ shì bú tài héshì.

You couldn't say it was a mistake for him to do that; just not very appropriate.

注 意 Notes:

“说不上”有三个意思：

There are three senses of “shuōbushàng”:

1.表示说不清楚。

It means “can't say for sure”.

① 老师什么时候来，我说不上。

Lǎoshī shénme shíhou lái, wǒ shuōbushàng.

I can't say for sure when the teacher's coming.

② 这个地方将会发生地震，但是什么时候，谁也说不上。

Zhège dìfang jiāng huì fāshēng dìzhèn, dànshì shénme shíhou, shuí yě shuōbushàng.

There's going to be an earthquake here but no one can say for sure when.

2.表示没达到一定的数目。

It suggests that a particular number has not been reached.

③ 我们俩一天说不上三句话。

Wǒmen liǎ yì tiān shuōbushàng sān jù huà.

The two of us don't manage to say three sentences to each other in a day.

3.表示“可以算作”。

It indicates that it is reasonable to regard something in some way.

④ 我的成绩说不上好，但是也不算很差。

Wǒ de chéngjì shuōbushàng hǎo, dànshì yě bú suàn hěn chà.

I can't say my grades are good, but I can't say they're that bad either.

5.3 犯得/不上
"Fàn de/bu shàng"

表示“值得/不值得”。

It has the sense of "worthwhile" or "not worthwhile".

① 这么点儿小事，你犯得上浪费这么多时间吗？

Zhème diǎnr xiǎoshì, nǐ fàndeshàng làngfèi zhènme duō shíjiān ma?

For such a minor thing, is it worth spending all that time?

② 你犯不上跟一个小孩子生这么大的气。

Nǐ fànbushàng gēn yí ge xiǎoháizi shēng zhème dà de qì.

It's not worth getting angry with a child.

1. 趋向意义
Directional sense

1.1 趋向意义（一）
Directional sense (1)

表示由低处向高处移动，参照点在高处。

Expressing movement from low to high, with the high point being the point of reference.

① 孩子走上楼来。

Háizi zǒushàng lóu lai.

The child came up the stairs.

② 来不及了，你快跑上来吧。

Láibují le, nǐ kuài pǎo shanglai ba.

There's no time; quick, run up here.

③ 你把茶给我送上楼来吧。

Nǐ bǎ chá gěi wǒ sòngshàng lóu lai ba.

Bring the tea upstairs for me, please.

④ 她从楼下带上一个人来。

Tā cóng lóu xià dàishàng yí ge rén lai.

She brought someone up from downstairs.

⑤ 这时我看见从山下走上来一个人。

Zhè shí wǒ kànjiàn cóng shān xià zǒu shanglai yí ge rén.

Then I saw someone walking up here from the foot of the hill.

⑥ 你给我搬一把椅子上来。

Nǐ gěi wǒ bān yì bǎ yǐzi shànglai.

Bring a chair up here.

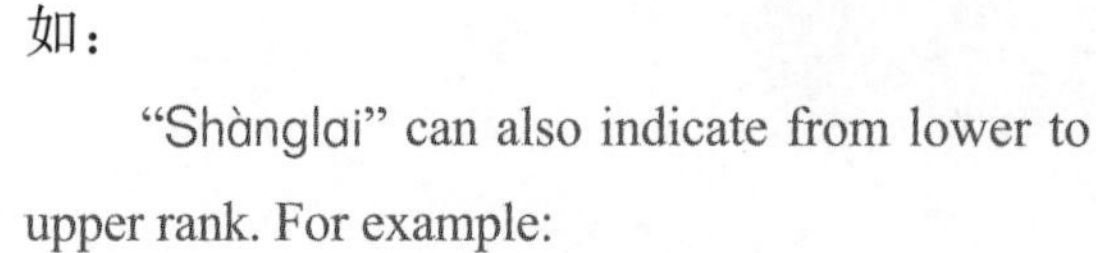

"上来"也可以表示由下级到上级。如：

"Shànglai" can also indicate from lower to upper rank. For example:

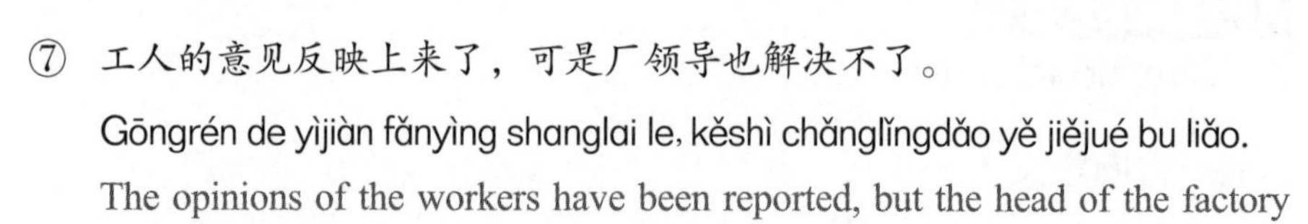

⑦ 工人的意见反映上来了，可是厂领导也解决不了。

Gōngrén de yìjiàn fǎnyìng shanglai le, kěshì chǎnglǐngdǎo yě jiějué bu liǎo.

The opinions of the workers have been reported, but the head of the factory still hasn't been able to solve the problem.

⑧ 学费都收上来了吗？

Xuéfèi dōu shōu shanglai le ma?

Has the tuition been received?

⑨ 公司现在很需要管理人才，他很能干，就把他调上来了。

Gōngsī xiànzài hěn xūyào guǎnlǐ réncái, tā hěn nénggàn, jiù bǎ tā diào shanglai le.

The company is in great need of management talent; he is very capable, so they promoted him.

⑩ 老师：把你们的作业都交上来吧！

Lǎoshī: Bǎ nǐmen de zuòyè dōu jiāo shanglai ba!

Teacher: Turn in your assignments!

注 意 Notes:

关于宾语的位置：

On the position of the object:

1."上来"后边可以有表示移动终点的处所词，处所词只能放在"上"和"来"中间，见例①、③。

As illustrated in examples ① and ③ above, a place word indicating a destination has to be placed between "shàng" and "lái".

2. 如果动词后边是名词宾语，宾语有三种位置：

An object noun phrase appearing after the verb can appear in three possible positions:

（1）可以位于"上"和"来"中间，如例④，这时名词宾语的位置和处所词宾语的位置一样，也就是说无论是名词还是处所词作宾语，都可以放在"上"和"来"中间，这种句式最好记，可以先教、先学。

It can be placed between "shàng" and "lái", as in example ④ above; in which case, the position of the noun object is the same as that of a place-word object. That is to say, regardless of whether it is a noun object or a place-word object, it is placed between "shàng" and "lái". This sentence type should be noted. It can be taught first and learned first.

（2）名词宾语可以位于"上来"之后，如例⑤。

A noun object can be placed after "shànglai", as in ⑤ above.

（3）名词宾语也可以位于"上来"前，多用于祈使句，如例⑩。

A noun object can also be placed in front of "shànglai", especially in imperatives, as in ⑩ above.

其他复合趋向补语与宾语的位置和"上来"一样，后面不再重复。

The position of objects with other compound directional complements behave like "shànglai", so additional examples will not be provided later.

1.2 趋向意义（二）
Directional sense (2)

表示向参照点（说话人或正在叙述的人或事物）移动。

Expressing movement towards a person or place, from the perspective of the speaker.

① 我看见人们围上来了，想走来不及了。（参照点是"我"）

Wǒ kànjiàn rénmen wéi shanglai le, xiǎng zǒu láibují le.

I saw people gathering round; there was no time to get away. (gathering round the speaker)

② 客人从外边进来，看见我，就走上来跟我握手。（参照点是"我"）

Kèren cóng wàibian jìnlai, kànjiàn wǒ, jiù zǒu shanglai gēn wǒ wò shǒu.

The guests came in from outside and on seeing me, they walked up and shook hands. (walked up to the speaker)

③ 后边的人追上来了，我只好快跑。（参照点是"我"）

Hòubian de rén zhuī shanglai le, wǒ zhǐhǎo kuài pǎo.

The people behind were catching up; I had to run faster. (catching up with the speaker)

④ 我叫服务员现在就把菜端上桌来。（参照点是"我"）

Wǒ jiào fúwùyuán xiànzài jiù bǎ cài duānshàng zhuō lai.

I told the waitress to bring the food to the table right away. (towards the speaker, who is at the table)

2. 结果意义
Resultative sense

2.1 结果意义(一)——基本结果意义
Resultative sense (1) — basic resultative sense

表示一个次要事物与主要事物的接触、附着。着眼点在主要事物。

Expresses a connection between a secondary object and a primary, with the focus on the primary.

① 这根绳子不够长，你把那根短绳子接上来。

Zhè gēn shéngzi bú gòu cháng, nǐ bǎ nà gēn duǎn shéngzi jiē shanglai.

This piece of string isn't long enough; attach this short piece to it.

这个句子说话人着眼于“这根绳子”，是主要事物。

In this sentence, the speaker is focused on “zhè gēn shéngzi” — that is the primary thing.

② 名单上人不够，再加上来几个。

Míngdān shang rén bú gòu, zài jiā shanglai jǐ ge.

There aren't enough people on the list; add a few more names.

这个句子说话人着眼于主要事物“名单”。

In this sentence, the speaker is focused on “míngdān” — that is the item of interest.

“上来”的结果意义（一）和“上”的结果意义（一）意思一样，但是可以结合的动词较少，没有“上”常用。

The 1st resultative sense of “shànglai” is the same as the 1st resultative sense of “shàng”, but it occurs with fewer verbs; it is not as common as “shàng”.

2.2 结果意义（二）
Resultative sense (2)

表示成功、正确完成，可能补语用得较多。

Expresses successful completion; more common in the potential form.

① 今天的考试我考得不错，所有的题都答上来了。

Jīntiān de kǎoshì wǒ kǎo de búcuò, suǒyǒu de tí dōu dá shanglai le.

I did quite well on today's test, I managed to answer all the questions.

② 这个句子我知道是什么意思，可是翻译不上来。

Zhège jùzi wǒ zhīdào shì shénme yìsi, kěshì fānyì bu shànglái.

I know what this sentence means, but I can't translate it.

③ 这么简单的题你都答不上来，太不应该了。

Zhème jiǎndān de tí nǐ dōu dá bu shànglái, tài bù yīnggāi le.

You can't even answer such easy questions — that's just not right.

④ 他跑得太累了，都喘不上气来了。

Tā pǎo de tài lèi le, dōu chuǎn bu shàng qì lai le.

He's exhausted from running, he can hardly get his breath.

3. 状态意义

Stative sense

"上来"用在形容词后，表示进入新的状态。可结合的形容词仅有"热、凉、黑"等少数几个与天气、天色有关的。

"Shànglai" is also used after the adjectives "rè" "liáng" and "hēi" — all related to weather or to the color of the sky. In such cases "shànglai" indicates the onset of a new situation.

天气慢慢凉上来了。

Tiānqì mànmàn liáng shanglai le.

The weather starts to get cooler.

1. 趋向意义

Directional sense

1.1 趋向意义（一）
Directional sense (1)

表示由低处向高处移动，参照点在低处。

Signifies movement upwards, from the lower perspective.

① 虽然他的腿不好，但还是坚持不坐电梯，自己慢慢走上去。（说话人在楼下）

Suīrán tā de tuǐ bù hǎo, dàn háishì jiānchí bú zuò diàntī, zìjǐ mànmàn zǒu shangqu.

Even though he's got a bad leg, he still insists on walking up rather than taking the elevator. (speaker is downstairs)

② 你把这张桌子搬上楼去吧。（说话人在楼下）

Nǐ bǎ zhè zhāng zhuōzi bānshàng lóu qu ba.

Take the table upstairs. (speaker is downstairs)

③ 小松鼠看见人来了，就很快地爬上树去。（松鼠原来在地上）

Xiǎo sōngshǔ kànjiàn rén lái le, jiù hěn kuài de páshàng shù qu.

When the little squirrel saw people coming, it quickly climbed up the tree. (the squirrel fled up the tree, away from the people on the ground)

④ 气球飞上天空去了。（说话人在地上）

Qìqiú fēishàng tiānkōng qu le.

The balloon flew up into the sky. (observed from the ground)

"上去"也可以用于由下级到上级。如：

"Shàngqu" can also mean from a lower rank to a higher one. For example:

⑤ 大家的意见反映上去了，可是没有人重视。

Dàjiā de yìjiàn fǎnyìng shangqu le, kěshì méiyǒu rén zhòngshì.

Everyone's opinions were reported but no one paid any attention to them.

⑥ 这些材料你快交上去吧，领导马上要。

Zhèxiē cáiliào nǐ kuài jiāo shangqu ba, lǐngdǎo mǎshàng yào.

Submit this material quickly — the boss needs it right away.

⑦ 参加这次活动的学生名单报上去了。（报到上一级）

Cānjiā zhè cì huódòng de xuésheng míngdān bào shangqu le.

The list of students attending this event has been submitted. (to a superior)

1.2 趋向意义（二）
Directional sense (2)

表示向前面的目标移动，参照点在移动的人或物体。

Expresses motion forwards towards a more distant goal, from the perspective of the person or thing doing the moving.

① 看见爷爷回来了，我走上前去帮他脱下大衣。

Kànjiàn yéye huílai le, wǒ zǒushàng qián qu bāng tā tuōxia dàyī.

When I saw grandpa coming back, I walked up to him and helped him take off his overcoat.

② 一个很有名的演员来我们学校，看见他，大家都围了上去。

Yí ge hěn yǒumíng de yǎnyuán lái wǒmen xuéxiào, kànjiàn tā, dàjiā dōu wéile shangqu.

A famous actor came to our school; when people saw him, they all gathered round.

③ 小李走了，我赶紧追了上去。

Xiǎo Lǐ zǒu le, wǒ gǎnjǐn zhuīle shangqu.

Xiao Li left and I ran after him right away.

2.结果意义
Resultative sense

表示次要物体接触或附着于主要物体。

Expresses the joining or attachment of a secondary object to a primary one.

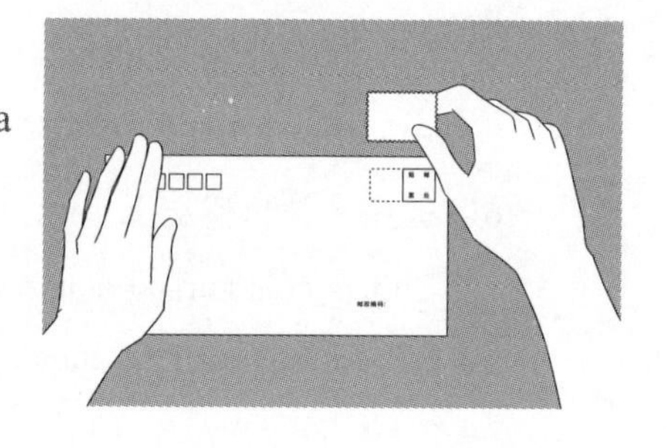

① 信封还没贴邮票，你把这张贴上去吧。（邮票接触信封）

Xìnfēng hái méi tiē yóupiào, nǐ bǎ zhè zhāng tiē shangqu ba.
The envelope still doesn't have a stamp; stick this one on. (stamp placed on envelope)

② 姐姐刚说完，妹妹就接上去说："后来的事情我说吧。"（妹妹的话接着姐姐的话）
Jiějie gāng shuōwán, mèimei jiù jiē shangqu shuō: "Hòulái de shìqing wǒ shuō ba ."
Older sister had just finished talking when younger sister went on to say: "Let me talk about what happened afterwards." (younger sister's words connect to older sister's)

③ 绳子太短，把这段接上去就够了。（一段绳子接触另一段绳子）
Shéngzi tài duǎn, bǎ zhè duàn jiē shangqu jiù gòu le.
The string's too short; tie this piece to it and it'll be enough. (two pieces of string brought together)

④ 前面地上有一堆垃圾，他没看见，一脚踩了上去。（脚接触垃圾）
Qiánmian dìshang yǒu yì duī lājī, tā méi kànjiàn, yì jiǎo cǎile shangqu.
There was a pile of trash on the ground ahead of him; he didn't notice and stepped in it. (foot touches trash)

⑤ 这张纸有油，字写不上去。（字接触纸）
Zhè zhāng zhǐ yǒu yóu, zì xiě bu shàngqù.
There's oil on this sheet of paper; you can't write on it. (words touch paper)

3.熟语

Idiom

"看上去"

"kàn shangqu"

意思是从人或事物的外表来观察，常用于人或物体。

Often used in the sense of observing the outer form of someone or something.

① 他看上去五十多岁。

Tā kàn shangqu wǔshí duō suì.

He looks over 50.

② 这个人看上去高大健壮，可是实际上身体很不好。

Zhège rén kàn shangqu gāodà jiànzhuàng, kěshì shíjìshang shēntǐ hěn bù hǎo.

This person looks big and strong, but in fact he's not in good health.

③ 这件衣服看上去很一般，实际上很贵。

Zhè jiàn yīfu kàn shangqu hěn yìbān, shíjìshang hěn guì.

This item of clothing looks quite ordinary, but in fact, it was expensive.

④ 你看上去精神不太好，是病了还是昨天没睡好觉？

Nǐ kàn shangqu jīngshen bú tài hǎo, shì bìngle háishì zuótiān méi shuìhǎo jiào?

You don't look very well; is it an illness or didn't you sleep very well last night?

"看上去"和"看起来"比较，见"起来"（第204页）。

For a comparison of "kàn shangqu" and "kàn qilai", see the section on "qǐlai" (p.204).

（一）"上"组趋向意义、结果意义、状态意义之间的意义联系

Semantic relationships among the directional sense, the resultative sense, and the stative sense of the "shàng" group

下面表中可以显示"上"组趋向意义（一）、状态意义、趋向意义（二）与结果意义（一）之间的关系。

The following chart shows that the 1st directional sense, the stative sense, the 2nd directional sense and the 1st resultative sense of the "shàng" group.

"上"组 "shàng" group	趋向意义（一） directional sense (1)	状态意义 stative sense	趋向意义（二） directional sense (2)	结果意义（一） resultative sense (1)
上 shàng	由低到高，参照不确定。 From low to high; no explicit point of reference.	动作、状态开始。 Initiation of an action or state.	向前面的目标移动。 Movement forwards towards a goal.	接触、附着。 Contact, proximity.
上来 shànglai	由低到高，参照点在高处。 From low to high, with "high" as point of reference.	状态开始。 Initiation of a state.	向前面的目标移动，参照点在目标。 Movement forwards towards a goal, viewed from the goal.	接触、附着，着眼点在主要物体。 Contact, proximity, with the focus on the primary object.
上去 shàngqu	由低到高，参照点在低处。 From low to high, with "low" as point of reference.	——	向前面的目标移动，参照点在移动的人或物体。 Movement forwards towards a goal, with person or thing doing the moving as point of reference.	接触、附着，着眼点在次要物体。 Contact, proximity, with the focus on the secondary object.

（二）"上"组意义小结

Summary of senses of the "shàng" group

	上 shàng	上来 shànglai	上去 shàngqu
趋向意义（一） directional sense (1) 由低到高移动。 Movement from low to high.	参照点不确定。 No explicit point of reference. 我看见他走上楼。（"我"在楼上或在楼下） Wǒ kànjiàn tā zǒu-shang lóu. (speaker upstairs or downstairs)	参照点在高处。 "High" as point of reference. 我看见他走上楼来。（"我"在楼上） Wǒ kànjiàn tā zǒu-shàng lóu lai. (speaker upstairs)	参照点在低处。 "Low" as point of reference. 我看见他走上楼去。（"我"在楼下） Wǒ kànjiàn tā zǒushàng lóu qu. (speaker downstairs)

（续表）

	上 shàng	上来 shànglai	上去 shàngqu
趋向意义（二） directional sense (2) 向前面的目标移动。 Movement forwards towards a goal.	参照点不确定。 No explicit point of reference. 他走上前，把作业交给老师。（说话人可能在“老师”旁边，也可能在“他”旁边） Tā zǒushang qián, bǎ zuòyè jiāogěi lǎoshī. (the speaker may be near the teacher or near him)	参照点在目标。 Destination as point of reference. 你再走上来一步，让我仔细看看。（参照点是“我”） Nǐ zài zǒu shanglai yí bù, ràng wǒ zǐxì kànkan. (moving towards the speaker)	参照点在移动的人或物体。 The person or thing doing the moving as point of reference. 我走上前去，把作业交给了老师。（参照点是“老师”） Wǒ zǒushàng qián qu, bǎ zuòyè jiāogěile lǎoshī. (moving forward to where the teacher is)
结果意义（一） resultative sense (1) 次要物体或物体的一部分向主要物体或整体接触、附着以致固定。 Indicating the connection between a primary object and a secondary.	着眼点不确定，可在主要物体、整体，也可在次要物体、物体的一部分。 Even weighting of primary and secondary objects. 把这两段绳子接上。（着眼点不确定） Bǎ zhè liǎng duàn shéngzi jiēshang. (neutral)	着眼点在主要物体或整体。 The focus on the primary object. 这段绳子不够长，把那段短绳子接上来。（着眼点在“这段绳子”） Zhè duàn shéngzi bú gòu cháng, bǎ nà duàn duǎn shéngzi jiē shanglai. (focus on the string that is not quite long enough)	着眼点在次要物体或物体的一部分。 The focus on the secondary object. 那段绳子不够长，把这段短绳子接上去吧。（着眼点在“这段短绳子”） Nà duàn shéngzi bú gòu cháng, bǎ zhè duàn duǎn shéngzi jiē shangqu ba. (focus on the piece added)

（续表）

	上 shàng	上来 shànglai	上去 shàngqu
结果意义(二) resultative sense (2) 表示实现了预期的目的或希望实现的目的。 Expresses the realization of an anticipated or hoped for goal.	工作三年，他买上了自己喜欢的车。 Gōngzuò sān nián, tā mǎishangle zìjǐ xǐhuan de chē.	——	——
结果意义（三） resultative sense (3) 表示成功地完成。 Expresses successful completion.	这道题太难了，我答不上。 Zhè dào tí tài nán le, wǒ dá bu shàng.	这道题太难了，我答不上来。 Zhè dào tí tài nán le, wǒ dá bu shànglái.	——
状态意义 stative sense 表示动作、状态开始。 Expresses the begining of an action or a state.	表示动作、状态开始。 Expresses the onset of an action or a state. 你不看书也不睡觉，怎么玩上电子游戏了，明天的考试怎么办? Nǐ bú kàn shū yě bú shuì jiào, zěnme wánshang diànzǐ yóuxì le, míngtiān de kǎoshì zěnme bàn?	表示状态开始。 Signifies the onset of a new state or situation. 天气慢慢凉上来了。 Tiānqì mànmàn liáng shanglai le.	——

“下”组

“Xià” group

“下”组包括“下”“下来”和“下去”。

The “xià” group includes “xià” “xiàlai” and “xiàqu”.

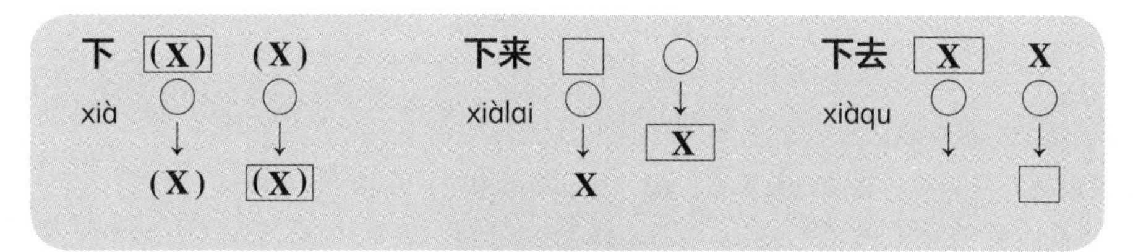

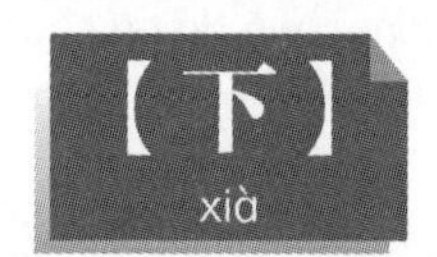

1. 趋向意义

Directional sense

1.1 趋向意义（一）

Directional sense (1)

表示由高处向低处移动，参照点不确定。“下”后的处所词表示的处所如果高于地平线，就表示动作的起点，否则，表示动作的终点。

Expresses movement from high to low, with no explicit point of reference. If the place word that follows “xià” is above the plane of sight, then it represents the starting point; if below the plane of sight, then it is the destination.

① 孩子们很快地跑下山。（山—动作起点）

Háizimen hěn kuài de pǎoxia shān.

The children ran quickly down the mountain. (the action begins up the mountain)

② 孩子们一个跟一个跳下水。

（水—动作终点）

Háizimen yí ge gēn yí ge tiàoxia shuǐ.

The children jumped into the water one by one. (water is the endpoint of the action)

③ 你病了，需要休息，快躺下。

Nǐ bìng le, xūyào xiūxi, kuài tǎngxia.

You're ill, you should rest; quick, lie down.

④ 喝下这碗汤，你会感觉好一些。

Hēxia zhè wǎn tāng, nǐ huì gǎnjué hǎo yìxiē.

Drink down this soup, you'll feel better.

⑤ 我放下电话，他在电话里的哭声好像还在我耳边响。

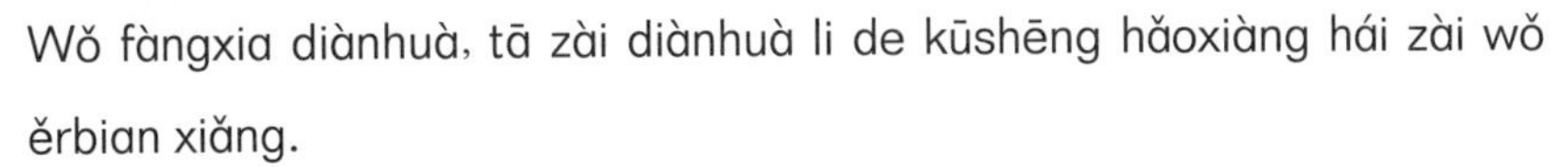

Wǒ fàngxia diànhuà, tā zài diànhuà li de kūshēng hǎoxiàng hái zài wǒ ěrbian xiǎng.

I put down the phone, but the sound of his cry seemed to be still ringing in my ears.

“下”也可以表示由上级到下级，如：

“Xià” can also indicate from a higher rank to a lower one. For example:

⑥ 这是上面派下的任务，不完成不行。

Zhè shì shàngmiàn pàixia de rènwù, bù wánchéng bù xíng.

This is a task that has been assigned by the higher-ups; it has to be completed.

⑦ 学校发下文件了，明年的工资不变。

Xuéxiào fāxia wénjiàn le, míngnián de gōngzī bú biàn.

The school has issued a document; salaries for next year won't change.

1.2 趋向意义（二）Directional sense (2)

表示退离前面的目标（人或物体）。

Expresses retreat or a shift backwards (for a person or thing).

① 教练叫8号运动员退下赛场。

Jiàoliàn jiào bā hào yùndòngyuán tuìxia sàichǎng.

The coach told player No.8 to leave the pitch.

② 他向司令报告完了，退下一步，敬了个礼。

Tā xiàng sīlìng bàogào wán le, tuìxia yí bù, jìngle ge lǐ.

After he reported to the commanding officer, he stepped back one pace and saluted.

2. 结果意义 Resultative sense

2.1 结果意义（一）——基本结果意义 Resultative sense (1) — basic resultative sense

表示次要物体或物体的一部分从主要物体或整体脱离、分离。着眼点不确定。

Expresses the complete separation or removal of a secondary item or part from a primary item; without explicit indication of a point of reference ("towards" or "away from").

① 天气很热，我脱下了外衣。（衣服与身体分离）

Tiānqì hěn rè, wǒ tuōxiale wàiyī.

It was hot, so I took off my outer garment. (clothes removed from body)

② 我从地里拔下一个萝卜。（萝卜与地分离）

Wǒ cóng dì li báxia yí ge luóbo.

I pulled a turnip out of the ground. (turnip removed from ground)

③ 她切下一块蛋糕，给小李送去了。（一块蛋糕与整个蛋糕分离）

Tā qiēxia yí kuài dàngāo, gěi Xiǎo Lǐ sòngqu le.

She cut off a piece of cake and brought it to Xiao Li. (slice removed from cake)

④ 这些是你朋友让我带给你的钱，你收下吧。（钱与带钱的人分离）

Zhèxiē shì nǐ péngyou ràng wǒ dài gěi nǐ de qián, nǐ shōuxia ba.

This is the money your friend asked me to bring to you; please accept it. (money removed from friend)

⑤ 十年时间，他买下了两套房子。（两套房子与原来的主人分离）

Shí nián shíjiān, tā mǎixiale liǎng tào fángzi.

He's bought two houses within 10 years. (houses removed from original owner)

⑥ 冰箱里还有剩下的菜，你热热吃吧。（剩下的菜与原来整盘的菜分离）

Bīngxiāng li háiyǒu shèngxia de cài, nǐ rère chī ba.

There's some leftover food in the refrigerator; heat it up and have it. (leftover food removed from original batch of food)

⑦ 这几年他妈妈存下一笔钱，给他上大学用。（存下的钱与原来收入的钱分离）

Zhè jǐ nián tā māma cúnxia yì bǐ qián, gěi tā shàng dàxué yòng.

The money that his mother put aside over these years is to be used for him to go to university. (money removed from the original sum)

"留、住、交（朋友）、定、答应"等动词与"下"结合，我们也归入此类结果意义。

When verbs such as "liú (stay, save, accept)" "zhù (stay, live)" "jiāo [péngyou] (be friends with, make friends)" "dìng (decide, subscribe)" and "dāying (reply, agree to, promise)" combine with "xià", they can be regarded as having the same type of resultative sense.

⑧ 中学时候交下的朋友，很多年以后还会互相帮助。

Zhōngxué shíhou jiāoxia de péngyou, hěn duō nián yǐhòu hái huì hùxiāng bāngzhù.

Friends made in middle school still help each other even after all these years.

⑨ 去欧洲旅行的时间已经定下了，你赶快准备准备吧。

Qù Ōuzhōu lǚxíng de shíjiān yǐjīng dìngxia le, nǐ gǎnkuài zhǔnbèi zhǔnbèi ba.

The time for our Europe trip is already set; please get ready right away.

⑩ 答应下的事情，一定要去做。

Dāyingxia de shìqing, yídìng yào qù zuò.

You have to do what you promised.

⑪ 他们两个人都觉得自己的想法对，争来争去，僵持不下。

Tāmen liǎng ge rén dōu juéde zìjǐ de xiǎngfǎ duì, zhēnglái-zhēngqù, jiāngchí bu xià.

Both of them feel they're right; they've been arguing back and forth and are quite deadlocked.

⑫ 今天晚上你住下吧，别走了。

Jīntiān wǎnshang nǐ zhùxia ba, bié zǒu le.

Stay here this evening — don't go.

从上面的例子可以看出来，表示结果意义的“下”可以结合的动词很多。有些动词后用“下”表示脱离、分离的意思很明显，如例①—⑦；例⑧以后的例子虽然和“脱离、分离”还有联系（或“脱离、分离”后已经固定），不过有的已经不那么明显，但是都表示动作有结果，这是无疑的。也正因为如此，我们提出学习趋向补语的结果意义时，要把动词和后边的趋向补语作为一个整体来记，像记一个词那样记。

These examples show that “xià” in its resultative sense combines with a great many verbs. In some cases, as in sentences ① to ⑦ above, “xià” after the main verb clearly indicates separation or removal. For sentences after ⑧, the sense of separation or removal may not be so obvious. However, such combinations do, without a doubt, indicate a clear consequence of the action of the verb. It is precisely because of this that when we consider learning about the resultative sense of directional complements, we treat the verb and the complement as a unit to be memorized as a semantic whole.

2.2 结果意义（二）
Resultative sense (2)

表示“凹陷”。前面可以用的动词有限，如“凹、陷、瘪、塌”等。

Signifies hollow or sunken. It combines with a limited number of verbs, such as “āo (dent), xiàn (fall into), biě (shrivel)” and “tā (collapse)”.

① 他开车撞在了树上，车头凹下一块。

Tā kāi chē zhuàngzàile shù shang, chētóu āoxia yí kuài.

He drove his car into a tree and dented the front.

② 大雨下了好几天，邻居家的房顶塌下了一片。

Dà yǔ xiàle hǎojǐ tiān, línjū jiā de fángdǐng tāxiale yí piàn.

It rained hard for days; the roof of the neighbor’s house collapsed.

2.3 结果意义（三）
Resultative sense (3)

表示“容纳”。

“Have the capacity for, hold”.

① 你的房间能不能放下两张床？

Nǐ de fángjiān néng bu néng fàngxia liǎng zhāng chuáng?

Can two beds fit in your room?

② 我的书包装不下十本书。

Wǒ de shūbāo zhuāng bu xià shí běn shū.

My schoolbag won’t hold ten books.

③ 这个餐厅虽然很大，但是也坐不下1000人。

Zhège cāntīng suīrán hěn dà, dànshì yě zuò bu xià yìqiān rén.

This cafeteria may be large but it won’t seat 1000.

3. 状态意义
Stative sense

表示由动态进入静态，在动词后有“停止”的意思。

Expresses a shift from a dynamic state to a static situation, from motion to stop.

① 红灯亮了，快停下！

Hóngdēng liàng le, kuài tíngxia!

The light's red — quick, stop!

② 最近你玩疯了，快考试了，你得静下心好好儿复习了。

Zuìjìn nǐ wánfēng le, kuài kǎoshì le, nǐ děi jìngxia xīn hǎohāor fùxí le.

You've been playing around like crazy recently. There's a test coming up; you need to calm down and start revising.

③ 你安下心住在我这里吧，不要想丢工作的事了。

Nǐ ānxia xīn zhùzài wǒ zhèli ba, bú yào xiǎng diū gōngzuò de shì le.

Why don't you relax and stay with me? Don't think anymore about losing your job.

1. 趋向意义
Directional sense

1.1 趋向意义（一）
Directional sense (1)

表示由高处向低处移动，参照点在低处。

Expresses movement from high to low, with "low" being the point of reference.

① 听见楼下有人敲门，妈妈很快地走下楼来。（楼下—动作起点）

Tīngjiàn lóuxià yǒu rén qiāo mén, māma hěn kuài de zǒuxià lóu lai.

Hearing someone downstairs knocking at the door, mother quickly went downstairs. (action begins downstairs)

② 不知道什么时候，正在睡觉的孩子滚下地来。（地—动作终点）

Bù zhīdào shénme shíhou, zhèngzài shuì jiào de háizi gǔnxià dì lai.

Not sure when, a child who was fast asleep rolled out of bed onto the floor. (movement ends on the floor)

③ 大家帮助他从楼上搬下很多东西来。

Dàjiā bāngzhù tā cóng lóu shàng bānxià hěn duō dōngxi lai.

Everyone helped him to move a bunch of things down from upstairs.

④ 你别着急，坐下来说。

Nǐ bié zháojí, zuò xialai shuō.

Don't worry, sit down and talk about it.

⑤ 雨太大了，从头上浇下来，我眼睛都睁不开了。

Yǔ tài dà le, cóng tóu shàng jiāo xialai, wǒ yǎnjing dōu zhēng bu kāi le.

It was pouring with rain and swilling off my head so much that I couldn't even open my eyes.

"下来"也可以表示由上级到下级或由地位高到地位低，如：

"Xiàlai" can also indicate a higher rank to a lower one, or a higher status to a lower one. For example:

⑥ 学校给系里拨下来一笔研究经费。

Xuéxiào gěi xì li bō xialai yì bǐ yánjiū jīngfèi.

The school came up with a chunk of research funds for the department.

⑦ 文件已经从教育部发下来了，你们学校应该收到了。

Wénjiàn yǐjīng cóng jiāoyùbù fā xialai le, nǐmen xuéxiào yīnggāi shōudào le.

The document's already been sent from the bureau of education; your school should have received it.

⑧ 因为犯了错误，他从总经理的位置降下来了。

Yīnwèi fànle cuòwu, tā cóng zǒngjīnglǐ de wèizhì jiàng xialai le.

Because he made a mistake, he was demoted from his position as general manager.

1.2 趋向意义（二）Directional sense (2)

表示退离前面的人或物体，参照点在移动的人或物体。

Signifies the retreat or removal of a person or thing; viewed from the person or thing doing the moving.

① 他太累了，教练把他换下场来。

Tā tài lèi le, jiàoliàn bǎ tā huànxià chǎng lai.

He was exhausted; the coach took him out of the game.

② 跟总经理说完话，他退下来一步，然后转身走了。

Gēn zǒngjīnglǐ shuōwán huà, tā tuì xialai yí bù, ránhòu zhuǎn shēn zǒu le.

When he finished talking with the general manager, he stepped back, turned and left.

2. 结果意义 Resultative sense

2.1 结果意义（一）——基本结果意义 Resultative sense (1) — basic resultative sense

表示次要物体或物体的一部分从主要物体或物体整体脱离、分离。着眼点在次要物体或物体的一部分。

Expresses the complete separation or removal of a secondary item or part from a primary item; with the secondary item as the point of reference.

① 小张从本子上撕下来一张纸，写上他的电话号码，交给了我。

Xiǎo Zhāng cóng běnzi shang sī xialai yì zhāng zhǐ, xiěshang tā de diànhuà hàomǎ, jiāogěile wǒ.

Xiao Zhang tore a page out of his notebook, wrote his telephone number on it and gave it to me.

在这个句子中，“下来”表示“纸”跟“本子”脱离，而且小张要用这张纸写电话号码，所以“纸”在这里是着眼点。

In this sentence, “xiàlai” indicates that the paper is separated from the notebook and that Xiao Zhang wants to use the paper to write his phone number on, so attention is focused on the sheet of paper.

② 鸟饿了，你把面包掰下来一小块，喂喂它吧。（面包的一小块和整个面包分离）

Niǎo è le, nǐ bǎ miànbāo bāi xialai yì xiǎo kuài, wèiwei tā ba.

The bird’s hungry; break off a small chunk of bread from the loaf and feed it. (a piece is removed from the loaf)

③ 房间很热，你快把外面的衣服脱下来吧。

Fángjiān hěn rè, nǐ kuài bǎ wàimian de yīfu tuō xialai ba.

It’s hot in the room; quick, please take your outer clothes off.

④ 这张图片没贴好，你得把它揭下来，再重新贴。（图片与贴图片的物体分离）

Zhè zhāng túpiàn méi tiēhǎo, nǐ děi bǎ tā jiē xialai, zài chóngxīn tiē.

This photograph hasn’t been properly attached; you need to remove it and stick it on again. (photograph removed from its backing)

⑤ 你们把刚刚听完的故事写下来，这就是今天的作业。（“写下来的故事”与原型“听到的故事”分离）

Nǐmen bǎ gānggāng tīngwán de gùshi xiě xialai, zhè jiùshì jīntiān de zuòyè.

Write down the story you've just heard — that's the assignment for today. (story to be written, removed from the original one heard)

⑥ 妈妈常常把好吃的东西留下来一些，等我回家的时候给我吃。

Māma chángcháng bǎ hǎochī de dōngxi liú xialai yìxiē, děng wǒ huí jiā de shíhou gěi wǒ chī.

Mother often saves some tasty things for me to eat when I get home.

⑦ 你这么多年一定存下来很多钱吧？

Nǐ zhème duō nián yídìng cún xialai hěn duō qián ba?

Over so many years, no doubt you've saved up a lot of money.

⑧ 他真的需要你的帮助，你就答应下来他的请求吧。

Tā zhēnde xūyào nǐde bāngzhù, nǐ jiù dāying xialai tā de qǐngqiú ba.

He really needs your help; please respond to his request.

⑨ 开会的时间已经定下来了，但在什么地方开，还定不下来。

Kāihuì de shíjiān yǐjīng dìng xialai le, dàn zài shénme dìfang kāi, hái dìng bu xiàlái.

The time of the meeting's already been fixed, but where it'll take place still hasn't been decided.

从上面的句子可以看出，像“下”一样，“下来”前可以用的动词很多，在有些动词后，“下来”表示分离、脱离的意思很明显，比如例①—④；有的虽然不太明显，但是还可以分析出来，比如例⑥“留下来”意思是“留下来的东西”和整体分离，例⑦“存下来”是“存的钱”与整个收入分离；有的例句只能看作表示“固定”，如例⑧、⑨。此外“住、延迟、拖、拖延、僵”等后边的“下来”也归入此类结果意义。

These sentences show that, just like “xià”, “xiàlai” can follow a lot of different verbs. In some cases, for instance, in sentences ①—④, the sense of separation or removal is quite clear. In other cases, although that sense is not so obvious, it can still be detected: thus in sentence ⑥ above, "liú xialai" ('what is saved') indicates that the things saved is removed from the original batch; in ⑦, the sense of "cún xialai" is that the money saved is separated from the rest of the income. But in some sentences, such as ⑧、⑨, the sense is "to fix" or "determine". Similarly, "xiàlai" following "zhù (stay, live), yánchí (delay, postpone), tuō (delay), tuōyán (delay, stall)" and "jiāng (frozen, deadlocked)" also belong to the same type of resultative sense.

2.2 结果意义（二）
Resultative sense (2)

表示"凹陷"，可以用的动词很少，比如"瘪、瘦"等。

Signifies "sunken" or "reduced"; combines with a relatively small number of verbs such as "biě (shrivel)" and "shòu (be thin, tight)".

① 他运动了一个月，瘦下来5公斤。

Tā yùndòngle yí ge yuè, shòu xialai wǔ gōngjīn.

He exercised for a month and lost 5 kg.

② 篮球漏气了，瘪了下来。

Lánqiú lòu qì le, biěle xialai.

The basketball's leaking air; it's gone flat.

2.3 结果意义（三）
Resultative sense (3)

表示完成了一个比较费时费力或需要克服一定困难才能完成的动作行为。可以用在动词后。

Indicates an activity or behavior that cannot be completed without expending a relatively large amount of time and effort in order to overcome serious difficulties. It can be used after a verb.

① 这次的任务总算拿下来了，真不容易呀。

Zhè cì de rènwù zǒngsuàn ná xialai le, zhēn bù róngyì ya.

At long last, this job's been accomplished — it really wasn't easy.

② 经过医生的努力，老李总算活下来了。

Jīngguò yīshēng de nǔlì, Lǎo Lǐ zǒngsuàn huó xialai le.

Through the efforts of the doctor, Lao Li's reviving at last.

③ 困难太多了，我们真有点儿坚持不下来了。

Kùnnan tài duō le, wǒmen zhēn yǒudiǎnr jiānchí bu xiàlái le.

There are so many difficulties; we really feel unable to carry on.

④ 他基础太差，大学念不下来了。

Tā jīchǔ tài chà, dàxué niàn bu xialai le.

His foundation's too weak; he can't continue at university.

也可以用在时间词后。如：

"Xiàlai" can also be used after a time word. For example:

⑤ 我在这个公司每天都早来晚走，很辛苦，可是一年下来，也没存下什么钱。

Wǒ zài zhège gōngsī měi tiān dōu zǎo lái wǎn zǒu, hěn xīnkǔ, kěshì yì nián xiàlai, yě méi cúnxia shénme qián.

I worked at this company every day from dawn to dusk, it was really tough. But at the end of the year, I still hadn't saved much money.

⑥ 四年大学下来，他不但学到了知识，人也成熟多了。

Sì nián dàxué xiàlai, tā búdàn xuédàole zhīshi, rén yě chéngshú duō le.

At the end of four years of university, he not only gained a lot of knowledge, he also matured a lot.

3. 状态意义

Stative sense

表示由动态进入静态，可以用在动词和形容词后。

Expresses a shift from a dynamic state to a static state; can be used after verbs or adjectives.

① 前面红灯亮了，我很快地把车停下来。

Qiánmian hóngdēng liàng le, wǒ hěn kuài de bǎ chē tíng xialai.

The light in front turned red and I quickly brought the car to a stop.

② 事情太多了，他想歇几天，可是歇不下来。

Shìqing tài duō le, tā xiǎng xiē jǐ tiān , kěshì xiē bu xiàlái.

There was too much to do; he wanted to rest for a few days but couldn't afford to stop.

③ 什么事都不要想，你就安下心来在我这里休息休息吧。

Shénme shì dōu bú yào xiǎng, nǐ jiù ānxià xīn lai zài wǒ zhèli xiūxi xiūxi ba.

Don't think about anything, just take it easy and stay at my place and rest.

④ 上课了，老师进来以后，学生很快就安静下来了。

Shàng kè le, lǎoshī jìnlai yǐhòu, xuésheng hěn kuài jiù ānjìng xialai le.

It was time for class and after the teacher entered, the students quickly calmed down.

⑤ 拉上窗帘，房间里立刻暗了下来。

Lāshang chuānglián, fángjiān li lìkè ànle xialai.

The curtains were drawn and the room quickly grew dark.

⑥ 火车快到站了，速度慢了下来。

Huǒchē kuài dàozhàn le , sùdù mànle xialai.

As the train got close to the station, it slowed down.

⑦ 他们俩在一起谈了很长时间，原来紧张的关系缓和下来了。

Tāmen liǎ zài yìqǐ tánle hěn cháng shíjiān, yuánlái jǐnzhāng de guānxi huǎnhé xialai le.

The two of them talked for a long time and their once tense relationship relaxed.

⑧ 他在这个小城市工作，闲下来的时候常去附近的湖边钓鱼。

Tā zài zhège xiǎo chéngshì gōngzuò, xián xialai de shíhou cháng qù fùjìn de húbiān diào yú.

He worked in this little town and in his free time, he often went to the neighboring lake to fish.

1. 趋向意义

Directional sense

1.1 趋向意义（一）

Directional sense (1)

表示由高处向低处移动，参照点在高处。

Expresses movement from high to low, with "high" being the point of reference.

① 听说姐姐回来了，弟弟很快地从楼上跑下去。

Tīngshuō jiějie huílai le, dìdi hěn kuài de cóng lóushàng pǎo xiaqu.

Hearing that older sister had returned, younger brother quickly ran downstairs.

② 空姐们微笑地看着乘客们走下飞机去。（飞机—动作起点）

Kōngjiěmen wēixiào de kànzhe chéngkèmen zǒuxià fēijī qu.

The airhostesses smiled as they watched the passengers disembark from the plane. (viewed from the plane)

③ 小运动员一点儿也不怕，一个接着一个跳下水去。（水—动作终点）

Xiǎo yùndòngyuán yìdiǎnr yě bú pà, yí ge jiēzhe yí ge tiàoxià shuǐ qu.

Without the slightest fear, the young athletes jumped into the water one by one. (with the water as the endpoint)

④ 孩子知道自己错了，把头低了下去。

Háizi zhīdào zìjǐ cuò le, bǎ tóu dīle xiaqu.

The child knew he had made a mistake and lowered his head.

⑤ 他病了，吃不下东西去。

Tā bìng le, chī bu xià dōngxi qu.

He's ill and can't eat any food.

⑥ 你怎么能从窗户把垃圾扔下去？太不像话了！

Nǐ zěnme néng cóng chuānghu bǎ lājī rēng xiaqu? Tài bú xiàng huà le!

How can you throw the trash out of the window? That makes no sense at all!

也可以表示由上级到下级。如：

It can also indicate a higher rank to a lower one. For example:

⑦ 市长叫救援人员把物资给灾民发下去。

Shìzhǎng jiào jiùyuán rényuán bǎ wùzī gěi zāimín fā xiaqu.

The mayor told the relief workers to distribute supplies to the disaster victims.

⑧ 教育部要求各学校把新的招生办法立即传达下去。

Jiāoyùbù yāoqiú gè xuéxiào bǎ xīn de zhāoshēng bànfǎ lìjí chuándá xiaqu.

The Ministry of Education asked every school to immediately pass on new ways of recruiting students.

1.2 趋向意义（二）

Directional sense (2)

表示退离前面的人或物体，参照点在前面的人或物体。

Signifies the retreat or removal of a person or thing; viewed from the person or thing front.

① 他对工作人员说："这里没事了，你们都退下去吧！"

Tā duì gōngzuò rényuán shuō: "zhèli méi shì le, nǐmen dōu tuì xiaqu ba!"

He said to the workers: "There's

nothing to do here anymore, you all go back down, okay?"

② A队有一个队员犯了5次规，被罚下场去。

A-duì yǒu yí ge duìyuán fànle wǔ cì guī, bèi fáxià chǎng qu.

There's a player on the A team who has committed 5 rule infractions; he's been thrown out of the game.

2. 结果意义

Resultative sense

2.1 结果意义（一）——基本结果意义

Resultative sense (1) — basic resultative sense

表示次要物体或物体的一部分从主要物体或整体脱离、分离，着眼点在主要物体或整体。

Expresses the complete separation or removal of a secondary item or part from a primary item, with the primary item being the point of reference.

① 进了房间，里边很热，我把帽子摘了下去。

Jìnle fángjiān, lǐbian hěn rè, wǒ bǎ màozi zhāile xiaqu.

Entering the room, I found it quite hot inside and took my hat off.

② 下课了，老师把自己写在黑板上的字擦下去以后走出教室。

Xià kè le, lǎoshī bǎ zìjǐ xiězài hēibǎn shang de zì cā xiaqu yǐhòu zǒuchu jiàoshì.

After class, the teacher erased what he'd written on the board and walked out of the classroom.

③ 这儿有很多杂草，你快拔下去吧。

Zhèr yǒu hěn duō zácǎo, nǐ kuài bá xiaqu ba.

There are a lot of weeds here; please be quick and pull them out.

从上边的句子可以看出，动词后用“下去”之后，次要物体是动作者不想留存原处的，如例①和例③；有时次要物体甚至消失不存在了，如例②。这和“下来”不同。比较下面的句子：

The examples such as ① and ③ above show that adding “xiàqu” to the verb indicates that secondary object (hat, weeds) is not intended to remain in its usual place. In cases such as ②, the secondary object (what was written on the board) ceases to exist. This is different from “xiàlai”, as the following sentences show:

④ 这幅画我很喜欢，你摘下来给我吧。（“保留”画）

Zhè fú huà wǒ hěn xǐhuan, nǐ zhāi xialai gěi wǒ ba.

I like this painting; could you take it down and give it to me? (it'll stay with me)

这幅画太难看了，你摘下去扔了算了。（不“保留”画）

Zhè fú huà tài nánkàn le, nǐ zhāi xiaqu rēngle suàn le.

This painting is awful; take it down and get rid of it. (it'll be eliminated)

⑤ 他从本子上撕下来一张纸，写了几句话，让我交给小李。（“保留”纸）

Tā cóng běnzi shang sī xialai yì zhāng zhǐ, xiěle jǐ jù huà , ràng wǒ jiāo gěi Xiǎo Lǐ.

He tore a sheet of paper out of the notebook, wrote a couple of sentences on it and had me give it to Xiao Li. (Xiao Li will keep the paper)

他写了几个字，觉得不好看，就把那张纸撕了下去。（不“保留”纸）

Tā xiěle jǐ ge zì, juéde bù hǎokàn, jiù bǎ nà zhāng zhǐ sīle xiaqu.

He wrote a few words, but felt they didn't look good and tore the page out. (the paper is destroyed)

因此，分离的物体如果是要保留的，就用“下来”；不想保留的，就用“下去”。

So if the thing that gets removed is preserved, “xiàlai” is used; if it is discarded, “xiàqu” is used.

2.2 结果意义（二）
Resultative sense (2)

表示“凹陷”，可以用在“凹、陷、瘪、塌、瘦”等动词后。

Expresses “sunken”; combines with verbs such as “āo (be concave), xiàn (cave in), biě (shrivel), tā (collapse)” and “shòu (be thin, tight)”.

① 他大病了一场，眼窝都塌下去了。

Tā dàbìngle yì chǎng, yǎnwō dōu tā xiaqu le.

He got very ill and his eyes sunk in their sockets.

② 一场大雨以后，路中间陷下去一个大坑。

Yì chǎng dàyǔ yǐhòu, lù zhōngjiān xiàn xiaqu yí ge dà kēng.

After a big storm, a large pothole formed in the road.

③ 几天不见，他瘦下去一圈儿，是在减肥吗？

Jǐ tiān bú jiàn, tā shòu xiaqu yì quānr, shì zài jiǎn féi ma?

We hadn’t seen him for a few days and he’d lost a load of weight; has he been dieting?

3. 状态意义
Stative sense

3.1 状态意义（一）
Stative sense (1)

表示由动态进入静态，常用在表示声音、光线、人的意志情绪等形容词后边。

Expresses a shift from a dynamic state to a static state. Commonly used after adjectives which indicate a change in intensity of sound, light or emotion.

① 我在门外听见里边有人吵架，开始声音很大，后来小下去了。

Wǒ zài mén wài tīngjiàn lǐbian yǒu rén chǎo jià, kāishǐ shēngyīn hěn dà, hòulái xiǎo xiaqu le.

Outside the door I heard people arguing inside; at first, it was very noisy, then it diminished.

② 我把电灯开关转动了一下，灯光渐渐暗下去了。

Wǒ bǎ diàndēng kāiguān zhuàndòng le yí xià, dēngguāng jiànjiàn àn xiaqu le.

I turned the light switch a bit and the light gradually diminished.

③ 等他心情平静下去了，我才开始跟他讨论问题。

Děng tā xīnqíng píngjìng xiaqu le, wǒ cái kāishǐ gēn tā tǎolùn wèntí.

I waited until his mood calmed down before starting to discuss the problems with him.

虽然“下来”“下去”都表示由动态进入静态，但还是有不同。“下来”表示近处的变化，“下去”则表示远处的变化。比较：

Although both “xiàlai” and “xiàqu” indicate a shift to a lower degree of intensity, they have their differences. “Xiàlai” indicates local changes; “xiàqu” indicates more distant ones. Compare:

④ 老师敲了几下桌子，教室才安静下来。

Lǎoshī qiāole jǐ xià zhuōzi, jiàoshì cái ānjìng xialai.

The teacher pounded on the table a few times before the class calmed down.

旁边的房间里有人吵架，开始声音很大，后来慢慢低下去了。

Pángbiān de fángjiān li yǒu rén chǎo jià, kāishǐ shēngyīn hěn dà, hòulái mànmàn dī xiaqu le.

There were people arguing in the room next door; it started out loud then slowly diminished.

⑤ 我拧了一下电灯开关，房间一下子暗下来了。

Wǒ nǐngle yí xià diàndēng kāiguān, fángjiān yíxiàzi àn xialai le.

I twisted the light switch and the room suddenly grew darker.

远处的灯光一点儿一点儿暗下去了。

Yuǎnchù de dēngguāng yìdiǎnr yìdiǎnr àn xiaqu le.

The light in the distance gradually diminished.

3.2 状态意义（二）

Stative sense (2)

表示动作继续进行或状态继续保持。

Expresses continuation of an action or persistence of a state.

① 你课文念得不错，接着念下去。

Nǐ kèwén niàn de búcuò, jiēzhe niàn xiaqu。

You're reading the lesson very nicely; continue reading.

② 你也不找工作，每天闲逛，再这样混下去，生活就成问题了。

Nǐ yě bù zhǎo gōngzuò, měi tiān xiánguàng, zài zhèyàng hùn xiaqu, shēnghuó jiù chéng wèntí le.

You don't look for work but wander around each day; if you continue muddling along like this, your life's going to have problems.

③ 学生的作业写得太差了，老师改了几页，就改不下去了。

Xuésheng de zuòyè xiě de tài chà le, lǎoshī gǎile jǐ yè, jiù gǎi bu xiàqù le.

The student didn't do a good job with his homework; the teacher corrected a few pages, but couldn't correct any more.

④ 你们工作做得不错，长期坚持下去，一定会有好成绩。

Nǐmen gōngzuò zuò de búcuò，chángqī jiānchí xiaqu, yídìng huì yǒu hǎo chéngjì.

You've done a good job; persevere over the long run and you're sure to have success.

⑤ 问题应该尽快解决，拖下去不是办法。

Wèntí yīnggāi jǐnkuài jiějué，tuō xiaqu bú shì bànfǎ.

The problems should be solved as quickly as possible; putting them off isn't an option.

⑥ 你不去医院，自己乱吃药，这样下去会出问题的。

Nǐ bú qù yīyuàn, zìjǐ luàn chī yào, zhèyàng xiaqu huì chū wèntí de.

If you go on avoiding going to the hospital and just take medicine randomly on your own, you're going to have some problems.

（一）"下"组趋向意义、结果意义、状态意义之间的意义联系

Semantic relationship among the directional sense, resultative sense and the stative sense of the "xià" group

下表可以显示"下"组趋向意义（一）、状态意义、趋向意义（二）与结果意义（一）之间的关系。

The following chart shows that the 1st directional sense, the stative sense, the 2nd directional sense and the 1st resultative sense of the "xià" group.

"下"组 "xià" group	趋向意义（一） directional sense (1)	状态意义 stative sense	趋向意义（二） directional sense (2)	结果意义（一） resultative sense (1)
下 xià	由高到低移动，参照点不确定。 Movement from high to low, with no explicit point of reference.	由动态进入静态、停止。 From a dynamic state to a static or stationary state.	退离前面的目标，参照点不确定。 Retreating from a prior position, with no explicit point of reference.	脱离、分离，参照点不确定。 Complete separation or removal, with no explicit point of reference.
下来 xiàlai	由高到低移动，参照点在低处。 Movement from high to low, with "low" as point of reference.	由动态进入静态、停止。 From a dynamic state to a static or stationary state.	退离前面的目标，参照点在移动的人或物体。 Retreating from a prior position; from the perspective of the person or thing doing the moving.	脱离、分离，着眼点在次要物体。 Complete separation or removal, with the secondary item as the point of reference.

（续表）

"下"组 "xià" group	趋向意义（一） directional sense (1)	状态意义 stative sense	趋向意义（二） directional sense (2)	结果意义（一） resultative sense (1)
下去 xiàqu	由高到低移动，参照点在高处。 Movement from high to low, with "high" as point of reference.	1.由动态进入静态； 2.继续。 1.From a dynamic state to a static state; 2.Continuing.	退离前面的目标，参照点在前面的人或物体。 Retreating from a prior position; from the perspective of the person or thing in front.	脱离、分离，着眼点在主要物体。 Complete separation or removal, with the primary item as the point of reference.

（二）"下"组意义小结

Summary of senses of the "xià" group

	下 xià	下来 xiàlai	下去 xiàqu
趋向意义（一） directional sense (1) 由高到低移动。 Movement from high to low.	参照点不确定。 No explicit point of reference. 我看见他走下楼。（我—在楼上或在楼下） Wǒ kànjiàn tā zǒuxia lóu. (speaker upstairs or downstairs)	参照点在低处。 With "low" as the point of reference. 我看见他走下楼来。（我—在楼下） Wǒ kànjiàn tā zǒuxià lóu lai. (speaker downstairs)	参照点在高处。 With "high" as the point of reference. 我看见他走下楼去。（我—在楼上） Wǒ kànjiàn tā zǒu xià lóu qu. (speaker upstairs)

（续表）

	下 xià	下来 xiàlái	下去 xiàqù
趋向意义（二） directional sense (2) 退离前面的目标。 To retreat or remove.	参照点不确定。 No explicit point of reference. 他把作业交给老师，退下一步，走了。（说话人可能在“老师”旁边，也可能在“他”旁边） Tā bǎ zuòyè jiāogěi lǎoshī, tuìxia yí bù, zǒu le. (the speaker could be near the teacher or him)	参照点在移动的人或物体。 From the point of view of the person or thing doing the moving. 他退下足球场来，坐在旁边休息。（参照点是“球场”外） Tā tuìxià zúqiúchǎng lai, zuòzài pángbiān xiūxi. (outside the football pitch)	参照点在前面的人或物体。 From the prespective of the person or thing in front. 这里没事了，你退下去吧。（参照点在说话人） Zhèli méi shì le, nǐ tuì xiaqu ba. (away from the speaker)
结果意义（一） resultative sense (1) 次要物体或物体的一部分从主要物体或整体脱离、分离。 Secondary item or part of item is completely separated or removed from the main item.	着眼点不确定，可在主要物体、整体，也可在次要物体、物体的一部分。 No explicit point of reference; focus could be on the primary object or the secondary. 他从行李上解下绳子。 Tā cóng xíngli shang jiě xia shéngzi.	着眼点在次要物体或物体的一部分。 The secondary object is the focus of interest. 你把行李上的绳子解下来。(着眼点在次要物体“绳子”) Nǐ bǎ xíngli shang de shéngzi jiě xialai. (the string is the focus of interest)	着眼点在主要物体或整体。 The primary object is the focus of interest. 你打开行李吧，把绳子解下去。(着眼点在主要物体“行李”) Nǐ dǎkāi xíngli ba, bǎ shéngzi jiě xiaqu. (the suitcase is the focus of interest)
结果意义(二) resultative sense (2) 表示“凹陷”。 Indicating sunken or collapsed.	车头撞得凹下一块。 Chētóu zhuàng de āoxia yí kuài.	几天不吃饭，他瘦下来5斤。 Jǐ tiān bù chī fàn, tā shòu xialai wǔ jīn.	车头撞得凹下去一块。 Chētóu zhuàng de āo xiaqu yí kuài.

（续表）

	下 xià	下来 xiàlái	下去 xiàqù
结果意义（三） resultative sense (3)	表示“容纳”。 Indicating capacity. 教室里坐不下100个学生。 Jiàoshì li zuò bu xià yìbǎi ge xuésheng.	表示完成了一个比较费时费力或需要克服一定困难的动作行为。 Indicating an activity or behavior that cannot be completed without expending a relatively large amount of time and effort or overcoming serious difficulties. 课文虽然很难，他还是念下来了。 Kèwén suīrán hěn nán, tā háishi niàn xialai le.	—
状态意义 stative sense	表示由动态进入静态。 Indicating a shift from a dynamic state to a static state 把车停下！ Bǎ chē tíngxia!	表示由动态进入静态。 Indicating a shift from a dynamic state to a static state. 天空暗下来了。 Tiānkōng àn xialai le.	1.表示由动态进入静态。 Indicating a shift from a dynamic state to a static state. 声音低下去了。 Shēngyīn dī xiaqu le. 2.表示继续。 Indicates continuity. 说下去！ Shuō xiaqu!

（三）“上”组和“下”组之间的对应关系

Correspondences between the “shàng” group and the “xià” group

“上”组中的“上”“上来”“上去”和“下”组中的“下”“下来”“下去”在参照点或着眼点不变的情况下，相互之间存在对应关系。我们用下表表示：

In contexts where the point of reference or the point of view is the same, the “shàng” group (“shàng” “shànglai” and “shàngqu”) and the “xia” group (“xià” “xiàlai” and "xiàqu") show correspondences.

	趋向意义（一） directional sense (1)	趋向意义（二） directional sense (2)	结果意义（一） resultative sense (1)	状态意义 stative sense
上 shàng	走上楼。（参照点不确定） zǒushang lóu. (neutral)	走上前。（参照点不确定） zǒushang qián. (neutral)	贴上邮票。（着眼点不确定） tiēshang yóupiào. (neutral)	他唱上歌了。 Tā chàngshang gē le.
下 xià	走下楼。（参照点不确定） zǒuxia lóu. (neutral)	退下一步。（参照点不确定） tuìxia yí bù. (neutral)	撕下邮票。（着眼点不确定） sīxia yóupiào. (neutral)	车停下了。 Chē tíngxia le.
上来 shànglai	走上楼来。（参照点在楼上） zǒushàng lóu lai. (with "high" as the point of reference)	走上前来。（参照点在前面的目标） zǒushàng qián lai. (viewed from the front goal)	给这个班补上两个人来。（着眼点在"这个班"） Gěi zhège bān bǔ shàng liǎng gè rén lai. (focus on "zhège bān")	天气慢慢凉上来了。 tiānqì mànmàn liáng shanglai le.
下去 xiàqu	走下楼去。（参照点在楼上） zǒuxià lóu qu. (with "high" as the point of reference)	退下去一步。（参照点在前面的目标） tuì xiaqu yí bù. (viewed from the front goal)	把这个班的人减下去两个。（着眼点在"这个班"） Bǎ zhège bān de rén jiǎn xiaqu liǎng ge. (focus on "zhège bān")	声音低下去了。 shēngyīn dī xiaqu le .
上去 shàngqu	走上楼去。（参照点在楼下） zǒushàng lóu qu. (with "low" as the point of reference)	走上前去。（参照点在移动的人或物体） zǒushàng qián qu. (with reference the moving person or thing)	墙上不干净，把这张纸贴上去。(着眼点是"纸") Qiáng shang bù gànjìng, bǎ zhè zhāng zhǐ tiē shangqu。 (focus on "zhǐ")	——

（续表）

	趋向意义（一）directional sense (1)	趋向意义（二）directional sense (2)	结果意义（一）resultative sense (1)	状态意义 stative sense
下来	走下楼来。（参照点在楼下）zǒuxià lóu lai. (with "low" as the point of reference)	退下来一步。（参照点在移动的人或物体）tuì xialai yí bù. (with reference the moving person or thing)	撕下来一张纸，写上你的电话号码给我。（着眼点是"纸"）Sī xialai yì zhāng zhǐ, xiěshang nǐ de diàn huà hàomǎ gěi wǒ. (focus on "zhǐ")	天空暗下来了。Tiānkōng àn xialai le .

“进”组

“Jìn” group

“进”组包括“进”“进来”“进去”。

The “jìn” group consists of “jìn” “jìnlai” and “jìnqu”.

进	进来	进去
jìn	jìnlai	jìnqu
(X) ○ ⟶ [(X)]	○ ⟶ [X]	X○ ⟶ [ ]

1. 趋向意义

Directional sense

表示由处所外面向里面移动。参照点不确定。

Signifies movement from outside to inside; no explicit point of reference.

① 上课了，学生们都走进教室。

Shàng kè le, xuéshengmen dōu zǒujin jiàoshì.

Time for class; the students are all going into the classroom.

② 我走进他的房间时，他正在打电话。

Wǒ zǒujin tā de fángjiān shí , tā zhèngzài dǎ diànhuà.

When I walked into his room, he was on the phone.

③ 看见老师走进教室，我们都站了起来。

Kànjiàn lǎoshī zǒujin jiàoshì , wǒmen dōu zhànle qilai.

When we saw the teacher walked into the classroom, we all stood up.

④ 我把手伸进书包里找手机。

Wǒ bǎ shǒu shēnjin shūbāo li zhǎo shǒujī.

I reached my hand into my schoolbag to feel for my mobile phone.

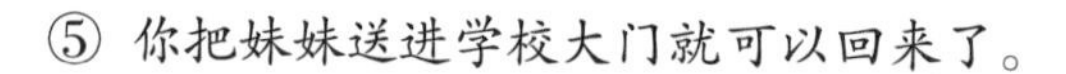

⑤ 你把妹妹送进学校大门就可以回来了。

Nǐ bǎ mèimei sòngjin xuéxiào dàmén jiù kěyǐ huílai le.

Take your younger sister to the door of the school and then you can come back.

也可以表示领有关系的改变，如：

It can also indicate a change of ownership. For example:

⑥ 现在你应该买进一些好的股票。

Xiànzài nǐ yīnggāi mǎijin yìxiē hǎo de gǔpiào.

Now is the time to invest in some good stocks.

还可以用在“看、读、念、听”等动词后，表示动作的结果，一般用可能补语形式，如：

It can also be used after verbs such as “kàn” “dú” “niàn” and “tīng” to express the result of an action; generally with potential complements. For example:

⑦ 这几天我老想着回家，看不进书。

Zhè jǐ tiān wǒ lǎo xiǎngzhe huí jiā, kàn bu jìn shū.

These last few days, I’ve been dreaming of going home; I can’t do any studying.

⑧ 他这个人只相信自己，听不进别人的意见。

Tā zhège rén zhǐ xiāngxìn zìjǐ, tīng bu jìn biérén de yìjiàn.

He only believes in himself; he doesn’t consider other people’s views.

2. 结果意义

Resultative sense

表示“凹陷”，用在“凹、瘪”等具有凹陷意义的动词后。

After verbs of "collapse", such as "āo (be concave, sunken)" or "biě (shrivel)", the resultative sense is "caved in" .

① 他的车门旁边瘪进一块，是被别人撞的。

Tā de chēmén pángbiān biějin yí kuài, shì bèi biérén zhuàng de.

The side of his car was dented in; it was smashed by someone.

② 这个房子比旁边的凹进很多，前面有一大块空地。

Zhège fángzi bǐ pángbiān de āojin hěn duō, qiánmian yǒu yí dà kuài kòngdì.

This house has sunk in much more than the one next to it; there's a large gap in the front.

趋向意义

Directional sense

表示由处所外面向里面移动。参照点在处所里面。

Signifies movement from outside to inside, with the inside being the point of reference.

① 我们正在上课的时候，有一个同学急急忙忙走进教室来。

Wǒmen zhèngzài shàng kè de shíhou, yǒu yí ge tóngxué jíjí-mángmáng zǒujìn jiàoshì lai.

Just as we were starting class, a classmate walked quickly into the classroom.

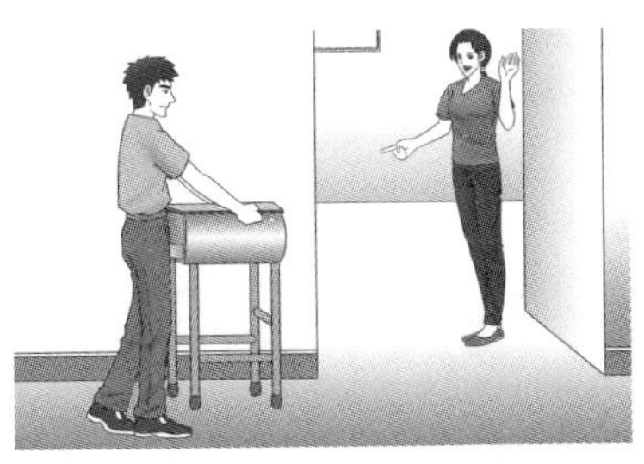

② 你把外边的桌子搬进来吧。

Nǐ bǎ wàibian de zhuōzi bān jinlai ba.

Move the outside table inside please.

③ 弟弟从窗户外边把头伸进来告诉我，我的好朋友来了。

Dìdi cóng chuānghu wàibian bǎ tóu shēn jinlai gàosu wǒ, wǒ de hǎo péngyou lái le.

Younger brother put his head in through the window and told me that my good friend had arrived.

④ 那个孩子我认识，你把他带进来吧。

Nàge háizi wǒ rènshi, nǐ bǎ tā dài jinlai ba.

I know that child, show him inside.

也可以表示领有关系的改变，如：

It can also signify a change of ownership. For example:

⑤ 最近他买进来很多股票。

Zuìjìn tā mǎi jinlai hěn duō gǔpiào.

Recently he's bought in a lot of stocks.

1. 趋向意义

Directional sense

表示由处所外面向里面移动。参照点在处所外面。

Signifies movement from outside to inside, with the outside being the point of reference.

① 上课了，老师走进教室去。

Shàng kè le, lǎoshī zǒujìn jiàoshì qu.

Class started and the teacher walked into the classroom.

② 在饭馆儿吃完饭，我把手伸进衣兜去，钱包不见了！

Zài fànguǎnr chīwán fàn, wǒ bǎ shǒu shēnjìn yīdōu qu, qiánbāo bú jiàn le!

After I finished eating at the restaurant, I put my hand into my pocket and my wallet wasn't there!

③ 里边正在开会，过一会儿你把这封信送进去吧。

Lǐbian zhèngzài kāi huì, guò yíhuìr nǐ bǎ zhè fēng xìn sòng jinqu ba.

Inside there's a meeting going on; in a while, take this letter in, okay?

可以用在“看、念、听”等动词后，表示动作结果，如：

It can also be used after verbs such as “kàn” “niàn” and “tīng” to express the result of an action. For example:

④ 上课的时候我一直想别的事，老师讲的我一句也没听进去。

Shàng kè de shíhou wǒ yìzhí xiǎng biéde shì, lǎoshī jiǎngde wǒ yí jù yě méi tīng jinqu.

All through class, I was thinking of other things and didn't take in a thing of what the teacher was talking about.

⑤ 周围很吵，我根本看不进去书。

Zhōuwéi hěn chǎo, wǒ gēnběn kàn bu jìnqù shū.

It's noisy around here; I simply can't manage to read anything.

⑥ 我告诉他这样做很危险，可是他听不进去。

Wǒ gàosu tā zhèyàng zuò hěn wēixiǎn, kěshì tā tīng bu jìnqù.

I told him that doing it that way was dangerous but he didn't take any heed.

2. 结果意义

Resultative sense

表示“凹陷”。

Signifies “collapse (sunken, caved in, hollow)”.

① 他两天没睡觉了，眼睛都凹进去了。

Tā liǎng tiān méi shuì jiào le, yǎnjing dōu āo jinqu le.

He hasn't slept for two days; his eyes have a hollow look.

② 你的车这儿怎么瘪进去一块？

Nǐ de chē zhèr zěnme biě jinqu yí kuài?

How come your car has a dent here?

"进"组小结

Summary of the "jìn" group

	进 jìn	进来 jìnlai	进去 jìnqu
趋向意义 directional sense	表示由处所外面向里面移动。参照点不确定。 Signifies movement from outside to inside; no explicit point of reference. 走进教室 zǒujin jiàoshì	表示由处所外面向里面移动。参照点在处所里面。 Signifies movement from outside to inside, with the inside being the point of reference. 已经上课5分钟了，他才走进教室来。 Yǐjīng shàng kè wǔ fēnzhōng le, tā cái zǒujìn jiàoshì lai.	表示由处所外面向里面移动。参照点在处所外面。 Signifies movement from outside to inside, with the outside being the point of reference. 上课了，我们走进教室去。 Shàng kè le, wǒmen zǒujìn jiàoshì qu.
结果意义 resultative sense	表示"凹陷"。 Signifies "collapse". 他的车头瘪进一块。 Tā de chētóu biějin yí kuài.	——	表示"凹陷"。 Signifies "collapse". 他的车头瘪进去一块。 Tā de chētóu biě jinqu yí kuài.

“出”组

“Chū” group

“出”组包括“出”“出来”“出去”。

The “chū” group consists of “chū” “chūlai” and “chūqu”.

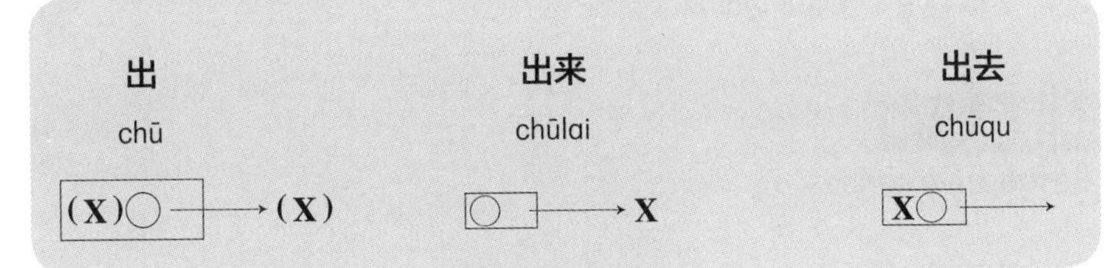

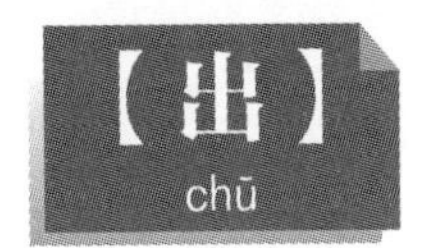

1. 趋向意义

Directional sense

表示由处所里面向外面移动，参照点不确定。

Signifies movement from inside to outside, with no explicit point of reference.

① 下课了，学生走出教室。

Xià kè le, xuésheng zǒuchu jiàoshì.

Class is over and the students are walking out of the classroom.

② 大门里跑出一匹马。

Dàmén li pǎochu yì pǐ mǎ.

A horse ran out of the main gate.

③ 她从书包里拿出了几本书。

Tā cóng shūbāo li náchule jǐ běn shū.

She took a few books out of her schoolbag.

④ 公司派出两个人到国外学习。

Gōngsī pàichu liǎng ge rén dào guówài xuéxí.

The company sent a couple of people abroad to study.

“出”也可以表示领有关系的转移，如：

It can also indicate a change of possession or ownership. For example:

⑤ 他让出一部分股份。

Tā ràngchu yí bùfen gǔfèn.

He let go a part of his stocks.

2. 结果意义

Resultative senses

2.1 结果意义（一）

Resultative sense (1)

表示突出、凸起的意思。

Signifies protrusion or projection.

① 这个房子比周围的高出有十米。

Zhège fángzi bǐ zhōuwéi de gāochu yǒu shí mǐ.

This house is about 10 meters taller than the surrounding ones.

② 他的牙长得不太齐，上边比下边突出不少。

Tā de yá zhǎng de bú tài qí, shàngbian bǐ xiàbian tūchu bù shǎo.

His teeth haven't grown out very evenly; the upper ones protrude quite a bit over the lower ones.

③ 这个操场真大，比我们学校的能大出两个足球场。

Zhège cāochǎng zhēn dà, bǐ wǒmen xuéxiào de néng dàchu liǎng ge zúqiúchǎng.

This playing field is really big — probably two football fields bigger than the one at our school.

这个意义跟趋向意义关系很密切，可以用在“突、鼓、凸”等动词和“高、大、宽”等形容词的后边。

This sense is very close to the directional sense; it can be used after verbs (of protrusion) like “tū (project)” “gǔ (be bulging)” and “tū (protrude)” and adjectives such as “gāo (tall)” “dà (big)” and “kuān (wide)”.

2.2 结果意义（二）Resultative sense (2)

表示由无到有，由隐蔽到显露，由不清楚到清楚。

Signifies a change from non-existence to existence, non-appearance to appearance, or obscurity to clarity.

① 这个问题虽然很难，但是最后我还是想出了解决的办法。（由没有办法到有办法）

Zhège wèntí suīrán hěn nán, dànshì zuìhòu wǒ háishi xiǎngchule jiějué de bànfǎ.

Although the problem is quite difficult, in the end, I was able to figure out a solution. (from not having a solution to having one)

② 春天了，树上长出了新叶。

Chūntiān le, shù shang zhǎngchule xīnyè.

Spring’s here; the trees are sprouting leaves.

③ 你应该说出不同意他的理由。

Nǐ yīnggāi shuōchu bù tóngyì tā de lǐyóu.

You should explain the reasons you don’t agree with him.

④ 听了我的话，她脸上露出了笑容。

Tīng le wǒ de huà, tā liǎnshang lòuchule xiàoróng.

When she heard what I said, her face broke out in a smile.

⑤ 你能看出这是谁写的字吗？

Nǐ néng kànchu zhè shì shuí xiě de zì ma?

Can you figure out who wrote this?

⑥ 听了半天，我才听出外边是我的同屋的声音。（由不清楚到清楚）

Tīngle bàntiān, wǒ cái tīngchu wàibian shì wǒ de tóngwū de shēngyīn.

After listening for a long time, I finally figured out that the noise outside was my roommate. (from uncertainty to clarity)

⑦ 雾散去了，渐渐显露出了远处的山。（由隐蔽到显露）

Wù sànqu le, jiànjiàn xiǎnlù chu le yuǎnchù de shān.

The fog lifted and gradually the distant mountains appeared. (from obscurity to clarity)

⑧ 这所大学培养出很多优秀人才。

Zhè suǒ dàxué péiyǎng chu hěn duō yōuxiù réncái.

This university has nurtured a large amount of talent.

我们也可以找到“出”的典型的结果意义与趋向意义之间的联系——“从里面到外面”自然就显露了，清楚了。

The connection between the prototypical resultative and directional sense of “chū” is easy to discern: both express “within” to “without”.

1. 趋向意义

Directional sense

“出来”的趋向意义和“出”一样，也表示由处所里面向外面移动，只是有确定的参照点，参照点在处所外面。

The directional sense of “chūlai” is the same as that of “chū”; it also expresses movement from inside to outside, except that in the case of “chūlai”, the point of reference is explicitly “outside”.

① 下课了，我看见学生走出教室来。

Xià kè le, wǒ kànjiàn xuésheng zǒuchū jiàoshì lai.

Class was over, I saw students leaving the classroom.

② 你把头从窗户伸出来看看，我们都在外边等你呢。

Nǐ bǎ tóu cóng chuānghu shēn chulai kànkan, wǒmen dōu zài wàibian děng nǐ ne.

Stretch your head out of the window and take a look, we're all outside waiting for you.

③ 你不用出来，把我的学生证从窗户扔出来吧。

Nǐ bú yòng chūlai, bǎ wǒ de xuéshēngzhèng cóng chuānghu rēng chulai ba.

No need to come out, just throw my student-card out of the window for me.

④ 我把老师请出来跟我们一起吃饭。

Wǒ bǎ lǎoshī qǐng chulai gēn wǒmen yìqǐ chī fàn.

I asked my teacher to come out and eat with us.

“出来”也可以表示领有关系的改变。如：

“Chūlai” can also indicate change in possession or ownership. For example:

⑤ 他从来不借给别人钱，我想你也借不出来。

Tā cónglái bú jiègěi biérén qián, wǒ xiǎng nǐ yě jiè bu chūlái.

He never lends money to other people; I don't think you can lend money out either.

⑥ 小张中午没有带饭，小李把自己带的午饭分出来一些给他。

Xiǎo Zhāng zhōngwǔ méiyǒu dài fàn, Xiǎo Lǐ bǎ zìjǐ dài de wǔfàn fēn chulai yìxiē gěi tā.

Xiao Zhang didn't bring any food for lunch, so Xiao Li took some of his and gave it to him.

2. 结果意义

Resultative senses

2.1 结果意义（一）

Resultative sense (1)

表示突出、凸起。

Signifying protrusion or projection.

① 你上衣的兜都鼓出来了，里边装的什么？

Nǐ shàngyī de dōu dōu gǔ chulai le, lǐbian zhuāng de shénme?

The pockets on your jacket are all bulging out — what are they filled with?

② 妹妹比姐姐高出来一头。

Mèimei bǐ jiějie gāo chulai yì tóu.

Younger sister's a head taller than her older sister.

③ 这条裤子我穿长出来一寸，不合适。

Zhè tiáo kùzi wǒ chuān cháng chulai yí cùn, bù héshì.

This pair of trousers are an inch too long for me; they don't fit.

2.2 结果意义（二）

Resultative sense (2)

表示从无到有，从隐蔽到显露，从不清楚到清楚。

Signifies a shift from non-existence to existence, non-appearance to appearance, or obscurity to clarity.

① 把你想说的话说出来。

Bǎ nǐ xiǎng shuō de huà shuō chulai.

Say what you're thinking.

② 他给刚出生的女儿想出来一个很好听的名字。

Tā gěi gāng chūshēng de nǚ'ér xiǎng chulai yí ge hěn hǎotīng de míngzi.

He thought up a nice sounding name for his daughter that was just born.

③ 院子里长出来很多草。

Yuànzi li zhǎng chulai hěn duō cǎo.

A lot of grass sprouted in the yard.

④ 哪个老师给我们考口试，你打听出来了吗？

Nǎ ge lǎoshī gěi wǒmen kǎo kǒushì, nǐ dǎtīng chulai le ma?

Have you inquired which teacher is giving us the oral exam?

⑤ 听了我的话，孩子的脸上露出来笑容。

Tīngle wǒ de huà, háizi de liǎn shang lòu chulai xiàoróng.

When she heard what I said, a smile appeared on the child's face.

⑥ 我听出来了，你是想跟我借钱？

Wǒ tīng chulai le, nǐ shì xiǎng gēn wǒ jiè qián?

Do I understand that you want to borrow money from me?

⑦ 这个谜语我猜不出来。

Zhège míyǔ wǒ cāi bu chūlái.

I can't guess this riddle.

⑧ 这所中学教育出来的学生大部分都很优秀。

Zhè suǒ zhōngxué jiàoyù chulai de xuésheng dà bùfen dōu hěn yōuxiù.

Most of the students being educated at this school are quite exceptional.

⑨ 学生们的作业老师还没改出来。

Xuéshengmen de zuòyè lǎoshī hái méi gǎi chulai.

The teacher hasn't yet corrected the students' homework.

【出去】chūqu

趋向意义 Directional sense

“出去”的趋向意义也和“出”一样，表示由处所里面向外面移动，只是有确定的参照点，参照点在处所里面。

The directional sense of “chūqu” is the same as that of “chū”. Both express movement from inside to outside, except that in the case of “chūqu”, the point of reference is explicitly “inside”.

① 下课以后，我很快地走出教室去。

Xià kè yǐhòu, wǒ hěn kuài de zǒuchū jiàoshì qu.

After class, I quickly walked out of the classroom.

② 水都淹到二楼了，你快从窗户跳出去吧。

Shuǐ dōu yān dào èrlóu le, nǐ kuài cóng chuānghu tiào chuqu ba.

The water's flooded up to the second floor; quick, jump out of the window.

③ 我把孩子带出去玩，你在家里等我们吧。

Wǒ bǎ háizi dài chuqu wán, nǐ zài jiā li děng wǒmen ba.

I'm taking the children out to play; you stay at home and wait for us, okay?

④ 他是学校派出去的，一切费用都由学校负责。

Tā shì xuéxiào pài chuqu de, yíqiè fèiyòng dōu yóu xuéxiào fùzé.

He's been sent by the school; all his expenses will be covered by the school.

“出去”也可以表示领有关系的改变。如：

“Chūqu” can also signify a change of ownership. For example:

⑤ 我的房子租出去了。（虽然领有关系没有变，但居住者改变了）

Wǒ de fángzi zū chuqu le.

My house has been rented out. (although there's been no change of owner, the resident has changed)

⑥ 她年龄不小了，妈妈老担心她嫁不出去。

Tā niánlíng bù xiǎo le, māma lǎo dānxīn tā jià bu chūqù.

She's not young anymore; her mother's always afraid she won't be able to get married.

（一）"出"组小结

Summary of the "chū" group

	出 chū	出来 chūlai	出去 chūqu
趋向意义 directional sense	表示由处所里面向外面移动，参照点不确定。 Signifies movement from inside to outside, with no explicit point of reference. 下课了，学生走出教室。 Xià kè le, xuésheng zǒuchu jiàoshì.	表示由处所里面向外面移动，参照点在处所外面。 Signifies movement from inside to outside, with the point of reference explicitly "outside". 下课了，我在操场上看见学生从教室里走出来。 Xià kè le, wǒ zài cāochǎng shang kànjiàn xuésheng cóng jiàoshì li zǒu chulai.	表示由处所里面向外面移动，参照点在处所里面。 Signifies movement from inside to outside, with the point of reference explicitly "inside". 下课了，我很快地走出教室去。 Xià kè le, wǒ hěn kuài de zǒuchū jiàoshì qu.

（续表）

	出 chū	出来 chūlai	出去 chūqu
结果意义 resultative sense	1.表示突出、凸起。 Signifies protrusion or projection. 那块地中间不知为什么鼓出一个大包。 Nà kuài dì zhōngjiān bù zhī wèi shénme gǔchu yí ge dàbāo. 2.表示由无到有，由隐蔽到显露，由不清楚到清楚。 Signifies a change from non-existence to existence, non-appearance to appearance, or obscurity to clarity. 我给孩子想出一个很好听的名字。 Wǒ gěi háizi xiǎngchu yí ge hěn hǎotīng de míngzi.	1.表示突出、凸起。 Signifies protrusion or projection. 那块地中间不知为什么鼓出来一个大包。 Nà kuài dì zhōngjiān bù zhī wèi shénme gǔ chulai yí ge dàbāo. 2.表示由无到有，由隐蔽到显露，由不清楚到清楚。 Signifies a change from non-existence to existence, non-appearance to appearance, or obscurity to clarity. 孩子叫什么名字好，你想出来了吗? Háizi jiào shénme míngzi hǎo, nǐ xiǎng chulai le ma?	——

（二）“进”组和“出”组之间的意义联系

Semantic relationships between the “jìn” and “chū” groups

在参照点不变的情况下，“进”组和“出”组的趋向意义和结果意义存在相对的关系。

Where the point of reference is consistent, the directional and resultative senses of the “jìn” group is opposite to that of the “chū” group.

	趋向意义 directional sense	结果意义 resultative sense
进 jìn	走进教室（参照点不确定） zǒujin jiàoshì (no explicit point of reference)	凹进一块 āojin yí kuài

（续表）

	趋向意义 directional sense	结果意义 resultative sense
出 chū	走出教室（参照点不确定） zǒuchu jiàoshì (no explicit point of reference)	突出一块 tūchu yí kuài 想出一个办法 xiǎngchu yí gè bànfǎ
进来 jìnlai	走进教室来（参照点在处所里面） zǒujìn jiàoshì lai (with point of reference inside)	——
出去 chūqu	走出教室去（参照点在处所里面） zǒuchū jiàoshì qu (with point of reference inside)	——
进去 jìnqu	走进教室去（参照点在处所外面） zǒujìn jiàoshì qu (with point of reference outside)	凹进去一块 āo jinqu yí kuài
出来 chūlai	走出教室来（参照点在处所外面） zǒuchū jiàoshì lai (with point of reference outside)	凸出来一块 tū chulai yí kuài 办法想出来了 bànfǎ xiǎng chulai le

“回”组

“Huí” group

“回”组包括“回”“回来”“回去”。

The “huí” group consists of “huí” “huílai” and “huíqu”.

趋向意义

Directional sense

表示向原来的处所（家、故乡、祖国、原来的出发地等）移动。参照点不确定。

Signifies movement back to an original place (home, birthplace, country and other points of origin); no explicit point of reference.

① 妈妈打电话说家里有事，我放下电话急忙跑回家。
Māma dǎ diànhuà shuō jiā li yǒu shì, wǒ fàngxia diànhuà jímáng pǎohui jiā.
Mother phoned to say that there was something going on at home, so I put down the phone and hastened home.

② 他把几年来在国外挣的钱都寄回国了。
Tā bǎ jǐ nián lái zài guówài zhèng de qián dōu jìhui guó le.
The money he earned abroad over the past

few years has all been repatriated.

③ 小李每天从宿舍跑到教室，下课以后再从教室走回家。

Xiǎo Lǐ měi tiān cóng sùshè pǎodào jiàoshì, xià kè yǐhòu zài cóng jiàoshì zǒuhui jiā.

Xiao Li runs from the dorm to the classroom every day, and then, after class, from the classroom, walks home again.

“回”也可以表示领有关系的转移。如：

“Huí” can also indicate a change of possession or ownership. For example:

④ 出租的房子我收回了，因为租房子的人好几个月不付房租。

Chūzū de fángzi wǒ shōuhui le, yīnwèi zū fángzi de rén hǎojǐ ge yuè bú fù fángzū.

The house that I was renting out, I’ve taken back, because the people who rented it didn’t pay the rent for several months.

⑤ 姐姐买的衣服太大，她只好把它退回商店。

Jiějie mǎi de yīfu tài dà, tā zhǐhǎo bǎ tā tuìhui shāngdiàn.

The clothes my older sister bought is too big; she’ll just have to return it to the shop.

趋向意义

Directional sense

表示向原处所（家、故乡、祖国、原来的出发地等）移动。参照点在原处所。

Signifies movement back to an original place (home, birthplace, country and other points of origin), with the point of reference at the original place.

① 弟弟早上去上学，刚出去几分钟，又跑了回来。

Dìdi zǎoshang qù shàng xué, gāng

chūqu jǐ fēn zhōng, yòu pǎole huilai.

Younger brother went to school this morning, but just a few minutes after he left, he ran back.

② 你把我的手机拿走了，到中国以后，快点儿给我寄回来。

Nǐ bǎ wǒ de shǒujī názǒu le, dào Zhōngguó yǐhòu, kuài diǎnr gěi wǒ jì huilai.

You took my mobile phone; when you get to China, mail it back to me right away.

③ 小妹妹自己出去很长时间了，我们找了很长时间才把她找回来。

Xiǎo mèimei zìjǐ chūqu hěn cháng shíjiān le, wǒmen zhǎole hěn cháng shíjiān cái bǎ tā zhǎo huilai.

Younger sister went out on her own for a long time and we had to search for her for a long time before we brought her back.

④ A：客人叫你气走了，你得把他请回来。

Kèren jiào nǐ qìzǒu le, nǐmen děi bǎ tā qǐng huilai.

You angered the guest so much that he left; you need to invite him back.

B：他本来就不想来，我怕请不回来了。

Tā běnlái jiù bù xiǎng lái, wǒ pà qǐng bu huílái le.

He didn't want to come in the first place; I'm afraid it won't be possible to ask him to return.

"回来"也可以表示领有关系的转移。如：

"Huílai" can also indicate a change of possession or ownership. For example:

⑤ 爸爸把房子卖了，几年以后，我把它买了回来。

Bàba bǎ fángzi mài le, jǐ nián yǐhòu, wǒ bǎ tā mǎile huilai.

Dad sold the house; a few years later, I bought it back.

⑥ 我们要努力工作，把浪费的时间补回来。

Wǒmen yào nǔlì gōngzuò, bǎ làngfèi de shíjiān bǔ huilai.

We need to work hard and make up for the time we wasted.

趋向意义

Directional sense

表示向原处所（家、故乡、祖国、原来的出发地等）移动。参照点不在原处所。

Signifies movement back to an original place (home, birthplace, country and other points of origin), with point of reference not at the original place.

① 太晚了，公共汽车没有了，我们只好走回家去。

Tài wǎn le, gōnggòng qìchē méiyǒu le, wǒmen zhǐhǎo zǒuhuí jiā qu.

It's too late; there are no more buses; we'll just have to walk back home.

② 你开车把张小姐送回去吧。

Nǐ kāi chē bǎ Zhāng xiǎojiě sòng huiqu ba.

Take the car and drive Miss Zhang back, okay?

③ 王明刚走出教室，老师就把他叫回去了。

Wáng Míng gāng zǒuchu jiàoshì, lǎoshī jiù bǎ tā jiào huiqu le.

Wang Ming had just walked out of the classroom when the teacher called him back.

④ 这双鞋你已经穿了好几天了，不合适也退不回去了。

Zhè shuāng xié nǐ yǐjīng chuānle hǎojǐ tiān le, bù héshì yě tuì bu huíqù le.

You've been wearing these shoes for days; even if they don't fit you can't return them.

“回去”也可以表示领有关系的转移。如：

“Huíqu” can also indicate a change of possession or ownership. For example:

⑤ 房东说这套房子她自己要住，所以下个月要收回去。

Fángdōng shuō zhè tào fángzi tā zìjǐ yào zhù, suǒyǐ xià ge yuè yào shōu huiqu.

The landlord said she wants to live in this apartment herself, so next month, she wants to reclaim it.

“过”组

“Guò” group

“过”组包括“过”“过来”“过去”。

The “guò” group consists of “guò” “guòlai” and “guòqu”.

过	过来	过去
guò	guòlai	guòqu
(X)○ ⟶ (X) □	○ ⟶ X □	X ○ ⟶ □

“过”的基本意义是从一个空间点移到另一个空间点，如“过桥”。“过”也可以表示从一个时间点移到另一个时间点，如“过年”。

The basic sense of “guò” is movement from one point to another (typically on the horizontal plane, over obstacles, etc.), e.g., “guò qiáo (cross a bridge)”. “Guò” can also express movement through time, e.g., “guò nián (pass the year; celebrate the new year)”.

1. 趋向意义

Directional sense

1.1 趋向意义（一）

Directional sense (1)

表示经过某处所或向某处所移动。如：

Indicates movement from one place to another, often, but not necessarily, over an obstacle. For example:

① 那个人跳过墙逃跑了。（经过“墙”）

Nàge rén tiàoguo qiáng táopǎo le.

That person jumped over the wall and ran away. (he crosses over the wall)

② 他递过一杯茶给我。（“茶”向“我”移动）

Tā dìguo yì bēi chá gěi wǒ.

He passed a cup of tea to me. (the tea moves across some space to me)

③ 学生排着队走过校长的办公室。（经过“校长的办公室”）

Xuésheng páizhe duì zǒuguo xiàozhǎng de bàngōngshì.

The students walked in a line past the principal's office. (they pass by the principal's office)

④ 医生从护士的手里接过病历。（“病历”向医生移动）

Yīshēng cóng hùshì de shǒuli jiēguo bìnglì.

The doctor took the medical records from the nurse's hand. (the medical records cross from the nurse to the doctor)

1.2 趋向意义（二）

Directional sense (2)

表示人或物体改变方向（转动），参照点不确定。

Signifying a person's turning around or a thing being turned over; no explicit point of reference.

① 你转过头看看谁来了。

Nǐ zhuǎnguo tóu kànkan shuí lái le.

Turn your head and see who's come.

② 你背过脸不要看。

Nǐ bèiguo liǎn bú yào kàn.

Turn your face away — don't look.

③ 我翻过几页书就找到了要看的那一页。

Wǒ fānguo jǐ yè shū jiù zhǎodàole yào kàn de nà yí yè.

I turned over a few pages and found the page I wanted to read.

2. 结果意义

Resultative sense

"过"的结果意义比较多，多来自"过"这个词本身的意义。

There are quite a number of resultative senses of "guò", most deriving from the basic sense of "guò" itself.

2.1 结果意义（一）

Resultative sense (1)

"度过"，即"过"的基本意义，从一个时间点向另一个时间点移动，通常用于表示度过一段艰难的时间或难关。这样用的"过"前面的动词具有"度过"的意思，后边的名词表示一段艰难的时间。

"To pass through", which is the basic sense of "guò"; i.e., to move from one point in time to another, often encountering some difficulty. This use of "guò" will be preceded by a verb with the sense of "pass through" and be followed by a noun phrase that indicates a difficulty or obstacle.

① 那一年，他们在山里挨饿受冻，好不容易挺过了漫长的冬天。

Nà yì nián, tāmen zài shān li ái'è-shòudòng, hǎo bù róngyì tǐngguole màncháng de dōngtiān.

In that year, they were in the mountains suffering from hunger and cold; it was really difficult to endure the long winter.

② 那一天他正好去外地，躲过了那场大地震。

Nà yì tiān tā zhènghǎo qù wàidì, duǒguole nà chǎng dà dìzhèn.

That day he just happened to have gone away, thereby dodging the big earthquake.

③ 我们熬过这个冬天就好了。

Wǒmen áoguo zhège dōngtiān jiù hǎo le.

As long as we get through the winter we'll be okay.

动词也可以是"骗、瞒、放"等。"骗过"的意思就是"骗"达到了目的，被骗的人相信了；"瞒过"的意思"瞒"达到了目的，被瞒的人不知道；"放过"的意思是不追究某人（错误、罪刑等）。后边的名词表示动作的对象。

Following verbs such as "piàn (deceive)" "mán (hide the truth)" and "fàng (put)", "guò" still has the general sense of "passing through". The meaning of "piànguo" is "to deceive so as to achieve a goal — to make the deceived person believe something"; the meaning of "mánguo" is "to hide the truth so as to achieve a goal — so the one deceived does not know"; the meaning of "fàngguo" is "to let it go, that is, not to investigate (a mistake, a crime, etc.)". The noun that follows indicates the goal of the action.

④ 他以为整了容，改了名字就能骗过别人。

Tā yǐwéi zhěngle róng, gǎile míngzi jiù néng piànguo biérén.

He thought that if he "had a face-lift" and changed his name, he'd be able to scam other people.

⑤ 你不要说谎，什么事都瞒不过我。

Nǐ bú yào shuō huǎng, shénme shì dōu mán bu guò wǒ.

Don't lie — nothing gets past me.

⑥ 我们不会放过一个坏人。

Wǒmen bú huì fàngguo yí ge huàirén.

We will not let a single bad guy escape.

2.2 结果意义（二）

Resultative sense (2)

“超过、超越”。这也是动词“过”的意义之一，如“过期”。“过”后边的名词表示合适的或者确定的点（空间的或时间的）。

“Exceed, pass by”. This is also one of the senses of the full verb “guò”, as in “guòqī (be overdue)”. The noun following “guò” expresses the original or intended place or time.

① 我一边开车一边想事情，结果开过了上班的公司。

Wǒ yìbiān kāi chē yìbiān xiǎng shìqing, jiéguǒ kāiguole shàng bān de gōngsī.

I was driving along lost in thought; as a result, I drove past the company where I work.

② 孩子下到游泳池，水快没过他的嘴了，他吓得哭了起来。

Háizi xià dào yóuyǒngchí, shuǐ kuài mòguo tā de zuǐ le, tā xià de kūle qilai.

The child got into the pool but as his mouth was about to go under the water, he got so afraid that he started to cry.

③ 昨天晚上睡得太晚，今天早上睡过了八点，上班迟到了。

Zuótiān wǎnshang shuì de tài wǎn, jīntiān zǎoshang shuìguole bā diǎn, shàng bān chídào le.

I went to bed too late last night; this morning I slept past 8 and was late for work.

④ 你写的字我看不见，你把纸再举高一点儿，举过头。

Nǐ xiě de zì wǒ kàn bu jiàn, nǐ bǎ zhǐ zài jǔ gāo yìdiǎnr, jǔguo tóu.

I cannot see what you wrote; lift the paper a little higher — lift it over your head.

⑤ 说话要实事求是，不要说过头儿。

Shuō huà yào shíshì-qiúshì, bú yào shuōguo tóur.

When you speak, seek to present the facts — don't exaggerate.

2.3 结果意义（三）Resultative sense (3)

“胜过”，这也是动词“过”的意义之一，如“聪明过人”。

“To excel, surpass” is also one of the citation meanings of the verb “guò” , e.g., “cōngming-guòrén (one whose knowledge surpasses other people’)”.

这个“过”多用于比赛、较量等方面，前面的动词一般表示比赛、竞争，如“比、打、斗、说、考、跑”等。

This sense of “guò” is often found after verbs that involve competitions or contests, such as “bǐ (compare), dǎ (beat), dòu (struggle), shuō (speak), kǎo (test), pǎo (run)”.

① 用英文演讲，你比不过她。

Yòng Yīngwén yǎnjiǎng , nǐ bǐ bu guò tā.

If you speak in English, you won’t be able to do better than her.

② 这场篮球赛，A队肯定打不过B队。

Zhè chǎng lánqiú sài, A duì kěndìng dǎ bu guò B duì.

In this basketball match, A team won’t be able to beat B team for sure.

③ 你太年轻了，斗不过你的老板。

Nǐ tài niánqīng le, dòu bu guò nǐ de lǎobǎn.

You’re too young; you can’t outdo your boss.

④ 你的嘴太厉害了，我说不过你。

Nǐ de zuǐ tài lìhai le, wǒ shuō bu guò nǐ.

Your tongue’s too sharp; I can’t compete with you.

⑤ 英文我考不过你，但是数学我一定考得比你好。

Yīngwén wǒ kǎo bu guò nǐ, dànshì shùxué wǒ yídìng kǎo de bǐ nǐ hǎo.

I can’t do better than you in the English exam but I’ll certainly beat you in maths.

⑥ 听你说这些话，胜过我读十年书了。

Tīng nǐ shuō zhèxiē huà, shèngguo wǒ dú shí nián shū le.

I benefit more from listening to you than I would reading for 10 years.

这个“过”也可以用在形容词后边，表示程度很高，如：

"Guò" in this sense can also be used after adjectives to express a superlative degree. For example:

⑦ 你这样做真是再好不过了。（没有比这样再好的了）
Nǐ zhèyàng zuò zhēnshì zài hǎo bu guò le.
You really can't beat doing it that way.

⑧ 这个孩子真是再聪明不过了。
Zhège háizi zhēnshì zài cōngming bu guò le.
There's really no one smarter than that kid.

⑨ 这件衣服再时髦不过了。
Zhè jiàn yīfu zài shímáo bu guò le.
There's nothing more fashionable than that item of clothing.

2.4 结果意义（四）
Resultative sense (4)

"完成、完结"。这个意义显然与"过"的基本意义"度过"有联系。

"To complete, accomplish". This sense is also obviously connected to the basic sense of "guò", that is, "to pass, go through".

① A：这本书你看看吧，非常有意思。
Zhè běn shū nǐ kànkan ba, fēicháng yǒu yìsi.
You should read this book — it's fascinating.
B：我早就看过了，是很有意思。
Wǒ zǎo jiù kànguo le, shì hěn yǒu yìsi.
I read it a long time ago — it certainly is interesting.

② 明天我吃过早饭就去新公司上班。
Míngtiān wǒ chīguo zǎofàn jiù qù xīn gōngsī shàng bān.
Tomorrow after I eat breakfast I'm going to start work at a new company.

★"过"结果意义（四）和"了"比较：

A comparison of the 4th resultative sense of "guò" and "le":

“过”结果意义（四）与动态助词“了”意义近似，但又有不同。

The 4th resultative sense of “guò” is similar, but not identical in meaning to that of the aspect particle “le”.

（1）“过”结果意义（四）的意思是“完成”，动态助词“了”的意思是“发生”，虽然它不排斥“完成”，但用“了”的句子可能只表示发生，而不表示“完成”。如：

The meaning of the 4th resultative sense of “guò” is “it’s complete”; the meaning of the aspect particle “le” is “it’s happened, occurred”. Although “le” may also imply “complete”, sentences with aspectual “le” probably signify occurrence rather than completeness, as for example:

③ 这个会已经开了两天了，再开一天就结束了。
Zhège huì yǐjīng kāile liǎng tiān le, zài kāi yì tiān jiù jiéshù le.
This meeting’s already been going on for two days, one more day and it’ll be over.

这个句子中的“了”不能用“过”替换：

“Guò” cannot be substituted for “le” in this sentence:

③’ * 这个会已经开过两天了，再开一天就结束了。
* Zhège huì yǐjing kāiguo liǎng tiān le, zài kāi yì tiān jiù jiéshù le.

（2）“过”结果意义（四）要求前面的动词表示已知信息，即动词所表示的动作是听话人知道的。如：例①，“看”在A的话中出现过；例②，一般人都会“吃早饭”，所以这种动作听话人会明白。

“Guò” in its 4th resultative sense requires the verbal action to have already been established, either by prior mention (as in example ① above, where “kàn shū” is mentioned in the A sentence), or by being an activity that is part of one’s daily routine (like “chī zǎofàn” in example ②).

用动态助词“了”不要求前面的动词表示已知信息。

Using the aspect particle “le” does not require that the verb to which it is attached expresses already established actions.

④ 我刚才买了一本书，很有意思，你想看吗？

Wǒ gāngcái mǎile yì běn shū, hěn yǒu yìsi, nǐ xiǎng kàn ma?

I've just bought a book, it's very interesting, do you want to read it?

这个句子中的“买书”对听话人来说显然不是已知信息，句中的“了”不能用“过”替换：

In this sentence, “mǎi shū (buy books)” is something that the addressee would assume from context, so “le” cannot be replaced by “guò”:

④’ * 我刚才买过一本书，很有意思，你想看吗？

* Wǒ gāngcái mǎiguo yì běn shū, hěn yǒu yìsi, nǐ xiǎng kàn ma?

不过由于“过”的结果意义（四）与动态助词“了”意义接近，所以如果句子中用了“过”，后边又用“了”，省去“过”，句子的意思不变。例如：

But because the 4th resultative sense of “guò” is similar to that of the aspect particle “le”, if “le” is added to a sentence with this sense of “guò”, “guò” can be omitted, and the meaning of the sentence will remain much the same. For example:

①’ A：这本书你看看吧，非常有意思。

Zhè běn shū nǐ kànkan ba, fēicháng yǒu yìsi.

B：我早就看（过）了，是很有意思。

Wǒ zǎo jiù kàn (guo) le, shì hěn yǒu yìsi.

②’ 明天我吃（过）了早饭就去新公司上班。

Míngtiān wǒ chī (guo) le zǎofàn jiù qù xīn gōngsī shàng bān.

动态助词“过”与“过”的结果意义（四）也不同。动态助词“过”表示“经验”，表示动作曾经发生，但是在说话时动作已经不再进行。而“过”的结果意义（四）表示完成。详见《趋向补语通释》第279—280页。

The aspect particle “guò” and the 4th resultative sense of “guò” are also different. The aspect particle “guò” signifies that the verbal action has happened before but has not happened again by the time of speaking. But the 4th resultative sense of “guò” signifies accomplishment. For details, see pp. 279–280 of *A Complete Explanation of Directional Complements*.

3. 特殊用法
Special usages

"V得过"
"V de guò"

"V得过"的意思是值得V，即值得做某事，口语。如"买得过、去得过、干得过、吃得过"。

The colloquial "V de guò" conveys the sense that something is "worth doing". Examples include: "mǎi de guo, qù de guo, gàn de guo, chī de guo".

① 这个房子地段好，价钱也便宜，买得过。

Zhège fángzi dìduàn hǎo, jiàqián yě piányi, mǎi de guo.

This house is in a good location and the price is inexpensive; it's worth buying.

② 这个菜别的饭馆儿没有，贵一点儿也吃得过。

Zhège cài biéde fànguǎnr méiyǒu, guì yìdiǎnr yě chī de guo.

Other restaurants don't have this dish; it's a bit more expensive, but worth it.

4. 熟语
Idioms

"信得/不过"
"Xìn de/bu guò"

"信得过"意思是"相信"，"信不过"意思是"不能相信"，用于口语。

A colloquial expression with the meaning of "trust" or "distrust".

① 这个人我们共事很多年了，我信得过他。

Zhège rén wǒmen gòngshì hěn duō nián le, wǒ xìndeguò tā.

I've worked with this person for years; I trust him.

② 把钱交给她，我信不过，还是你拿着吧。

Bǎ qián jiāogěi tā, wǒ xìnbuguò, háishi nǐ názhe ba.

I wouldn't hand the money over to her; you hold on to it.

1. 趋向意义

Directional sense

1.1 趋向意义（一）

Directional sense (1)

表示向参照点移动，可能经过一个处所，也可能不经过，参照点在说话人所在的位置。

Signifies horizontal movement, whether or not passing through a particular place; with the speaker's location as the point of reference.

① 汽车开过桥来。

Qìchē kāiguò qiáo lai.

The bus has crossed over the bridge.

② 汽车开过来了，大家准备上车。

Qìchē kāi guolai le, dàjiā zhǔnbèi shàng chē.

The car's been fetched; everyone gets ready to get on.

③ 那个人一步一步向我走过来。

Nàge rén yí bù yí bù xiàng wǒ zǒu guolai.

The man walked over to me step by step.

④ 你把那杯茶给我递过来。

Nǐ bǎ nà bēi chá gěi wǒ dì guolai.

Pass me that cup of tea.

⑤ 声音从远处传过来，还很清楚。

Shēngyīn cóng yuǎnchù chuán guolai, hái hěn qīngchu.

The sound is coming from far off but it's still quite clear.

⑥ 看见我拿着表格来了，大家围过来抢。

Kànjiàn wǒ názhe biǎogé lái le, dàjiā wéi guolai qiǎng.

On seeing me come with the forms in my hand, everyone surrounded me to take one.

⑦ 我看见一条大狗向我扑过来，非常害怕。

Wǒ kànjiàn yì tiáo dàgǒu xiàng wǒ pū guolai, fēicháng hàipà.

I saw a large dog sprang across towards me; it was scary.

⑧ 把手伸过来。

Bǎ shǒu shēn guolai.

Spread your arms.

⑨ 你去把那位先生请过来。

Nǐ qù bǎ nà wèi xiānsheng qǐng guolai.

Go and invite that man over.

⑩ 你去搬把椅子过来。

Nǐ qù bān bǎ yǐzi guolai.

Go and move the chair over here.

⑪ 把盐递过来。

Bǎ yán dì guolai.

Pass the salt.

“过来”也可以表示领有关系的转移。如：

“Guòlai” can also indicate a change of possession or ownership. For example:

⑫ 这是你家的地，你一定要从不法开发商手里夺过来。

Zhè shì nǐ jiā de dì, nǐ yídìng yào cóng bùfǎ kāifāshāng shǒuli duó guolai.

This is your family’s land; you must take it out of the hands of the illegal developers.

1.2 趋向意义（二）

Directional sense (2)

表示向参照点方向转动。

Signifies turning around, turning back from the original direction.

① 他转过脸来对我笑了笑。

Tā zhuǎnguò liǎn lai duì wǒ xiào le xiào.

He turned his face to me and smiled.

② 你转过身来看看谁来了。

Nǐ zhuǎnguò shēn lai kànkan shuí lái le.

Turn around and see who's arrived.

③ 你把车掉过头来。

Nǐ bǎ chē diàoguò tóu lai.

Turn the car right around.

2. 结果意义

Resultative sense

2.1 结果意义（一）

Resultative sense (1)

"度过"，像"过"的结果意义（一）一样，通常用于表示度过一段艰难的时期或难关。

"To pass through", like the 1st resultative sense of "guò", generally used to indicate passing through a time of difficulty or an obstacle.

这样用的"过来"前面的动词多表示度过的方式，如"熬、挺、闯、活、挣扎"。

This usage of "guòlai" occurs after verbs such as "áo (endure)" "tǐng (deal with)" "chuǎng (get through, charge)" "huó (live)" and "zhēngzhá (struggle)", which express the idea of getting through something.

① 在战争的年代，我们好不容易活过来了。

Zài zhànzhēng de niándài, wǒmen hǎo bù róngyì huó guolai le.

In the war years, it was very difficult to get by.

② 你一个人在国外，是怎么闯过来的？

Nǐ yí ge rén zài guówài, shì zěnme chuǎng guolai de?

Being all alone in a foreign land, how did you get through it?

③ 那些年家里非常困难，可是他们还是熬过来了。

Nàxiē nián jiāli fēicháng kùnnan, kěshì tāmen háishi áo guolai le.

Things were really hard at home during those years, but they still managed to make it through.

2.2 结果意义（二）

Resultative sense (2)

表示恢复或转变到正常的、积极的状态。

Signifies return to a normal or positive state.

常用的动词如“醒、清醒、活、救、明白、觉悟、暖和、改、改变、变、教育”等。

Often with verbs such as “xǐng (wake up)” “qīngxǐng (to come to, sober up)” “huó (live)” “jiù (save)” “míngbai (understand)” “juéwù (realize, see the light)” “nuǎnhuo”(warm)” “gǎi (change)” “gǎibiàn (change)” “biàn (change)” and “jiàoyù (educate, teach)”.

① 他昏迷了很久，终于醒过来了。

Tā hūnmíle hěn jiǔ, zhōngyú xǐng guolai le.

He was in a coma for a long time, but in the end he came out of it.

② 经过这件事，他明白过来，爸爸批评他，是为他好。

Jīngguò zhè jiàn shì, tā míngbai guolai, bàba pīpíng tā, shì wèi tā hǎo.

Having got through it, he came to understand that his dad’s criticism of him was for his own good.

③ 他病得很重，但是医生还是把他抢救过来了。

Tā bìng de hěn zhòng, dànshì yīshēng háishi bǎ tā qiǎngjiù guolai le.

He was seriously ill, but the doctor nevertheless managed to save him.

④ 前几年他的公司快要破产了，今年刚刚缓过来。

Qián jǐ nián tā de gōngsī kuài yào pòchǎn le, jīnnián gānggāng huǎn guolai.

A few years ago, his company was close to bankruptcy, but this year it's just got back on its feet.

⑤ 外边太冷了，我都快冻死了，现在暖和过来了。

Wàibian tài lěng le , wǒ dōu kuài dòngsǐ le, xiànzài nuǎnhuo guolai le.

It's so cold out; I was just about completely frozen, but now I'm thawing out.

⑥ 你们把练习当中的错误改过来。

Nǐmen bǎ liànxí dāngzhōng de cuòwù gǎi guolai.

Correct the mistakes in the exercises.

⑦ 这个孩子在错误的路上越走越远，老师说一定要把他教育过来。

Zhège háizi zài cuòwù de lù shàng yuè zǒu yuè yuǎn, lǎoshī shuō yídìng yào bǎ tā jiàoyù guolai.

As this kid goes farther and farther down the wrong road, the teacher says he's determined to school him back to the right path.

⑧ 我躺了好几天了，休息过来了。

Wǒ tǎngle hǎojǐ tiān le, xiūxi guolai le.

I've been lying down for several days and have now recovered.

⑨ 我不懂英文，你把这一段话翻译过来。

Wǒ bù dǒng Yīngwén, nǐ bǎ zhè yí duàn huà fānyì guolai.

I don't understand English; translate this passage for me.

2.3 结果意义（三）

Resultative sense (3)

表示尽数地完成。

Signifies total completion.

通常表示是否有完成某种数量的事物、工作的能力、条件，常用可能补语形式。

This sense generally signifies whether or not a task of some magnitude or requiring some strength has been or, more often, can be completed; usually in the potential.

① 慢点儿跑，我都喘不过气来了。

Màn diǎnr pǎo, wǒ dōu chuǎn bu guò qì lai le.

Slow down; I can't catch my breath.

② 这几天事情太多，我真有点儿忙不过来了。

Zhè jǐ tiān shìqing tài duō, wǒ zhēn yǒu diǎnr máng bu guòlái le.

There's been too much to do these few days; I really feel overwhelmed.

③ 我们公司的人太少，工作常常安排不过来。

Wǒmen gōngsī de rén tài shǎo, gōngzuò chángcháng ānpái bu guòlái.

Our company has too few people; it's often impossible to plan the work.

④ 我们的学生太多，我管不过来。

Wǒmen de xuésheng tài duō, wǒ guǎn bu guòlái.

We have too many students; I can't manage them all.

⑤ 老师让看的书很多，你看得过来吗？

Lǎoshī ràng kàn de shū hěn duō, nǐ kàn de guolai ma?

The teacher is making us read too many books; can you make it through them all?

⑥ 那个孩子还小，一百以内的数都数不过来。

Nàge háizi hái xiǎo, yìbǎi yǐnèi de shù dōu shǔ bu guòlái.

That child's still young; he can't even count up to a hundred.

⑦ 我们班50个学生，只有30本书，分不过来。

Wǒmen bān wǔshí ge xuésheng, zhǐ yǒu sānshí běn shū, fēn bu guòlái.

Only 30 books for 50 students in our class; no way to divide them up.

⑧ 你们每个人都提要求，我应付不过来。

Nǐmen měi ge rén dōu tí yāoqiú, wǒ yìngfu bu guòlái.

Each of you has a demand; there's no way for me to deal with them all.

1. 趋向意义
Directional sense

1.1 趋向意义（一）
Directional sense (1)

表示离开参照点，向另一处所移动，中间可能经过一个处所，也可能不经过。参照点不在说话人的位置，在远处。

Signifies horizontal movement from one place to another, whether or not passing through a particular place on the way; the point of reference is the more distant place, away from the speaker's location.

① 看见妹妹哭了，我就走过去安慰她。
Kànjiàn mèimei kū le, wǒ jiù zǒu guoqu ānwèi tā.
Seeing my younger sister crying, I walked over and consoled her.

② 这时一辆汽车开过桥去。
Zhèshí yí liàng qìchē kāiguò qiáo qu.
At that time, a car drove across the bridge.

③ 这个沟太宽，我迈不过去。
Zhège gōu tài kuān, wǒ mài bu guòqù.
This ditch is too wide; I can't make it across.

④ 看见那个演员来了，很多年轻人围过去请他签名。
Kànjiàn nàge yǎnyuán lái le, hěn duō niánqīngrén wéi guoqu qǐng tā qiān míng.
When they saw the actor arrive, a lot of young people gathered around him and asked him for his autograph.

⑤ 从这儿看过去，那所房子好像很大，很漂亮。

Cóng zhèr kàn guoqu, nà suǒ fángzi hǎoxiàng hěn dà, hěn piàoliang.

Looking across from here, that house seems quite large and attractive.

⑥ 你把这杯咖啡给爷爷递过去。

Nǐ bǎ zhè bēi kāfēi gěi yéye dì guoqu.

Pass that cup of coffee to grandpa.

⑦ 看见客人来了，校长伸过手去跟他们握手。

Kànjiàn kèren lái le, xiàozhǎng shēnguò shǒu qu gēn tāmen wò shǒu.

On seeing that the guests arrive, the principal extended his hand and shook hands with them.

⑧ 你把这件衣服给你哥哥送过去吧，他可能冷了。

Nǐ bǎ zhè jiàn yīfu gěi nǐgēge sòng guoqu ba, tā kěnéng lěng le.

Deliver this item of clothing to your older brother; he may be cold.

⑨ 小李让老师叫过去了。

Xiǎo Lǐ ràng lǎoshī jiào guoqu le.

Xiao Li was called over by the teacher.

"过去"也可以表示领有关系的转移。如：

"Guòqu" can also indicate a change of possession or ownership. For example:

⑩ 这次篮球比赛的冠军叫我们的对手夺过去了。

Zhè cì lánqiú bǐsài de guànjūn jiào wǒmen de duìshǒu duó guoqu le.

The championship of this basketball competition was taken by our competitor.

⑪ 你哥哥什么时候把你的宝马买过去了？

Nǐ gēge shénme shíhou bǎ nǐ de Bǎomǎ mǎi guoqu le?

When did your brother buy your BMW?

1.2 趋向意义（二）

Directional sense (2)

表示向背离参照点的方向转动。

Signifies turning around from the original direction.

① 听见后边有人叫我，我就回过头去。

Tīngjiàn hòubian yǒu rén jiào wǒ, wǒ jiù huíguò tóu qu.

Hearing someone calling me from behind, I turned my head around.

② 你把脸转过去，不要看。

Nǐ bǎ liǎn zhuǎn guoqu, bú yào kàn.

Turn your head away — don't look.

③ 前边没有路了，汽车只好掉过头去往回开。

Qiánbian méiyǒu lù le, qìchē zhǐhǎo diàoguò tóu qu wǎnghuí kāi.

There's no way through ahead, best to turn the car around and head back.

2. 结果意义

Resultative sense

2.1 结果意义（一）

Resultative sense (1)

“度过”。前面的动词表示度过的方式，如“熬、挺、闯、混、溜、拖延、流逝、耽误、等、坐”等。

“To pass through, spend [time]”. Occurs with prior verbs such as “áo (endure)” “tǐng (endure)” “chuǎng (get through, charge)” “hùn (drift along)” “liū (glide, sneak off)” “tuōyán (delay)” “liúshì (elapse)” “dānwu (waste)” “děng (wait)” and “zuò (sit)” that involve the passage of time.

① 最困难的日子熬过去了，我相信以后情况会越来越好。

Zuì kùnnan de rìzi áo guoqu le, wǒ xiāngxìn yǐhòu qíngkuàng huì yuè lái yuè hǎo.

You've made it through the hardest days; I believe that, hereafter, the situation will get better and better.

② 我相信你的能力，这一关你一定能闯过去。
Wǒ xiāngxìn nǐ de nénglì, zhè yì guān nǐ yídìng néng chuǎng guoqu.
I believe in your ability; you're sure to get through this impasse.

③ 他每天除了上课就是玩游戏，一个学期很快地混过去了。
Tā měi tiān chúle shàng kè jiùshì wán yóuxì, yí ge xuéqī hěn kuài de hùn guoqu le.
Everyday, all he does is go to class and play games, so a semester has drifted quickly by.

④ 你很年轻，应该好好儿学习，不要把这么宝贵的时间耽误过去。
Nǐ hěn niánqīng, yīnggāi hǎohāor xuéxí, bú yào bǎ zhème bǎoguì de shíjiān dānwu guoqu.
You're young; you should study hard and not waste such valuable time.

⑤ 我在椅子上坐着等你，一个下午就这样坐过去了。
Wǒ zài yǐzi shang zuòzhe děng nǐ, yí ge xiàwǔ jiù zhèyàng zuò guoqu le.
I'm sitting on a chair waiting for you; I've spent a whole afternoon like this.

⑥ 这件事你只能忍，忍过去就没事了，不然可能会更麻烦。
Zhè jiàn shì nǐ zhǐ néng rěn, rěn guoqu jiù méi shì le, bùrán kěnéng huì gèng máfan.
You just have to put up with it; if you put up with it, it'll go away, otherwise it may be even more trouble.

⑦ 这件事一定要搞清楚，不能马虎过去。
Zhè jiàn shì yídìng yào gǎo qīngchu, bù néng mǎhu guoqu.
This business needs to be dealt with carefully; it can't be done sloppily.

⑧ 他们很聪明，你骗不过去的。
Tāmen hěn cōngming, nǐ piàn bu guòqù de.
They're smart; you won't be able to con them.

⑨ 这么大的事你要瞒过父母去，我看很难。

Zhème dà de shì nǐ yào mánguò fùmǔ qu, wǒ kàn hěn nán.

I think it will be difficult to conceal such an important thing from your parents.

⑩ 事情既然发生了，你只能面对，躲是躲不过去的。

Shìqing jìrán fāshēng le, nǐ zhǐ néng miànduì, duǒ shì duǒ bu guòqù de.

Since it's happened, you can only face it; you can't hide from it.

★"过来"和"过去"比较：

Comparing "guòlai" and "guòqu":

（1）"过来"和"过去"都表示"度过"，"过去"可以用的动词比较广，因为"过来"表示度过一段艰难的时间，而"过去"表示度过的时间可能很艰难，也可能不那么艰难。

Both "guòlai" and "guòqu" express the sense of "pass by" or "pass through" but "guòqu" combines with a broader range of verbs. That is because "guòlai" implies going through a difficult period, whereas "guòqu" can, but need not, suggest that sense.

（2）用"过来"还是用"过去"，与说话的时间有关。"过来"只用于已经发生的动作行为，"过去"更多地用于还没有发生的动作行为，虽然也可以用于已经发生的动作行为。

When to use "guòlai" or "guòqu" also has to do with the time of speaking: "guòlai" is only used with actions or situations that have already happened, whereas "guòqu", though it can also be used in situations that have happened, is used more in situations that have not yet occurred.

2.2 结果意义（二）
Resultative sense (2)

表示失去正常的、积极的状态，进入不正常的、消极的状态。常用的动词如"晕、昏、死"等。

Signifies a shift from a normal or positive situation to an abnormal or negative one. Often used with verbs such as "yūn (to feel nauseous)" "hūn (faint)" "sǐ (die)".

① 他觉得眼前一黑，就晕过去了。

Tā juéde yǎn qián yì hēi, jiù yūn guoqu le.

He felt everything go dark and then he fainted.

② 你刚才死过去了，医生好不容易把你救过来了。

Nǐ gāngcái sǐ guoqu le, yīshēng hǎo bù róngyì bǎ nǐ jiù guolai le.

You just about died; the doctors barely managed to save you.

③ 小李昨天发高烧，昏迷过去了，一个小时以后才醒过来。

Xiǎo Lǐ zuótiān fā gāoshāo, hūnmí guoqu le, yí ge xiǎoshí yǐhòu cái xǐng guolai.

Yesterday, Xiao Li had a high temperature; he fainted and didn't come round for an hour.

一般不用可能补语形式。

Generally not used in the potential.

"过去"的这个结果意义和"过来"的结果意义（二）相反。正常、积极的状态显然离说话人更近，所以用"过来"，不正常、消极的状态显然离说话人更远，所以用"过去"，这与"过来""过去"的趋向意义有明显的联系。

In their resultative senses, "guòqu" is opposite to the 2nd sense of "guòlai". A normal or positive state tends, naturally, to be viewed as closer to the speaker; hence "guòlai". An abnormal or negative state tends to be viewed as more remote; hence "guòqu". So "guòlai" "guòqu" in their resultative senses still have a sort of directionality that make them clearly related to the directional senses of "guòlai" and "guòqu".

2.3 结果意义（三）
Resultative sense (3)

"胜过"。前面可以用的动词与"过"不完全相同。一般不能用表示比赛、竞争等方面的动词，如"打、说、考"等；但可以用形容词，如"厉害、聪明"等。

"To surpass". Verbs that occur with "guòqu" in this sense are not the same as those that appear with "guò" alone. Generally speaking, this sense is not compatible with verbs like "dǎ (fight)" "shuō (speak)" and "kǎo (test)" and other verbs that can involve competition. However adjectives such as "lìhai (tough, fierce)" and "cōngming (intelligent)" do allow it.

① 妹妹平时考试比哥哥好，这次让哥哥给比过去了。（这次哥哥考得比妹妹好）

Mèimei píngshí kǎo shì bǐ gēge hǎo, zhè cì ràng gēge gěi bǐ guoqu le.

Younger sister usually does better on tests than her older brother; this time she was outdone by her older brother. (older brother did better than younger sister on the exam)

② 那个人的功夫虽然很厉害，但是厉害不过我的老师去。

Nàge rén de gōngfu suīrán hěn lìhai, dànshì lìhai bu guò wǒ de lǎoshī qu.

That guy's martial arts are impressive, granted, but not as impressive as my teacher's.

③ 你还是按照老板的话去做吧，胳膊拧不过大腿去。

Nǐ háishì ànzhào lǎobǎn de huà qù zuò ba, gēbo nǐng bu guò dàtuǐ qu.

Better do it according to what the boss says; the arms can't win against the legs.

2.4 结果意义（四）
Resultative sense (4)

"完结"，与"过"的结果意义（四）意思类似，但没有"过"常用。

"To end or be over", similar to the 4th resultative sense of "guò" but not as frequent.

① 这件事说过去就完了，以后大家都别再提了。

Zhè jiàn shì shuō guoqu jiù wán le, yǐhòu dàjiā dōu bié zài tí le.

Now we've talked about it, that's it; don't anyone bring it up again.

② 一阵风刮过去，下起小雨来。

Yí zhèn fēng guā guoqu, xiàqǐ xiǎoyǔ lai.

A gust of wind blew by and it started to drizzle.

③ 我现在正在考试，等我这段时间忙过去，一定陪你去旅行。

Wǒ xiànzài zhèngzài kǎo shì, děng wǒ zhè duàn shíjiān máng guoqu, yídìng péi nǐ qù lǚxíng.

Right now I'm in the middle of an exam; wait until I'm done with this busy period and I'll travel with you for sure.

3. 特殊用法

Special usages

表示是否能让人接受。

Signifies that something can or cannot be excused or accepted.

3.1 "说得/不过去"：表示合理/不合理（能让人接受/不能让人接受）

"Shuō de/bu guòqù": "be reasonable / not reasonable" (i.e., be acceptable to someone or not)

① 你把他的车撞坏了，给他修好了，才说得过去。

Nǐ bǎ tā de chē zhuànghuài le, gěi tā xiūhǎo le, cái shuō de guoqu.

You've smashed up his car; the least you can do it repair it for him.

② 你不上课也不请假，这样做太说不过去了。

Nǐ bú shàng kè yě bù qǐng jià, zhèyàng zuò tài shuō bu guòqù le.

You're not in class and you haven't asked for leave; that's just unacceptable.

③ 今天是姐姐的生日，你连电话都不打，说不过去。

Jīntiān shì jiějie de shēngrì, nǐ lián diànhuà dōu bù dǎ, shuō bu guòqù.

It's your older sister's birthday today and you haven't even phoned her; that's inexcusable.

3.2 "看得/不过去"

"Kàn de/bu guòqù"

（1）表示"外观还可以，不太差"。如：

Outwardly okay, adequate. For example:

① 这件衣服的样子还看得过去，就是质量太差了。

Zhè jiàn yīfu de yàngzi hái kàn de guoqu, jiùshì zhìliàng tài chà le.

This item of clothing, it looks okay; it's just that its quality isn't very good.

② 这所房子外边还看得过去，不知道里边怎么样。

Zhè suǒ fángzi wàibian hái kàn de guoqu, bù zhīdào lǐbian zěnmeyàng.

On the outside this house looks okay, but I don't know what it's like inside.

（2）表示"感情上不能容忍"。如：

Being "emotionally intolerable". For example:

③ 这个人对父母太不好了，邻居们看不过去，都去批评他。

Zhège rén duì fùmǔ tài bù hǎo le, línjūmen kàn bu guòqù, dōu qù pīpíng tā.

This person hasn't been very nice to his parents; the neighbors can't take it and have all gone to criticize him.

④ 你这样打孩子，我实在看不过去，如果你再打，我就去找警察。

Nǐ zhè yàng dǎ háizi, wǒ shízài kàn bu guòqù, rúguǒ nǐ zài dǎ, wǒ jiù qù zhǎo jǐngchá.

I can't stand to see you hitting a child like that; if you do it again I'm going to get a policeman.

3.3 "听得/不过去"：表示听着还合理/不合理（可以接受、忍受/不能接受、忍受）

"Tīng de/bu guòqù": "to sound reasonable / not reasonable" (i.e., it sounds acceptable to someone or not)

① 他正在弹钢琴，虽然弹得不是特别好，还听得过去。

Tā zhèngzài tán gāngqín, suīrán tán de bú shì tèbié hǎo, hái tīng de guoqu.

He's playing the piano; although he doesn't play that well, it sounds okay.

② 他又吵又骂，站在一旁的老张实在听不过去了，制止了他。

Tā yòu chǎo yòu mà, zhàn zài yìpáng de Lǎo Zhāng shízài tīng bu guòqù le, zhìzhǐ le tā.

He was shouting and swearing; Mr. Zhang, who was standing by, couldn't stand it and stopped him.

3.4 "住得过去"：表示"（房子）不算很差，还可以住"
"Zhù de guoqu": "(for a house) to be liveable, bearable"

这个房子虽然很旧，但是还住得过去，你就租下吧。

Zhège fángzi suīrán hěn jiù, dànshì hái zhù de guoqu, nǐ jiù zūxia ba.

Although this house is old it's still liveable — go ahead and rent it.

"过"组小结
Summary of the "guò" group

	过 guò	过来 guòlai	过去 guòqu
趋向意义（一） directional sense (1)	表示经过某处所或向某处所移动，参照点不确定。 Expresses horizontal movement from one place to another, whether or not passing through a particular place; no explicit point of reference. ① 那个人跳过墙逃跑了。 Nàge rén tiàoguo qiáng táopǎo le. ② 他递过一杯茶给我。 Tā dìguo yì bēi chá gěi wǒ.	表示向参照点移动，参照点在说话人的位置，可能经过一个处所，也可能不经过。 Expresses horizontal movement towards the speaker, whether or not passing through a particular place. ① 我看见一个人跳过墙来。 Wǒ kànjiàn yí ge rén tiàoguò qiáng lai. ② 你看那边跑过来一个人。 Nǐ kàn nàbian pǎo guolai yí ge rén.	表示离开参照点移动，向另一处所移动，参照点在远处，中间可能经过一个处所，也可能不经过。 Expresses horizontal movement away from one place to another distant place, whether or not passing through a particular place. ① 我看见一个人跳过墙去。 Wǒ kànjiàn yí ge rén tiàoguò qiáng qu. ② 你给他递过一杯茶去。 Nǐ gěi tā dìguò yì bēi chá qu.

（续表）

	过 guò	过来 guòlai	过去 guòqu
趋向意义（二） directional sense (2)	表示人或物体改变方向，参照点不确定。 Signifies someone or something turning or twisting around; no explicit point of reference. 你转过头看看谁来了。（“头”可能转向说话人也可能背离说话人） Nǐ zhuǎnguo tóu kànkan shuí lái le. (the head could be turning towards or away from the speaker)	表示向参照点方向转动。 Expresses a turning or twisting towards a point of reference. 你转过头来看看（“头”转向说话人） Nǐ zhuǎnguò tóu lai kànkan. (the head turns in the direction of the speaker)	表示向背离参照点的方向转动。 Expresses a turning or twisting away from a point of reference. 你转过头去，别看！（头转向背离说话人的方向） Nǐ zhuǎnguò tóu qu, bié kàn! (the head turns away from the speaker)
结果意义（一） resultative sense (1)	度过一段艰难的时间或难关。 To pass through a time of difficulty. ① 熬过了那一年冬天，后来就不困难了。 Áoguole nà yì nián dōngtiān, hòulái jiù bú kùnnan le. ② 这件事你不要想骗过别人。 Zhè jiàn shì nǐ bú yào xiǎng piànguo biérén.	度过一段艰难的时期或难关。 To pass through a time of difficulty. 那年冬天特别困难，我们好不容易熬过来了。（前面不能用“骗、瞒、放”等动词） Nà nián dōngtiān tèbié kùnnan, wǒmen hǎo bù róngyì áo guolai le. (does not combine with verbs like “piàn (cheat)” “mán (deceive)” and “fàng (miss [opportunity]”)	度过。 To pass through, spend [time]. ① 艰难的日子熬过去了。 Jiānnán de rìzi áo guoqu le. ② 不要把这么好的机会错过去。（可以不是艰难的事） Bú yào bǎ zhème hǎo de jīhuì cuò guoqu. (it does not necessarily involve a difficulty) ③ 这件事你要想办法瞒过他去。 Zhè jiàn shì nǐ yào xiǎng bànfǎ mánguò tā qu.

（续表）

	过 guò	过来 guòlai	过去 guòqu
结果意义(二) resultative sense (2)	超过，超越。 To exceed, pass by. 今天早上睡过了八点，上班迟到了。 Jīntiān zǎoshang shuìguole bā diǎn, shàng bān chídào le.	表示恢复或转变到正常的、积极的状态。 To return to a normal or positive state of affairs. 他昏倒了很久才醒过来。 Tā hūndǎole hěn jiǔ cái xǐng guolai.	表示失去正常的、积极的状态，进入不正常的、消极的状态。 To change from a normal, positive situation to an abnormal, negative one. 他突然昏过去了。 Tā tūrán hūn guoqu le.
结果意义(三) resultative sense (3)	胜过。 To excel, surpass. A班打篮球打不过B班。 A bān dǎ lánqiú dǎ bu guò B bān.	表示尽数地完成。 To finish completely. 零钱太多了，我数不过来。 Língqián tài duō le, wǒ shǔ bu guòlái.	胜过。 To excel, surpass. 你这次考试成绩比不过他去。 Nǐ zhè cì kǎoshì chéngjì bǐ bu guò tā qu.
结果意义(四) resultative sense (4)	完成、完结。 To complete, be over. ① 这本书我看过了。 Zhè běn shū wǒ kàn guo le. ② 我吃过饭就去。 Wǒ chīguo fàn jiù qù.	——	完结。 To end, be over. 这件事说过去就算了，不必再提了。 Zhè jiàn shì shuō guoqu jiù suàn le, búbì zài tí le.
特殊用法 Special usages	V得过（值得） Verb de guò (worthwhile) 这件衣服又好又便宜，买得过。 Zhè jiàn yīfu yòu hǎo yòu piányi, mǎi de guo.	——	V得/不过去（能/不能接受） Verb de/bu guòqù (be acceptable, reasonable or not) ① 你借钱不还说不过去。 Nǐ jiè qián bú huán shuō bu guòqù. ② 这件衣服质量不太好，样子还看得过去。 Zhè jiàn yīfu zhìliàng bú tài hǎo, yàngzi hái kàn de guoqu.

（续表）

	过 guò	过来 guòlai	过去 guòqu
熟语 Idioms	信得/不过 Xìn de/bu guò 这个人我很了解，我信得过他。 Zhège rén wǒ hěn liǎojiě, wǒ xìndeguò tā.	——	——

“起”组

“Qǐ” group

“起”组包括“起”和“起来”。

The “qǐ” group includes “qǐ” and “qǐlai”.

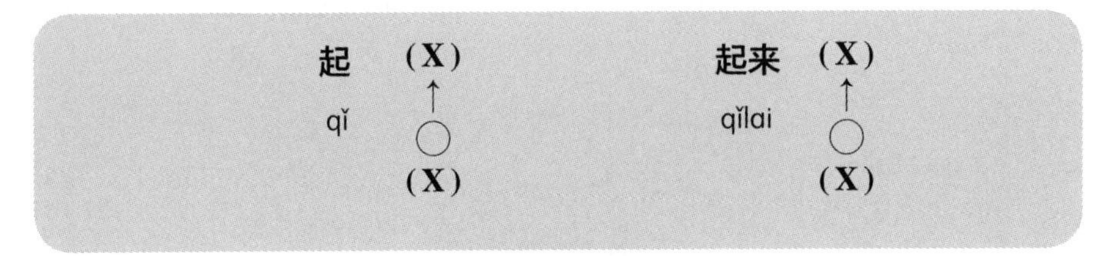

“起”组的意义和用法也是比较复杂的，尤其是结果意义。此外，还有不少特殊用法和熟语。

The function and usage of the “qǐ” group is also rather complicated, especially the resultative senses. In addition, there are also quite a lot of special usages and idioms.

“起”的趋向意义、基本结果意义都没有“起来”常用。

Neither the directional nor the basic resultative senses of “qǐ” are as common as those of “qǐlai”.

“起”组的趋向意义和基本结果意义与“上”组的趋向意义（一）及其基本结果意义有近似之处，我们将在适当的地方进行比较。

The directional and the basic resultative senses of “qǐ” are quite similar to the 1st directional sense and the basic resultative sense of the “shàng” group. We will compare the two at an appropriate time.

1. 趋向意义

Directional sense

动词“起”有“上升”的意义，作为趋向补语，其趋向意义是“由低处向高处移动”，参照点不确定。“上”的趋向意义也是“由低处向高处移动”，二者的不同在于用“上”时，动作所涉及的物体移动有终点，而“起”没有。

The meaning of the verb “qǐ” is “to rise”. As a directional complement, it tends to mean “to move from low to high”, with no explicit point of reference. The meaning of “shàng” is also “low to high”. The difference is that in the case of “shàng”, the movement effected by the verb has an endpoint; with “qǐ”, it does not.

① 你抬起头看着我。（“头”没有移动的终点）

Nǐ táiqi tóu kànzhe wǒ.

Lift up your head and look at me. (the head does not rise to a fixed point)

② 太阳从东方升起。（“太阳”没有移动的终点）

Tàiyáng cóng dōngfāng shēngqi.

The sun rises in the east. (the sun does not rise to a fixed point)

③ 我端起杯子喝了一口茶。（“杯子”没有移动的终点）

Wǒ duānqi bēizi hēle yì kǒu chá.

I raised my cup and drank a mouthful of tea. (the cup does not end up at a fixed point)

④ 我很快地走上楼。（“我”由“楼下”移动到“楼上”，“楼上”是终点）

Wǒ hěn kuài de zǒushang lóu.

I quickly walked upstairs. (upstairs is the endpoint)

⑤ 气球飞上天空。（“气球”移动的终点是“天空”）

Qìqiú fēishang tiānkōng.

The balloon rises into the sky. (the sky is the endpoint)

2. 结果意义

Resultative sense

2.1 结果意义（一）

Resultative sense (1)

连接、结合以致固定。动词后用“起”时，所涉及的名词表示的事物一定不止一个。

To join up, gather together. When “qǐ” is used after a verb, the noun involved must indicate more than one thing.

① 我看不清楚墙上的字，就眯起眼睛看。（涉及“上眼皮”与“下眼皮”）
Wǒ kàn bu qīngchu qiáng shang de zì, jiù mīqi yǎnjing kàn.
I couldn't read the words on the wall very well, so I squinted at them. (upper eyelids join with lower)

② 你快用绳子捆起行李走吧。（涉及“行李”和“绳子”）
Nǐ kuài yòng shéngzi kǔnqi xíngli zǒu ba.
Quick, tie your luggage up with string leave, okay? (string joined to luggage)

③ 我收起她给我的钱，说了声“谢谢”。（涉及“我”与“钱”）
Wǒ shōuqi tā gěi wǒ de qián, shuōle shēng “xièxie”.
I accepted the money she gave me and said “thanks”. (money joined to the speaker)

④ 我这时想起已经好几个星期没给妈妈打电话了。（涉及“我”与“已经好几个星期没给妈妈打电话”）
Wǒ zhèshí xiǎngqi yǐjīng hǎojǐ ge xīngqī méi gěi māma dǎ diànhuà le.
At this time I realized that it was already several weeks since I phoned my mother. (makes the connection about the speaker and not having made the telephone call)

⑤ 他每天晚上把电视开得声音非常大，引起了周围邻居的不满。（涉及“声音”与“引起周围邻居的不满”）

Tā měi tiān wǎnshang bǎ diànshì kāi de shēngyīn fēicháng dà, yǐnqile zhōuwéi línjū de bù mǎn.

Every evening he plays the TV very loud, which irritates the neighbors in the vicinity. (connects the sound and the neighbor' irritation)

⑥ 我家旁边最近盖起一个新的大楼。（涉及“我家旁边”与“新的大楼”）

Wǒ jiā pángbiān zuìjìn gàiqi yí ge xīn de dàlóu.

Recently, they've been building a new highrise next to our home. (indicates the connection between the house and the new building)

⑦ 很多年以前，他的爷爷在老家办起了一所小学。（涉及“他的爷爷”与“一所小学”）

Hěn duō nián yǐqián, tā de yéye zài lǎojiā bànqile yì suǒ xiǎoxué.

A number of years ago, his grandfather started an elementary school in his hometown. (grandfather connected to the school)

⑧ 高中毕业的时候，我们班的同学和老师已经建立起很深的感情。（涉及“我们班的同学”与“老师”）

Gāozhōng bì yè de shíhou, wǒmen bān de tóngxué hé lǎoshī yǐjīng jiànlì qi hěn shēn de gǎnqíng.

By the time we graduated from high school, our class had already developed strong emotional ties to our teachers. (ties between students and teachers)

“起”的结果意义（一）的反义补语是“开”，详见“开”（第209页）。

The verbal complement that is the opposite of the 1st resultative sense of “qǐ” is “kāi”; for details, see the section on “kāi” (p. 209).

2.2 结果意义（二）

Resultative sense (2)

突起、隆起。一般不用可能补语形式。

“To swell, bulge”; generally not in the potential mode.

① 他的眼睛上边肿起一个小包。

Tā de yǎnjing shàngbian zhǒngqi yí ge xiǎobāo.

He developed a small bump on his eye.

② 爸爸批评了她几句，她很不高兴，撅起了小嘴。

Bàba pīpíngle tā jǐ jù, tā hěn bù gāoxìng, juēqile xiǎo zuǐ.

Dad said a few critical words to her; she was not happy, and pouted.

③ 听见集合的号声，他挺起胸走了出去。

Tīngjiàn jíhé de hàoshēng, tā tǐngqi xiōng zǒule chuqu.

On hearing the call to fall in, he straightened his chest and walked out.

2.3 结果意义（三）
Resultative sense (3)

主观上是否能承受，只用可能补语形式。

Acceptance or rejection; only in the potential form.

（1）表示在经济方面是否能承受。

Signifying that something is affordable or not.

① 这么贵的衣服，我买不起。

Zhème guì de yīfu, wǒ mǎi bu qǐ.

I can't afford such expensive clothes.

② 那个地方房子太贵，你住得起吗？

Nàge dìfang fángzi tài guì, nǐ zhù de qǐ ma?

The houses there are really expensive; can you afford to live there?

③ 每天去饭馆儿吃饭，我吃不起。

Měi tiān qù fànguǎnr chī fàn, wǒ chī bu qǐ.

I can't afford to eat out at restaurants on a daily basis.

④ 他又付不起下个月的房租了。

Tā yòu fù bu qǐ xià ge yuè de fángzū le.

Once again, he can't pay next month's rent.

（2）表示在时间上是否能承受，动词如“花、陪、拖、浪费、耗”等。

Signifies that one cannot afford the time to do something; with verbs such as “huā (spend)” “péi (accompany)” “tuō (extend)” “làngfèi (waste)” and “hào (consume)”.

⑤ 他的病很重，得马上去医院，拖不起！

Tā de bìng hěn zhòng, děi mǎshàng qù yīyuàn, tuō bu qǐ!

His illness is very serious; he must get to the hospital right way, without delay!

⑥ 你让我每天陪你逛街，时间我花不起。

Nǐ ràng wǒ měi tiān péi nǐ guàng jiē, shíjiān wǒ huā bu qǐ.

You want me to go window shopping with you everyday; I don’t have the time.

⑦ 陪她买东西，太花时间了，我陪不起。

Péi tā mǎi dōngxi, tài huā shíjiān le, wǒ péi bu qǐ.

Taking her shopping is too time-consuming; I don’t have time to do it.

（3）表示是否能承受某种地位、资格、待遇等，动词如“承受、担待、担（责任）、消受”等。

Signifies whether or not a location, qualification, or treatment, etc. is acceptable, with verbs such as “chéngshòu (endure)” “dāndài (forbear)” “dān [zérèn] (undertake [responsibility])” “xiāoshòu (endure, bear)”.

⑧ 你这么夸我，我可承受不起。

Nǐ zhème kuā wǒ, wǒ kě chéngshòu bu qǐ.

I really don’t deserve such praise.

⑨ 我能力有限，负不起教育你孩子的责任。

Wǒ nénglì yǒu xiàn, fù bu qǐ jiàoyù nǐ háizi de zérèn.

I can only take on so much; I can’t take on the responsibility of teaching your child.

也可以用于“得罪、惹、劳驾”等动词后，有“不敢”的意思，如：

It also appears after verbs such as “dézuì (commit an offense)” “rě (rile, insult)” and "láo jià (trouble someone)" in the sense of "not dare to". For example:

⑩ 她是你的老板，你说话小心点儿，得罪不起。

Tā shì nǐ de lǎobǎn, nǐ shuō huà xiǎoxīn diǎnr, dézuì bu qǐ.

She's your boss, so be a bit careful when you talk, you don't want to insult her.

⑪ 这件事我劳不起你这个校长的大驾，还是自己办吧。

Zhè jiàn shì wǒ láo bu qǐ nǐ zhège xiàozhǎng de dàjià, háishi zìjǐ bàn ba.

I shouldn't bother you, principal, with this business; better I do it myself.

⑫ 他很凶？我惹不起，还躲不起嘛？

Tā hěn xiōng? Wǒ rě bu qǐ, hái duǒ bu qǐ ma?

He's fierce? Since I can't afford to rile him, I'd better hide from him.

（4）表示精神和体力上是否能承受，动词如"经、丢（人）、背（骂名）"。

With verbal meanings such as "jīng (undergo)" "diū [rén] (lose [face])" and "bēi [màmíng] (bear on one's back)", it signifies that something can or cannot be withstood (in physical or mental terms).

⑬ 她的心理素质太差了，经不起任何挫折 。（意思是：让她受挫折，她会受不了）

Tā de xīnlǐ sùzhì tài chà le, jīng bu qǐ rènhé cuòzhé.

She doesn't have much strength of character; she just can't deal with any sort of setback. (That is: If she gets frustrated, she can't deal with it.)

⑭ 做这种骗人的事，他说丢不起那个人。（意思是：让他"丢人"，他受不了；他怕丢人）

Zuò zhè zhǒng piàn rén de shì, tā shuō diū bu qǐ nàge rén.

He said if he did something so deceptive, he wouldn't be able to face the person. (That is: If something make him in disgrace, he feel ashamed.)

⑮ 我从来不做对不起人的事，因为背不起骂名。（意思是：怕别人骂）

Wǒ cónglái bú zuò duìbuqǐ rén de shì, yīnwèi bēi bu qǐ màmíng.

I've never do things that offend others because I can't stand to get a bad name. (meaning the speaker fears rejection)

3. 状态意义

Stative sense

表示进入新的状态或动作开始，只能用在动词后。

Signifies a change of state or the beginning of action; only after verbs.

① 听到这个消息，他高兴地唱起《今天是个好天气》。

Tīngdào zhège xiāoxi, tā gāoxìng de chàngqi “Jīntiān shì ge hǎo tiānqì”.

When he heard the news, he was so happy that he started to sing “What a lovely day it is today”.

② 下课以后，他们讨论起去南方旅行的事。

Xià kè yǐhòu, tāmen tǎolùn qi qù nánfāng lǚxíng de shì.

After class, they discussed their trip down south.

③ 妹妹一回家，就打开电脑写起了明天要给老师的作业。

Mèimei yì huí jiā, jiù dǎkāi diànnǎo xiěqile míngtiān yào gěi lǎoshī de zuòyè.

As soon as younger sister got home, she switched on her computer and did the homework that she needed to give to her teacher tomorrow.

④ 跟这个小男孩儿打了几次篮球以后，我开始喜欢起他了。

Gēn zhège xiǎo nánháir dǎle jǐ cì lánqiú yǐhòu, wǒ kāishǐ xǐhuan qi tā le.

After playing a few games of basketball with the young fellow, I grew to like him.

⑤ 下午外边下起了大雨，我们只好在家里看电视。

Xiàwǔ wàibian xiàqile dàyǔ, wǒmen zhǐhǎo zài jiāli kàn diànshì.

That afternoon it started to rain heavily outside, so all we could do was watch TV at home.

4. 特殊用法
Special usages

4.1 用来从某一方面说明、评论人或者事物
Commenting on a particular aspect of someone or something

① 说起中国文化，我很感兴趣，可是懂得不多。

Shuōqi Zhōngguó wénhuà, wǒ hěn gǎn xìngqù，kěshì dǒng de bù duō.

When it comes to Chinese culture, I'm interested, but I don't know much about it.

② 比起哥哥，他的功课差多了。

Bǐqi gēge, tā de gōngkè chà duō le.

Compared to his older brother, his school work isn't nearly as good.

4.2 用在表示说话的意思的动词后，引进所谈的人或事
Used after verbs of speaking, it introduces the person or thing to be talked about

① 昨天我和爸爸谈起毕业以后找工作的事。

Zuótiān wǒ hé bàba tánqi bì yè yǐhòu zhǎo gōngzuò de shì.

Yesterday I talked to Dad about finding work after graduating.

② 我哥哥常常问起你，他对你很关心。

Wǒ gēge chángcháng wènqi nǐ, tā duì nǐ hěn guānxīn.

My older brother often asks about you; he's very concerned about you.

③ 提起期末大考的事，我们都很紧张。

Tíqi qīmò dàkǎo de shì, wǒmen dōu hěn jǐnzhāng.

When the semester final exam is brought up, we get quite nervous.

4.3 表示动作的起点
Signifies onset of action

① 我们就从你为什么要来我们公司工作谈起吧。

Wǒmen jiù cóng nǐ wèi shénme yào lái wǒmen gōngsī gōngzuò tánqi ba.

Let's begin by talking about why it is that you want to come work for our company.

② 从我到这里工作那天算起，已经超过10年了。

Cóng wǒ dào zhèli gōngzuò nà tiān suànqi, yǐjīng chāoguò shí nián le.

Reckoning from the day I came to work here, it's already more than 10 years.

③ 环保，我们应该先从自己做起。

Huánbǎo, wǒmen yīnggāi xiān cóng zìjǐ zuòqi.

Environmental protection should start with us.

5. 熟语

Idioms

5.1 "看(瞧)得/不起"

"Kàn (qiáo) de/bu qǐ"

"看（瞧）不起"的意思是"轻视"，"看（瞧）得起"的意思是"不轻视"。"瞧得/不起"更加口语。

The sense of "kànbuqǐ" and "qiáobuqǐ" is "look down on", "kàndeqǐ" and "qiáodeqǐ" is "look up to, regard well". "Qiáo" is more colloquial.

① 我最看不起说谎的人。

Wǒ zuì kànbuqǐ shuō huǎng de rén.

I am most contemptuous of people who lie.

② 你别去求他，别人会瞧不起你的。

Nǐ bié qù qiú tā, biérén huì qiáobuqǐ nǐ de.

Don't entreat him; others will look down on you if you do.

③ 不应该看不起穷人。

Bù yīnggāi kànbuqǐ qióngrén.

You shouldn't look down on the poor.

5.2 “对得/不起”

“duì de/bu qǐ”

“对不起”的意思是对人愧疚，“对得起”的意思是对人无愧。

The meaning of “duìbuqǐ” is “to not be fair to, to let someone down”; “duìdeqǐ” is “not to feel bad about” or “not to let someone down”.

① 你对父母太不好了，你对不起他们。

Nǐ duì fùmǔ tài bù hǎo le, nǐ duìbuqǐ tāmen.

You’re not at all good to your parents; you’re letting them down.

② 我没有做对不起你的事。

Wǒ méiyǒu zuò duìbuqǐ nǐ de shì.

I’ve done nothing to offend you.

③ 你帮助过我，可是我也给你做了很多事，对得起你了。

Nǐ bāngzhù guo wǒ, kěshì wǒ yě gěi nǐ zuòle hěn duō shì，duìdeqǐ nǐ le.

You helped me before, but I’ve also done a lot for you, I don’t feel bad on your account.

“对不起”常用来表示道歉。如：

“Duìbuqǐ” is often used to express apologies. For example:

④ 对不起，我来晚了。

Duìbuqǐ, wǒ lái wǎn le.

Sorry, I’m late.

⑤ 对不起，请等一下。

Duìbuqǐ, qǐng děng yí xià.

Excuse me, please wait a minute.

5.3 “了不起”

“liǎobuqǐ”

意思是“不平常”“优点突出”。

“Liǎobuqǐ” means “not ordinary, extraordinary”.

① 她真了不起，才20多岁，公司就管得这么好。

Tā zhēn liǎobuqǐ, cái èrshí duō suì, gōngsī jiù guǎn de zhème hǎo.

She's amazing: only a little over 20 years of age and she manages a company so well.

② 她父亲是一个了不起的科学家。

Tā fùqīn shì yí ge liǎobuqǐ de kēxuéjiā.

Her father's an extraordinary scientist.

③ 考不上好大学我觉得没什么了不起的，你为什么这么伤心呀？

Kǎo bu shàng hǎo dàxué wǒ juéde méi shénme liǎobuqǐ de, nǐ wèi shénme zhème shāng xīn ya?

Not passing the exam to get into a top university — I don't feel it's such a big big deal; how come you're so upset?

1. 趋向意义

Directional sense

由低处向高处移动，也没有确定的参照点。如："你抬起头来"。

Movement from low to high. Despite the presence of "lái", "qǐlai" generally has no clear point of reference, as the following example illustrates: "Nǐ táiqǐ tóu lai (Lift up your head)".

① 国旗升起来了。

Guóqí shēng qilai le.

The flag is being raised.

② 他端起杯子来想喝水，可是杯子里没有水了。

Tā duānqǐ bēizi lai xiǎng hē shuǐ, kěshì bēizi li méiyǒu shuǐ le.

He raised the cup to drink some water but the cup had no water in it.

③ 你把照片挂起来吧。

Nǐ bǎ zhàopiàn guà qilai ba.

Hang the pictures up.

④ 下课了，学生们背起书包来走出教室。

Xià kè le，xuéshengmen bēiqǐ shūbāo lai zǒuchu jiàoshì.

Class is over; the students put on their backpacks and walk out of the classroom.

⑤ 这么晚了还在睡觉，把他叫起来。

Zhème wǎn le hái zài shuì jiào，bǎ tā jiào qilai.

Still sleeping this late in the day — wake him up.

与“上”组的不同，像“起”一样，用“上”组时，物体移动都有终点（在句子中可能出现，也可能不出现），而用“起来”时，句子中不能出现表示移动终点的词语。

Like “qǐ”, “qǐlai” differs from the “shàng” group in that for the latter, there is an end point to the movement — a destination (which may or may not be expressed). For “qǐlai” there is no implied endpoint.

⑥ 气球飞上房顶了。

Qìqiú fēishang fángdǐng le.

The balloon flew up to the ceiling.

* 气球飞起房顶了。

* Qìqiú fēiqi fángdǐng le.

⑦ 你快点儿跑上山来。

Nǐ kuài diǎnr pǎoshàng shān lai.

Run up to the top of the hill, quick.

* 你快点儿跑起山来。

* Nǐ kuài diǎnr pǎoqǐ shān lai.

2. 结果意义

Resultative sense

2.1 结果意义（一）

Resultative sense (1)

表示连接、结合以致固定。

To join up, gather together.

与“起”的结果意义（一）一样，所涉及的名词表示的事物也不止一个。

“Qǐlai” has the same meaning as the 1st resultative sense of “qǐ”; it usually implies bringing together several things or chosing from a selection of items.

① 你把图上这两条线连起来。

Nǐ bǎ tú shang zhè liǎng tiáo xiàn lián qilai.

Join up the two lines on the chart.

② 3和8 加起来是11。

3 hé 8 jiā qilai shì 11.

3 added to 8 is 11.

③ 你姐姐的男朋友叫什么名字，你想起来了吗？

Nǐ jiějie de nánpéngyou jiào shénme míngzi，nǐ xiǎng qilai le ma?

Have you remembered what the name of your older sister’s boyfriend is?

④ 我们两个班的同学应该团结起来，这样才能打败三班和四班的篮球队。

Wǒmen liǎng ge bān de tóngxué yīnggāi tuánjié qilai，zhèyàng cái néng dǎbài sān bān hé sì bān de lánqiúduì.

The students of both our classes should combine so that we can defeat the class 3 and class 4 basketball teams.

⑤ 对这个问题的解决办法，大家的意见不同，但是必须统一起来。

Duì zhège wèntí de jiějué bànfǎ，dàjiā de yìjiàn bù tóng，dànshì bìxū tǒngyī qilai.

People differ on how to solve this problem but we do need to come to an agreement.

⑥ 你把这些水果包起来带给你的同学吧。

Nǐ bǎ zhèxiē shuǐguǒ bāo qilai dàigěi nǐ de tóngxué ba.

Pack up this fruit and take it to your classmates.

⑦ 我把爸爸寄给我的钱存起来了。

Wǒ bǎ bàba jìgěi wǒ de qián cún qilai le.

I've deposited the money that Dad gave me.

⑧ 那个人犯了罪，被抓起来了。

Nàge rén fànle zuì，bèi zhuā qilai le.

That guy committed a crime and was caught.

⑨ 我们学校的教学大楼盖起来了。

Wǒmen xuéxiào de jiàoxué dàlóu gài qilai le.

The classroom building at our school is being constructed.

⑩ 最近中国在非洲建起来多条新铁路。

Zuìjìn Zhōngguó zài Fēizhōu jiàn qilai duō tiáo xīn tiělù.

Recently, in Africa, China has been constructing a number of railways.

“上”的结果意义（一）中的“接触”与“起”和“起来”的结果意义（一）的“连接”近似，但是不完全相同，比如“起”不表示“附着”意义。“起”组和“上”组可以用的动词有的相同，大部分不同，这也是我们一再强调动词和补语要作为一个短语一起记的原因。另外，“上”组所涉及的事物是两个，而且有主次之分，“起”组涉及的事物不限于两个，也没有主次之分，所以可以用的句式不同。例如“上”组可以用在下面的句式里：

N_1+V上+N_2 ……

The 1st resultative sense of “shàng”, that is, “to connect” or “to join”, is similar to the 1st resultative sense of “qǐ” and “qǐlai”; but they are not identical. For example, “qǐ” does not have the sense of “fùzhuó (to attach, adhere to something)”. The verbs that can be used with the “qǐ” group and the “shàng” group are mostly not from the same set; some can be used with both, others, not. This is another reason why we need to treat verbs and their complements as phrases to be learned as units. Moreover, the “shàng” group involves two things, one of which is primary; the “qǐ” group, on the other hand, may involve more than two things, no one of which is primary. So they appear in different sentence patterns. For example, the “shàng” group can be used in patterns such as the following:

N_1 + V shàng + N_2 ……

⑪ 5加上23等于28。

5 jiāshang 23 děngyú 28.

5 added to 23 makes 28.

不能说：＊5加起来23等于28。

But not: ＊5 jiā qilai 23 děngyú 28.

只能说： 5和23加起来等于28。

Only: 5 hé 23 jiā qilai děngyú 28.

5 and 23 added together make 28.

“起”的结果意义（一）的反义补语是“开”，详见“开”（第209页）。

The opposite sense of the 1st resultative sense of “qǐ” is “kāi”; see, “kāi” on p. 209.

2.2 结果意义（二）

Resultative sense (2)

“突起、隆起”。

“To swell, bulge”.

可以用的动词如“肿、鼓、高、膨胀”“碰、磨、撞”以及“撅（嘴）、挺（胸）”等。

This sense is associated with verbs such as “zhǒng (swell)” “gǔ (be bulging)” “gāo (be raised up)” “péngzhàng (inflate)”; “péng (bump into)” “mó (rub, grind)” “zhuàng (collide)”; “juē[zuǐ] (purse [the lips])” “tǐng[xiōng] (straighten [the chest])”.

① 你的脸怎么肿起来了？

Nǐ de liǎn zěnme zhǒng qilai le?

How come your face is swollen?

② 我不小心，头碰起一个包来。

Wǒ bù xiǎoxīn，tóu pèngqǐ yí ge bāo lai.

I wasn’t careful and got a bump on my head.

③ 小心点儿开，前面的路高起来一块。

Xiǎoxīn diǎnr kāi，qiánmiàn de lù gāo qilai yí kuài.

Drive carefully, there's a raised section of road ahead.

④ 我昨天走路走得太多了，脚上磨起来一个泡。

Wǒ zuótiān zǒu lù zǒu de tài duō le，jiǎo shang mó qilai yí ge pào.

I walked too much yesterday and got a blister on my foot.

3. 状态意义

Stative sense

表示进入新的状态，或动作开始并继续。可以用在动词和形容词后。

Signifies a new situation or the onset and continuation of action. Used after both verbs and adjectives.

① 我听见教室里的孩子唱起歌来，很好听。

Wǒ tīngjiàn jiàoshì li de háizi chàngqǐ gē lai，hěn hǎotīng.

I heard the children starting to sing in their classroom; they sounded wonderful.

② 她看着看着书，忽然笑了起来。

Tā kànzhe kànzhe shū，hūrán xiàole qilai.

She was reading a book when suddenly she started laughing.

③ 看见好久不见的老朋友，他高兴得叫了起来。

Kànjiàn hǎo jiǔ bú jiàn de lǎo péngyou，tā gāoxìng de jiàole qilai.

On seeing good friends that he hadn't seen for a long time, he called out happily.

④ 昨天天气很好，可是今天早上下起雨来了。

Zuótiān tiānqì hěn hǎo，kěshì jīntiān zǎoshang xiàqǐ yǔ lai le.

The weather was fine yesterday but this morning it's starting to rain.

⑤ 直到听到这个好消息，大家才高兴起来。

Zhí dào tīngdào zhège hǎo xiāoxi，dàjiā cái gāoxìng qilai.

It wasn't until they hear the good news that everyone got so excited.

⑥ 前些天没什么事，最近我忙起来了。

Qián xiē tiān méi shénme shì，zuìjìn wǒ máng qilai le.

The last few days there was nothing going on, but recently it's got quite busy.

⑦ 路上车少了，他开得快起来了。

Lùshang chē shǎo le，tā kāi de kuài qilai le.

The cars on the road thinned out and he started to drive faster.

“起来”前一般用表示积极意义的正向形容词，如“快、亮、忙、高兴、热闹”等。如果描写季节的正常变化，秋天、冬天用“冷”，春天用“暖和”，夏天用“热”。表示状态意义的“下来”前通常用负向意义的形容词，如“慢、暗、安静”等。如果“起来”前用负向形容词，“下来”前用正向形容词，就表示不正常的、出乎人意料的变化。如以下两例：

Generally speaking, “qǐlai” follows “positive” or “vivid” adjectives, such as “kuài (fast)” “liàng (bright)” “máng (busy)” “gāoxìng (happy)” or “rènao (lively)”. “Qǐlai” may also follow adjectives associated with a particular season: “lěng (cold)” for autumn and winter; “nuǎnhuo (warm)” for spring; “rè (hot)” for summer. By contrast, the stative sense of the complement “xiàlai” is associated with adjectives that express more “negative” or “quiescent” meanings, such as “màn (slow)” “àn (dark)” and “ānjìng (quiet)”. If, on the other hand, the roles are reversed, and “qǐlai” appears with “negative” verbs and “xiàlai” with “positive” ones, then they are expressing situations that are abnormal or unexpected. The following two examples illustrate:

⑧ 我叫他快点儿开，他却开得慢起来了。

Wǒ jiào tā kuài diǎnr kāi，tā què kāide màn qilai le.

I asked him to speed up but, instead, he slowed down.

⑨ 现在是中午一点钟，房间怎么突然暗起来了？

Xiànzài shì zhōngwǔ yī diǎn zhōng，fángjiān zěnme tūrán àn qilai le?

It's now only an hour after noon, how come the room's suddenly getting dark?

4. 特殊用法

Special usages

4.1 从某一方面评论人或事物

Commenting on a particular aspect of someone or something

① 饺子吃起来好吃，做起来很麻烦。（从“吃”和“做”的方面评论饺子）

Jiǎozi chī qilai hǎochī，zuò qilai hěn máfan.

Dumplings are great to eat but a lot of trouble to make. (from the point of view of “eating” and “making” them)

② 她看起来有点儿不高兴。

Tā kàn qilai yǒu diǎnr bù gāoxìng.

She looks rather unhappy.

③ 这件事听起来可以成功。

Zhè jiàn shì tīng qilai kěyǐ chénggōng.

It sounds like this business is going to succeed.

④ 跟她比起来，我的中文差多了。

Gēn tā bǐ qilai，wǒ de Zhōngwén chà duō le.

Compared to her, my Chinese is not nearly as good.

4.2 “想起来”“看起来”引进说话人的一种看法

“Xiǎng qilai” and “kàn qilai” make reference to an opinion or a viewpoint of the speaker

① 看起来，很快就要下雨了。

Kàn qilai，hěn kuài jiù yào xià yǔ le.

It looks like it’s about to rain.

② 昨天他说的那些话，现在想起来很可笑。

Zuótiān tā shuō de nàxiē huà，xiànzài xiǎng qilai hěn kěxiào.

Thinking back on what he said yesterday, it now seems quite funny.

"起"组小结
Summary of the "qǐ" group

	起 qǐ	起来 qǐlai
趋向意义 directional sense	由低处向高处移动，参照点不确定。 To move from low to high, with no explicit point of reference. 抬起头。 Táiqi tóu.	由低处向高处移动，参照点不确定。 To move from low to high, with no explicit point of reference. 抬起头来。 Táiqǐ tóu lai.
结果意义（一） resultative sense (1)	连接、结合以致固定。 To join up, gather together. ①想起这件事我就不高兴。 Xiǎngqi zhè jiàn shì wǒ jiù bù gāoxìng. ②你快收起电脑，该去机场了。 Nǐ kuài shōuqi diànnǎo, gāi qù jīchǎng le. ③我家旁边办起一所新的中学。 Wǒ jiā pángbiān bànqi yì suǒ xīn de zhōngxué.	连接、结合以致固定。 To join up, gather together. ①那件事我想不起来了。 Nà jiàn shì wǒ xiǎng bu qǐlái le. ②你快把电脑收起来，该去机场了。 Nǐ kuài bǎ diànnǎo shōu qilai，gāi qù jīchǎng le. ③我家旁边那家中学办起来了。 Wǒ jiā pángbiān nà jiā zhōngxué bàn qilai le.
结果意义（二） resultative sense (2)	突起、隆起。 To swell, bulge. 他的头碰起一个大包。 Tā de tóu pèngqi yí ge dàbāo.	突起、隆起。 To swell, bulge. 他的头碰起来一个大包。 Tā de tóu pèng qilai yí ge dàbāo.

（续表）

	起 qǐ	起来 qǐlai
结果意义（三） resultative sense (3)	主观上是否能承受，只用可能补语形式。 Acceptable, affordable, bearable or not; only in the potential. ①房子太贵，买不起。 Fángzi tài guì, mǎi bu qǐ. ②陪你逛街，我时间花不起。 Péi nǐ guàng jiē, wǒ shíjiān huā bu qǐ. ③他承担不起这么大的责任。 Tā chéngdān bu qǐ zhème dà de zérèn.	——
状态意义 stative sense	表示进入新的状态或动作开始，只能用在动词后。 Indicates a new situation or the onset of an action; only after verbs. 他突然唱起我们过去学过的一首老歌。 Tā tūrán chàngqi wǒmen guòqù xuéguo de yì shǒu lǎogē.	表示进入新的状态，或动作开始并继续，可以用在动词和形容词后。 Indicates a new situation or the onset and continuation of an action; after verbs or adjectives. ①我们一见面就激动得大叫起来。 Wǒmen yí jiàn miàn jiù jīdòng de dà jiào qilai. ②过去不忙，现在忙起来了。 Guòqù bù máng, xiànzài máng qilai le.
特殊用法（一） special usages (1)	从某一方面说明、评论人或者事物。 Commenting on a particular aspect of someone or something. 比起他，我的中文差多了。 Bǐqi tā, wǒ de Zhōngwén chà duō le.	从某一方面说明、评论人或者事物。 Commenting on a particular aspect of someone or something. ①比起他来，我的中文差多了。 Bǐqǐ tā lai, wǒ de Zhōngwén chà duō le. ②饺子吃起来好吃，做起来麻烦。 Jiǎozi chī qilai hǎochī, zuò qilai máfan.

（续表）

	起 qǐ	起来 qǐlai
特殊用法（二） special usages (2)	引进所谈的人或事。 Introducing a person or thing to be talked about. 我们常常谈起你。 Wǒmen chángcháng tánqi nǐ.	引进说话人的看法。 Making reference to an opinion or a viewpoint of the speaker. ①想起来、看起来 Xiǎng qilai; kàn qilai ②看起来今天他不会来了。 Kàn qilai jīntiān tā bú huì lái le. ③这件事现在想起来还觉得不是真的。 Zhè jiàn shì xiànzài xiǎng qilai hái juéde bú shì zhēn de.
特殊用法（三） special usages (3)	表示动作的起点。 Signfies onset of action. 我们应该先从自己做起。 Wǒmen yīnggāi xiān cóng zìjǐ zuòqi.	——
熟语 idioms	1.看（瞧）得/不起 Kàn(qiáo) de/bu qǐ 2.对得/不起 Duì de/bu qǐ 3.了不起 Liǎobuqǐ ①他很小气，我看不起他。 Tā hěn xiǎoqì，wǒ kànbuqǐ tā. ②我错了，对不起。 Wǒ cuò le，duìbuqǐ. ③这个人真了不起，会好几种语言。 Zhège rén zhēn liǎobuqǐ，huì hǎojǐ zhǒng yǔyán.	——

“开”组

“Kāi” group

“开”组包括“开”“开来”“开去”。

The “kāi” group consists of “kāi” “kāilai” and “kāiqu”.

开	开来	开去
kāi	kāilai	kāiqu
[(X)] ○ ⟶ (X)	□○ ⟶ X	[X] ○ ⟶

1. 趋向意义

Directional sense

表示离开某处所，参照点不确定。

Indicates clearing an area, moving things away from a place; no explicit point of reference.

① 走开，这里危险！

Zǒukai，zhèli wēixiǎn!

Leave — it’s dangerous here.

② 她很怕那个人看见自己，就躲开了。

Tā hěn pà nàge rén kànjiàn zìjǐ，jiù duǒkai le.

She was afraid that person would see her so she hid.

③ 车来了，让开路！

Chē lái le，ràngkai lù！

A car's coming, clear the road!

④ 吃饭了，把桌子上的东西挪开。

Chī fàn le，bǎ zhuōzi shang de dōngxi nuókai.

Time to eat; clear the things off the table.

2. 结果意义

Resultative sense

2.1 结果意义（一）

Resultative sense (1)

"分离、分裂"。这与"开"的趋向意义有明显的联系。

"To separate, divide". This sense is obviously related to the directional sense of "kāi".

① 你睁开眼睛看看。

Nǐ zhēngkai yǎnjing kànkan.

Open your eyes and look around.

② 到了图书馆，我推开门走了进去。

Dàole túshūguǎn，wǒ tuīkai mén zǒule jinqu.

Once I got to the library, I opened the door and walked inside.

③ 太热了，我把衣服扣子解开。

Tài rè le，wǒ bǎ yīfu kòuzi jiěkai.

It was so hot that I undid the buttons on my clothing.

④ 我打开抽屉把钱拿了出来。

Wǒ dǎkai chōuti bǎ qián nále chulai.

I opened the drawer and took out the money.

★“开”与“下/下来”比较：

Comparison of “kāi” and “xià/xiàlai”:

“下/下来”表示次要物体与主要物体（或部分与整体）分离，“开”只表示“分离”，分离的物体没有主要和次要的分别。

“Xià/xiàlai”expresses the parting or removal of a secondary item (or part of an item) from a primary, whereas “kāi” does not involve a ranking of items.

⑤ 你把面包切开。（可以是从中间切开）

Nǐ bǎ miànbāo qiēkai.

Slice open the loaf. (could be in the middle)

⑥ 你把面包切下来一块给我。

Nǐ bǎ miànbāo qiē xialai yí kuài gěi wǒ.

Slice off a piece of bread for me.

⑦ 你把这两根绳子解开。

Nǐ bǎ zhè liǎng gēn shéngzi jiěkai.

Separate these two pieces of string.

⑧ 你把绳子从行李上解下来。

Nǐ bǎ shéngzi cóng xíngli shang jiě xialai .

Take the string off the luggage.

2.2 结果意义（二）

Resultative sense (2)

“舒展、分散”。

“To unfold, spread”.

① 做这个运动的时候，两只胳膊要伸开。

Zuò zhège yùndòng de shíhou，liǎng zhī gēbo yào shēnkai.

To do this exercise you need to extend your arms.

② 鸟儿展开翅膀飞了。

Niǎor zhǎnkai chìbǎng fēi le.

The birds spread open their wings to fly.

③ 你把这张画儿打开。

Nǐ bǎ zhè zhāng huàr dǎkai.

Unroll this scroll.

④ 这个消息很快传开了。

Zhège xiāoxi hěn kuài chuánkai le.

The news spread rapidly.

2.3 结果意义（三）

Resultative sense (3)

空间是否能容纳某一物体或某一动作施展。口语。

Signifies whether a thing or action fits in a space or not. Colloquial.

① 这个房间放不开两张床。

Zhège fángjiān fàng bu kāi liǎng zhāng chuáng.

Two beds won't fit in this room.

② 厨房太小，两个人做饭转不开身。

Chúfáng tài xiǎo, liǎng ge rén zuò fàn zhuǎn bu kāi shēn.

The kitchen's too small; two people cooking won't be able to turn around.

★“开”与“下”比较：

Comparison of “kāi” and “xià”:

“下”也表示“容纳”，与“开”的不同之处：

“Xià” can also mean “accommodate, fit”, but differs from “kāi” in the following ways:

（1）“下”可以表示一个容器是否可以容纳，“开”不行。

Only “xià” can express the notion of a container having a certain capacity. That cannot be expressed with “kāi”.

③ 这个瓶子盛不下三斤油。

Zhège píngzi chéng bu xià sān jīn yóu.

This bottle won't hold 3 catties of oil.

* 这个瓶子盛不开三斤油。

* Zhège píngzi chéng bu kāi sān jīn yóu.

（2）“开”可以表示某处所是否容许动作施展，“下”不行。

“Kāi” can express the notion that a place is large enough to permit certain actions. That cannot be expressed with “xià”.

④ 这个厨房太小，两个人做饭就转不开了。

Zhège chúfáng tài xiǎo，liǎng ge rén zuò fàn jiù zhuàn bu kāi le.

The kitchen's too small; two people cooking won't be able to turn around.

* 这个厨房太小，两个人做饭就转不下了。

* Zhège chúfáng tài xiǎo，liǎng ge rén zuò fàn jiù zhuàn bu xià le.

2.4 结果意义（四）
Resultative sense (4)

“清楚、彻悟”，只与“想、看、说、解释”等动词一起用。

“To be clear, fully understood”; used with verbs like “xiǎng (think)” “kàn (see)” “shuō (speak)” and “jiěshì (explain)”.

① 经过这件事，我想开了，不要太舍不得花钱，钱花了才是你的。

Jīngguò zhè jiàn shì，wǒ xiǎngkai le，bú yào tài shěbudé huā qián，qián huāle cái shì nǐ de.

After this business, it became clear to me that it wasn't necessary to be so careful with money; after all, the money spent is yours.

② 你要看开点儿，什么困难都会过去的。

Nǐ yào kànkai diǎnr，shénme kùnnan dōu huì guòqu de.

You need to open your eyes a bit; any difficulty can be overcome.

③ 你们俩有些误会，把事情说开了就好了。

Nǐmen liǎ yǒuxiē wùhuì，bǎ shìqing shuōkaile jiù hǎo le.

You two had a few misunderstandings; talk things out and all will be well.

3. 状态意义
Stative sense

由静态进入动态，口语。

To go from a static state to a more active one; colloquial.

① 孩子们一出学校就打开架了。

Háizimen yì chū xuéxiào jiù dǎkai jià le.

The children started fighting once they got out of school.

② 我听了他的话就琢磨开了：他为什么告诉我这些？

Wǒ tīngle tā de huà jiù zuómo kai le: tā wèi shénme gàosu wǒ zhèxiē？

When I heard what he had to say, I started wondering how come he told me those things?

③ 他今天很高兴，一回家就唱开了。

Tā jīntiān hěn gāoxìng，yì huí jiā jiù chàngkai le.

He was so happy today that once he got home he started to sing.

④ 前些天没有什么事，这几天忙开了。

Qián xiē tiān méiyǒu shénme shì，zhè jǐ tiān mángkai le.

A few days ago there was nothing much going on, but these few days have got busy.

“开”可以结合的动词没有“起来”广，也没有“起来”常用。

“Qǐlai” follows a wider range of verbs and is more common than “kāi”.

4. 熟语
Idioms

4.1 “吃得/不开”
“chī de/bu kāi”

“吃得/不开”表示能不能为人接受，或受不受人欢迎，口语。

“Chī de/bu kāi” signifies whether or not someone or something is acceptable or popular; colloquial.

① 请客送礼那一套，在这儿吃得开。

Qǐng kè sòng lǐ nà yí tào，zài zhèr chīdekāi.

The business of inviting people out and giving presents is acceptable here.

② 他过去权力很大，现在不当官了，吃不开了。

Tā guòqù quánlì hěn dà，xiànzài bù dāng guān le，chībukāi le.

In the past he was quite powerful, but now he's no longer an official, he's not so popular.

4.2 "磨不开"

"mòbukāi

意思是"不好意思"，口语。

The meaning of "mòbukāi" is "to feel embarrassed, feel ashamed"; colloquial.

① 别磨不开，想说什么就说吧。

Bié mòbukāi，xiǎng shuō shénme jiù shuō ba.

Don't be shy, say what you want.

② 在他家吃饭，我有点儿磨不开，没吃饱。

Zài tā jiā chī fàn，wǒ yǒudiǎnr mòbukāi，méi chībǎo.

Eating at his place I felt a bit uncomfortable; I didn't eat my fill.

4.3 "找得/不开（钱）"

"zhǎo de/bu kāi (qián)"

① 五十块钱你找得开吧?

Wǔshí kuài qián nǐ zhǎodekāi ba?

Do you have change for 50 yuan?

② 一百块，我找不开。

Yì bǎi kuài，wǒ zhǎobukāi.

I don't have change for a 100 yuan.

1. 趋向意义

Directional sense

离开某处所，参照点不在某处所。

"To leave a place", with the original place not the point of reference.

① 好事传得很慢，坏事很快就传开来了。

Hǎoshì chuánde hěn màn，huàishì hěn kuài jiù chuán kailai le.

Good news travels slowly; bad news travels fast and wide.

② 他得奖的消息在朋友中间传开来，大家都很高兴。

Tā dé jiǎng de xiāoxi zài péngyou zhōngjiān chuán kailai，dàjiā dōu hěn gāoxìng.

News of his award spread among his friends; everyone was very happy.

2. 结果意义

Resultative sense

2.1 结果意义（一）

Resultative sense (1)

"分离、分裂"。没有"开"常用。

"To separate, divide"; not as common as "kāi".

① 打了针不久，老张就慢慢睁开眼来，感觉好多了。

Dǎle zhēn bù jiǔ，Lǎo Zhāng jiù mànmàn zhēngkāi yǎn lai，gǎnjué hǎo duō le.

Soon after the injection, Zhang slowly opened his eyes and felt much better.

② 这两件事没关系，要分开来解决。

Zhè liǎng jiàn shì méi guānxi，yào fēn kailai jiějué.

These two things don't have anything to do with each other; we'll deal with them separately.

2.2 结果意义（二）
Resultative sense (2)

"舒展、分散"。

"To unfold, spread".

① 你把这几本被雨淋湿的书摊开来晾一晾。

Nǐ bǎ zhè jǐ běn bèi yǔ línshī de shū tān kailai liàng yi liàng.

These books that have been soaked by the rain, spread them out to dry.

② 火越来越大，蔓延开来，非常危险。

Huǒ yuè lái yuè dà，mànyán kailai，fēicháng wēixiǎn.

The fire is getting bigger and bigger, it's spreading and is extremely dangerous.

趋向意义
Directional sense

表示离开某处所，参照点在某处所。较少使用。

"To leave a place", viewed from the place left. Rather rare.

① 这件事从这座小城市传开去，传到工厂，传到乡村。

Zhè jiàn shì cóng zhè zuò xiǎo chéngshì chuán kaiqu，chuándào gōngchǎng，chuándào xiāngcūn.

The news travelled from this small town to factories and villages.

② 白云从我脚下飘开去，很有意思。

Báiyún cóng wǒ jiǎo xià piāo kaiqu，hěn yǒu yìsi.

White clouds wafted away from beneath my feet, it was very interesting.

（一）“开”组小结

Summary of the “kāi” group

	开 kāi	开来 kāilai	开去 kāiqu
趋向意义 directional sense	离开某处所，参照点不确定。 Indicates movement away from a place, with no explicit point of reference. 走开！ Zǒukai!	离开某处所，参照点不在某处所。 To leave a place, with the original place not the point of reference. 那个消息很快传开来。 Nàge xiāoxi hěn kuài chuán kailai.	离开某处所，参照点在某处所。 To leave a place, viewed from the place left. 那个消息很快向各地传开去。 Nàge xiāoxi hěn kuài xiàng gèdì chuán kaiqu.
结果意义（一） resultative sense (1)	分离、分裂。 To separate or divide. ①睁开眼睛看看。 Zhēngkai yǎnjing kànkan. ②木板裂开了一条缝。 Mùbǎn lièkaile yì tiáo fèng.	分离、分裂。 To separate or divide. 把西瓜切开来一看，很不错。 Bǎ xīguā qiē kailai yí kàn, hěn búcuò.	——
结果意义（二） resultative sense (2)	舒展、分散。 To unfold, spread. ①床有点儿短，伸不开腿。 Chuáng yǒudiǎnr duǎn, shēn bu kāi tuǐ. ②把队伍散开。 Bǎ duìwǔ sànkai.	舒展、分散。 To unfold, spread. 大家分散开来隐蔽。 Dàjiā fènsàn kailai yǐnbì.	——

（续表）

	开 kāi	开来 kāilai	开去 kāiqu
结果意义（三） resultative sense (3)	空间是否能容纳、施展。 Whether there is space enough to fit, stretch out. ①这个房间摆不开一张大床。 Zhège fángjiān bǎi bu kāi yì zhāng dà chuáng. ②这个厅很小，打不开太极拳。 Zhège tīng hěn xiǎo，dǎ bu kāi tàijíquán.	——	——
结果意义（四） resultative sense (4)	（思想）清楚、彻悟。 Clear, comprehensible, transparent. ①想开了。 Xiǎngkai le. ②看开了。 Kànkai le.	——	——
状态意义 stative sense	由静态进入动态，动作开始。 Shift from a static state to a more active state; onset of action. ①一回家他就唱开了。 Yì huí jiā tā jiù chàngkai le. ②客人来了以后，他就忙开了。 Kèren láile yǐhòu，tā jiù mángkai le.	——	——

（续表）

	开 kāi	开来 kāilai	开去 kāiqu
熟语 idioms	1.吃得/不开 chī de/bu kāi 2.磨不开 mòbukāi 3.找得/不开 zhǎo de/bu kāi	——	——

（二）“起”组与“开”组的语义联系
Semantic relationships between the “qǐ” group and the “kāi” group

1．“起/起来”的结果意义（一）表示连接、结合以致固定，“开”的结果意义（一）表示分离、分裂，“起”与“开”呈现反义关系。例如：

The 1st resultative sense of “qǐ/qǐlai” is “to connect” or “join up”; the 1st resultative sense of “kāi” is to “separate” or “divide”. So “qǐ” and “kāi” are in opposition. For example:

① 用绳子把行李捆起来。

Yòng shéngzi bǎ xíngli kǔn qilai.

Tie the luggage up with string.

② 把行李上的绳子解开。

Bǎ xíngli shang de shéngzi jiěkai.

Undo the string on the luggage.

③ 把眼睛闭起来。

Bǎ yǎnjīng bì qilai.

Close your eyes.

④ 把眼睛睁开。

Bǎ yǎnjīng zhēngkai.

Open your eyes.

2. “起/起来”和“开”都可以表示由静态进入动态或动作的开始，但是二者还是不同：

Both “qǐ/qǐlai” and “kāi” indicate a shift from state to action or the start of an action; nevertheless, the two are not equivalent:

（1）“起/起来”不仅可以表示由静态进入动态，还可以表示相反的状态，即由动态进入静态。

“Qǐ/qǐlai” not only indicates a shift from state to action; it also indicates the converse, from action to state.

（2）“起/起来”前可以用的动词和形容词很广，“开”前可以用的动词和形容词有限。形容词如“忙、乱”等。“开”前的动词一般表示可以感知的，而且往往表示动作者对自己的动作不加控制、约束的变化。

“Qǐ/qǐlai” can follow a wide range of verbs and adjectives. “Kāi”, on the other hand, combines with a much more restricted set of verbs and adjectives — adjectives, such as “máng (busy)” and “luàn (chaotic)”. Verbs that combine with “kāi” generally express the ability to perceive, and frequently imply a response over which the agent has no control, or feels no restraint.

⑤ 孩子发现妈妈不见了，便“哇”地一声哭开了。
Háizi fāxiàn māma bú jiàn le，biàn “wā” de yì shēng kūkai le.
When the child noticed he couldn’t see his mum anymore, he started to wail.

⑥ 那个女汉子一进门就大声嚷嚷开了。
Nàge nǚhànzi yí jìn mén jiù dà shēng rǎngrang kai le.
That “tomboy”, as soon as she came in the door, she let out a loud holler.

“到”组

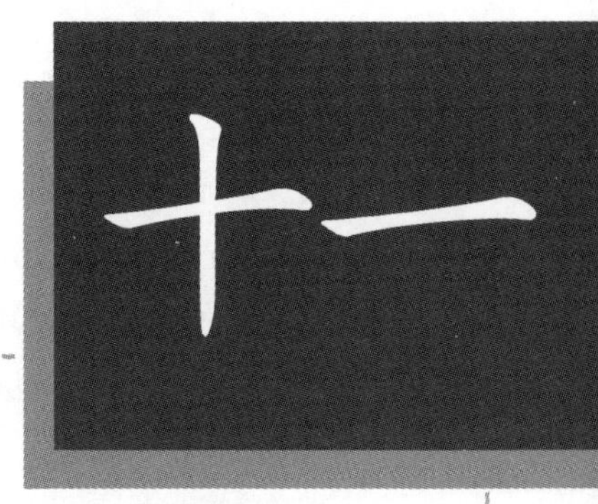

“Dào” group

“到”组包括“到”“到……来”“到……去”。“到……来”“到……去”之间要插入处所词语。

The “dào” group consists of “dào” “dào……lai” and “dào……qu”. A location phrase can be placed between the two parts of the construction.

到	到……来	到……去
dào	dào……lai	dào……qu
(X)○ ⟶ [(X)]	○ ⟶ [X]	X○ ⟶ □

1. 趋向意义

Directional sense

表示移动到某一处所，参照点不确定。

Signifies movement to another place, with no explicit point of reference.

① 下班以后我马上回到家。

Xià bān yǐhòu wǒ mǎshàng huídao jiā.

After work I’m going right home.

② 你把这张邮票贴到信封上。

Nǐ bǎ zhè zhāng yóupiào tiēdao xìnfēng shang.

Stick this stamp on the envelope.

③ 校长叫我把新来的老师带到学生活动中心看一看。

Xiàozhǎng jiào wǒ bǎ xīn lái de lǎoshī dàidao xuésheng huódòng zhōngxīn kàn yi kàn.

The principal told me to take the newly arrived teacher to the student union to look around.

④ 我们学到第十二课了。

Wǒmen xuédao dì shí' èr kè le.

We've studied up to lesson 12.

⑤ 他很不好意思，脸一下子红到耳根。

Tā hěn bù hǎo yìsi，liǎn yíxiàzi hóngdao ěrgēn.

He was very embarrassed and right away his face turned red up to his ears.

比喻用法：

Metaphorical extensions :

（1）表示动作持续到某一时间。

Signifies that the action or situation lasts up to a certain time.

⑥ 我昨天晚上玩电脑玩到12点。

Wǒ zuótiān wǎnshang wán diànnǎo wándao shí' èr diǎn.

Last night, I played computer games till midnight.

⑦ 他们请你吃晚饭，等你等到9点你还没去，他们很不高兴。

Tāmen qǐng nǐ chī wǎnfàn，děng nǐ děngdao jiǔ dian nǐ hái méi qù，tāmen hěn bù gāoxìng.

They invited you to dinner; then they waited till 9 but you didn't show up, which made them very unhappy.

⑧ 这个地方一直冷到5月才开始暖和一点儿。

Zhège dìfang yìzhí lěngdao wǔyuè cái kāishǐ nuǎnhuo yìdiǎnr.

This place stays cold until May at which point it starts to warm up.

（2）表示动作涉及的事物达到的数量。

Signfies to "a certain degree" or "to a certain number".

⑨ 我考英文考到90分，妈妈还不满意。

Wǒ kǎo Yīngwén kǎodao jiǔshí fēn，māma hái bù mǎnyì.

I got a 90 on my English test but mother still wasn't satisfied.

⑩ 今天的生词我已经写到第10遍了，还记不住。

Jīntiān de shēngcí wǒ yǐjīng xiědao dì-shí biàn le，hái jì bu zhù.

I've written today's vocabulary items out for the 10th time and still they won't stick.

⑪ 你活到50岁了，这么简单的道理还不懂。

Nǐ huódao wǔshí suì le，zhème jiǎndān de dàolǐ hái bù dǒng.

You've lived till 50 and you still don't comprehend such basic principles.

（3）表示事情、状态发展变化所达到的程度。

Signifies a level that has been reached (after some growth or development).

⑫ 那个地方的就业率刚刚恢复到经济衰退以前的水平。

Nàge dìfang de jiùyèlǜ gānggāng huīfù dao jīngjì shuāituì yǐqián de shuǐpíng.

That place's employment rate has just recovered to the level it was before the downturn.

⑬ 那年他穷到快没有饭吃了。

Nànián tā qióngdao kuài méiyǒu fàn chī le.

That year he grew so poor he almost didn't have food to eat.

⑭ 他竟然傻到被一个小孩子给骗了。

Tā jìngrán shǎdao bèi yí ge xiǎoháizi gěi piàn le.

I didn't think he'd be so stupid as to get cheated by a young kid.

2. 结果意义

Resultative sense

动作达到目的或有结果。

Signifies that the action has been successful or has reached its goal.

① 这本书我跑了好几个书店才买到。

Zhè běn shū wǒ pǎole hǎojǐ ge shūdiàn cái mǎidao.

I had to run around to lots of bookshops before I could get this book.

② 你的车钥匙找到了吗?

Nǐ de chēyàoshi zhǎodao le ma?

Have you managed to find your car keys?

上面两例都表示一个不太容易实现的结果。再如：

The previous two examples both express results that are not very easy to achieve. Here are more examples:

③ 我刚才在篮球场碰到了小王。

Wǒ gāngcái zài lánqiúchǎng pèngdaole Xiǎo Wáng.

I just met Xiao Wang on the basketball court.

④ 我刚躺下，想到还有中文作业没做，就赶紧起来了。

Wǒ gāng tǎngxia, xiǎngdao háiyǒu Zhōngwén zuòyè méi zuò, jiù gǎnjǐn qǐlai le.

I had just lain down when I remembered that I hadn't done some Chinese homework, so I hurriedly got up.

⑤ 好几年没有工作了，现在刚刚看到一点儿希望。

Hǎojǐ nián méiyǒu gōngzuò le, xiànzài gānggāng kàndao yìdiǎnr xīwàng.

I haven't worked for years, but recently I've just glimpsed a bit of hope.

⑥ 我们昨天聊天儿，说到一些毕业以后去了中国的学生。

Wǒmen zuótiān liáo tiānr, shuōdao yìxiē bì yè yǐhòu qùle Zhōngguó de xuésheng.

Yesterday we were gossiping and got to talking about some students who'd gone to China after graduating.

⑦ 我们到处找你，想不到你在这里。

Wǒmen dàochù zhǎo nǐ，xiǎng bu dào nǐ zài zhèli.

We were looking all over for you; didn't expect you to be here.

⑧ 他很有办法，没有他办不到的事情。

Tā hěn yǒu bànfǎ，méiyǒu tā bàn bu dào de shìqing.

He'll find a way; there's nothing he can't deal with.

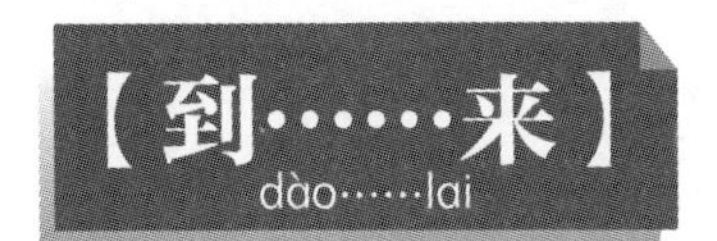

趋向意义

Directional sense

表示由远处移动到参照点所在的处所。

Signifies movement from a more distant place towards the location of the speaker.

① 王朋搬到我们宿舍来了。

Wáng Péng bāndào wǒmen sùshè lai le.

Wang Peng's moved to our dorm.

② 听说中国的手机卖到美国来了。

Tīngshuō Zhōngguó de shǒujī màidào Měiguó lai le.

I've heard that Chinese mobile phones are sold in America now.

③ 你快去把刚来的那位客人请到我这儿来。

Nǐ kuài qù bǎ gāng lái de nà wèi kèren qǐngdào wǒ zhèr lai.

Quickly go and ask the guest that's just arrived to come over to me.

趋向意义
Directional sense

表示离开参照点移动到另一处所。

Signifies movement from a place close at hand to one more distant.

① 那个人跑到山上去了。

Nàge rén pǎodào shān shang qu le.

That man's run up the mountain.

② 他把车开到外地去了。

Tā bǎ chē kāidào wàidì qu le.

He drove the car out of town.

③ 我们想问题想到一起去了。

Wǒmen xiǎng wèntí xiǎngdào yìqǐ qu le.

We thought about it and came to the same conclusion.

比喻用法：表示程度，用在形容词后，一般用否定形式"adj.+不到哪儿去"。

Metaphorical extensions: used after adjectives to expresses degree. Generally used in the negative: "adj. + bú dào nǎr qù".

④ 我觉得那个演员演的电影好不到哪儿去。

Wǒ juéde nàge yǎnyuán yǎn de diànyǐng hǎo bu dào nǎr qu.

I don't think that actor's films are much good.

⑤ 他父母都这么瘦，他也胖不到哪里去吧。

Tā fùmǔ dōu zhème shòu, tā yě pàng bu dào nǎli qu ba.

His parents are so thin, there's no way he's going to get too fat.

“到”组小结
Summary of the “dào” group

	到 dào	到……来 dào……lai	到……去 dào……qu
趋向意义 directional sense	表示移动到某一处所，参照点不确定。 Signifies movement to a particular place, with no explicit point of reference. 比喻用法： Can be used metaphorically: 1.表示动作持续到某一时间。 Indicates that the action lasts up to a particular time. 2.表示动作涉及的事物达到的数量。 Indicates amount, i.e., to a certain degree or to a certain number. 3.表示事情、状态发展变化所达到的程度。 Indicates a level that has been reached.	表示由远处移动到参照点所在的处所。 Signifies movement from some more distant place to one closer to the speaker.	表示离开参照点移动到另一处所。 Signifies movement from a place close at hand to one more distant. 比喻用法：表示程度。 Metaphorically, it may indicate degree.
结果意义 resultative sense	动作达到目的或有结果。 Signifies that the action has been successful or has reached its goal.	——	——

第三节 趋向补语教学建议

Suggestions for teaching directional complements

趋向意义学生学习汉语早期就需要用，所以教材中应尽早安排。趋向意义最直观，很容易形象化，可以利用教室等周围环境，也可以利用本书所给的图片。全部趋向补语的趋向意义可以分两次教完。

Students of Chinese need to use directional complements quitc early in their study of Chinese, so that should be reflected in the choice of teaching materials. The directional senses that are most needed can easily be represented by using the classroom environment or the pictures included in this book. They can be covered more or less completely in two or three class periods.

趋向补语的结果意义是最复杂的。我们建议把动词和表示结果意义的趋向补语作为一个整体（就像一个词汇单位）来教，特别是第一次教某个趋向补语的结果意义时。比如“吃完、听懂、连起来、看出来”等。开始阶段不必告诉学生每个表示结果意义的趋向补语的语法意义，因为有的太抽象（比如“起、出来”等）。

The resultative senses of directional complements are the most complicated. We recommend teaching verbs and their corresponding resultative complements as units (i.e., as vocabulary items), particularly when encountering them for the first time. For example: combinations such as “chīwán” “tīngdǒng” “lián qilai” and “kàn qilai” should be learned as units. In the first stage, there is no reason to explain to students the grammatical and semantic functions of all resultative senses of directional complements, because some, such as “qǐ” and “chūlai”, are too abstract to grasp and are better learned by example.

趋向补语是一个成系统的语法现象，老师最好能清楚地了解。这样当遇到某一个“动+趋”短语时，能立即判断出其意义，不至于讲错。这也是本书的目的。千万不要把本书的内容照本宣科地教给学生。

Directional complements form a coherent grammatical system. Teachers need to understand this clearly. That way, when they encounter a combination of verb plus directional complement, they perceive its type and function quickly and correctly. This is one of the goals of this book. It is important that teachers not just parrot the contents of the book back to the students.

当学生对某一个趋向补语的结果意义学了较多之后，可以归纳其结果意义，以使学生加深这种语法现象的了解（可能要到汉语学习的高级阶段）。

When students have become familiar with a particular directional sense of a complement, teachers can guide them towards a generalization, which will allow students to build a deeper understanding of the grammar (though, to be sure, full understanding may not come until a higher level of Chinese is achieved).

状态意义不太难，可以遇到一个教一个。

Stative senses are not so difficult and can be taught as they are encountered.

第四章 Chapter 4

可能补语
Potential complements

可能补语是指由“动词+不/得+结果补语/趋向补语”或只由“动词+不得”构成的短语。可能补语意义中心在“不/得”上。按照结构，我们把可能补语分为三类：

Potential complements are phrases whose construction is of the following form:

“V + bu/de + RC/DC”; or simply “V+bude”. The key component is the “bu/de” that appears infixed in the middle of the construction. Potential complements can be divided into three types, according to their construction:

1. 由“动词+不/得+结果补语/趋向补语”构成的，叫A类可能补语；
   The A-type that has the form: “V + bu/de + RC/DC”.
2. 由“动词+不/得+了”构成的，叫B类可能补语；
   The B-type that has the form: “V + bu/de + liǎo”.
3. 只由“动词+不得”构成的，叫C类可能补语。
   The C-type that has the form: “V + bude”.

A类可能补语是最典型、最重要的可能补语，其否定形式是不能用其他语言结构代替的；B类可能补语是一种口语用法，一般可以用“能/不能+动词”形式代替；C类可能补语在实际语言中，用得比较有限。

The A-type is the most prototypical of the three; its negative is particularly important since, unlike most positives, there is no exact paraphrase for it. The B-type is a colloquial usage that is more or less equivalent to “néng/bù néng+V”. In actual usage, the C-type is quite restricted.

一般语法书都用“动词+得/不+结果补语/趋向补语”表示A类可能补语。我们把“得/不”改为“不/得”，是因为可能补语的否定形式比肯定形式重要得多，这样写是为了突出可能补语的否定形式。

Most books on Chinese grammar state the potential formula with its positive form first, then its negative: “de/bu”. We state the negative first: “bu/de”, because in actual speech, the negative potential construction is much more common than the positive.

第一节 A类可能补语

A-type potential complements

从A类可能补语的构成成分看，它历史上似乎来源于结果补语和趋向补语，但很多学者的研究表明，它们之间不存在历史渊源关系。但是在现代汉语中，结果补语和趋向补语是A类可能补语的重要组成部分，所以我们要先讨论结果补语和趋向补语，然后再讨论可能补语。在教学中也必须按照这个顺序。

Although A-type potential complements suggest that they derive historically from resultative and directional complements, some research shows that this is not actually the case. However, in modern Chinese, the most prominent components of A-type potential complements are resultative and directional complements. It is for this reason that we have waited until now — after the presentation of resultative and directional complements — to deal with potential complements. We recommend the same order be followed in teaching.

1. A类可能补语的语法意义

The grammatical sense of A-type potential complements

“可能补语”是一般语法著作沿用的术语，但是实际上，可能补语在意义上并不包含“可能”的意思。比如：

Most authors make use of the term “potential complement”; but in fact, the term “potential”, in the sense of “have the potential to” or “be possible”, is not really appropriate. Observe the following examples:

① 外面太黑，我什么都看不见。

Wàimiàn tài hēi，wǒ shénme dōu kàn bu jiàn.

It’s too dark outside; I can’t see anything at all.

这句话的意思显然是“看”了，但是没有结果“见”，而不是“不可能看见”。

The meaning of “kàn bu jiàn” is “look but not perceive”. It does not really mean “not possible to perceive”.

② A: 你看得见外边的风景吗？

Nǐ kàn de jiàn wàibian de fēngjǐng ma?

Can you see the scenery outside?

B: 外边有月光，看得见外边有树、湖、山……

Wàibian yǒu yuèguāng, kàn de jiàn wàibian yǒu shù, hú, shān……

There's a moon so I can see that outside there are trees, lakes, mountains…

这句话的意思是“看”而有结果“见”，而不是“可能看见”。

In this interchange, the sense is "look" and as a result, "be able to see". It does not really mean "possible to see".

因此在学习可能补语时，一定不要按照名称理解意义。

For this reason, when we study potential complements, we should be wary of interpreting them in terms of the name; they are not literally "potential".

A类可能补语表示主、客观条件是否容许实现某种结果。例如：

The A-type potential complements signify whether or not a particular result is achievable under the subjective or objective conditions stated. For example:

③ 我没学过英文，看不懂英文书。

Wǒ méi xuéguo Yīngwén, kàn bu dǒng Yīngwénshū.

I've never studied English and can't read English books.

④ 他的耳朵有问题，听不见声音了。

Tā de ěrduo yǒu wèntí, tīng bu jiàn shēngyīn le.

He's got a problem with his ears and can't hear very well.

⑤ 我走得很慢，从宿舍走十分钟也走不到教室。

Wǒ zǒu de hěn màn, cóng sùshè zǒu shí fēn zhōng yě zǒu bu dào jiàoshì.

I walk very slowly; even if I walk for 10 minutes from the dorm, I won't get to the classroom.

以上三例都表示由于主观条件、能力的限制，不能实现“懂、（听）见、（走）到”的结果。

The above three examples express the fact that owing to subjective conditions or limitations on ability, "understanding" "perception" or "arrival" was not realized.

⑥ 天黑了，看不清楚外面的人是谁。

Tiān hēi le，kàn bu qīngchu wàimiàn de rén shì shuí.

It's getting dark; I can't see clearly who the person outside is.

⑦ 这个房间太小，坐不下二十个人。

Zhège fángjiān tài xiǎo，zuò bu xià èrshí ge rén.

This room's too small; it won't seat 20 people.

⑧ 教室里坐满了人，你进不去了。

Jiàoshì li zuòmǎnle rén，nǐ jìn bu qù le.

The seats in the classroom are all taken; you can't go in.

以上三例都表示由于客观条件的限制，不能实现“（看）清楚、（坐）下、（进）去”的结果。

The above three examples express the fact that, owing to the objective conditions stated, the intended results (i.e. "seeing clearly" "seating twenty" "entering the classroom to get a seat") could not be realized.

2. A类可能补语的否定形式和肯定形式的不对应性

The incompatibility of the positive and negative forms of A-type potential complements

虽然我们常用“动词+得/不+结果补语/趋向补语”来表示可能补语的肯定形式和否定形式，但是实际上否定形式比肯定形式更常用，而表示肯定的意义时，一般更常用“能+动词+结果补语/趋向补语”。如：

Although we often present the formula for potential complements as a pairing of positive and negative ("V + de/bu + RC/DC"), the negative form is, in fact, far more common than the positive. The positive sense is more often expressed with "néng": "néng + V + RC/DC", as in the following examples:

① 你不用这么大声说话，声音小一点儿我能听见。

Nǐ bú yòng zhème dà shēng shuō huà，shēngyīn xiǎo yìdiǎnr wǒ néng tīngjiàn.

No need to shout; if you speak more softly I'll be able to understand.

② 她的中文不错，不用词典就能看懂中文报。

Tā de Zhōngwén búcuò，bú yòng cídiǎn jiù néng kàndǒng Zhōngwénbào.

Her Chinese is pretty good; she can read a Chinese newspaper without a dictionary.

③ 老师讲得很清楚，我都能听懂。

Lǎoshī jiǎng de hěn qīngchu，wǒ dōu néng tīngdǒng.

The teacher speaks very clearly; I can understand everything.

由于"听得懂"是"能听懂"的意思，而"能听懂"对于学习者来说非常简单，而"听得懂"则是一个完全陌生的表达方式，所以他们喜欢用"能/不能+动词+结果补语/趋向补语"来代替可能补语。当表示肯定的意思时，这没有问题。

Because "tīng de dǒng" has the same meaning as "néng tīngdǒng" and because, for students, the potential construction "tīng de dǒng" is less familiar, they often prefer to use the "néng/bù néng + V + RC/DC" pattern instead of the positive potential complement (tīng de dǒng). For the positive, they are free to do so.

④ A: 我小声说话你能听见吗？

Wǒ xiǎoshēng shuō huà nǐ néng tīngjiàn ma?

If I speak softly, will you be able to hear me?

B: 我能听见。

Wǒ néng tīngjiàn.

Sure, I will.

⑤ A: 他的中文怎么样？不用词典就能看懂中文报吗？

Tā de Zhōngwén zěnmeyàng? Bú yòng cídiǎn jiù néng kàndǒng Zhōngwénbào ma?

How's his Chinese? Can he read the Chinese newspaper without using a dictionary?

B: 他的中文不错，不用词典也能看懂。

Tā de Zhōngwén búcuò，bú yòng cídiǎn yě néng kàndǒng.

His Chinese is pretty good; he can read without using a dictionary.

⑥ A: 上课的时候，你能听懂老师讲的语法吗？

Shàng kè de shíhou，nǐ néng tīngdǒng lǎoshī jiǎng de yǔfǎ ma?

In class, can you understand the grammar the teacher talks about?

B: 老师讲得很清楚，我都能听懂。

Lǎoshī jiǎng de hěn qīngchu，wǒ dōu néng tīngdǒng.

The teacher speaks very clearly; I understand everything.

但是对上面的问句如果回答是否定的，一般就只能用可能补语形式：

However, if the answers to the previous questions were negative, then it would be more usual to use the potential form:

⑦ A: 我小声说话你能听见吗？

Wǒ xiǎoshēng shuō huà nǐ néng tīngjiàn ma?

If I speak softly, will you be able to hear me?

不能说：

Rather than:

B：*我不能听见。

*Wǒ bù néng tīngjiàn.

而要说：

You would say:

B：我听不见。

Wǒ tīng bu jiàn.

No, I can't hear you.

如果要表达因为声音小，没有实现“听见”这个结果，只能用“听不见”，“*不能听见”这种回复在汉语中是不存在的。

So if you want to express the fact that because it was so soft, it could not be heard, you can only use “tīng bu jiàn”; “*bù néng tīngjiàn” is simply not said.

⑧ A: 他的中文怎么样？不用词典就能看懂中文报吗？

Tā de Zhōngwén zěnmeyàng? Bú yòng cídiǎn jiù néng kàndǒng Zhōngwénbào ma?

How's his Chinese? Can he read the Chinese newspaper without using a dictionary?

B: 他的中文不太好，不用词典看不懂中文报。

Tā de Zhōngwén bú tài hǎo, bú yòng cídiǎn kàn bu dǒng Zhōngwénbào.

His Chinese isn't very good; he can't read a Chinese newspaper without using a dictionary.

"*不能看懂中文报"在汉语中也是一个不正确的句子。

"* Bù néng kàndǒng Zhōngwénbào" is not an acceptable sentence in Chinese.

"能"有不止一个意思，有时"不能+动词+结果补语/趋向补语"是可以说的，但有另外的意思：

"Néng" has a number of senses: sometimes it is possible to say "bù néng + V+RC/DC", but it has a different meaning:

⑨ 每天晚饭不能吃饱，不然你会胖起来。

Měi tiān wǎnfàn bù néng chībǎo, bùrán nǐ huì pàng qilai.

You shouldn't fill up at dinner everday; if you do, you'll get fat.

这里的"不能"是"不应该"的意思。

In this context, "bù néng" has the sense of "shouldn't".

⑩ A: 我能进去吗？

Wǒ néng jìnqu ma?

Can I go in?

B: 里面正在开一个很重要的会，主任说谁都不能进去。

Lǐmiàn zhèngzài kāi yí ge hěn zhòngyào de huì, zhǔrèn shuō shuí dōu bù néng jìnqu.

There's an important meeting going on in there; the director says no one can enter.

这里的"不能"是"不准许"的意思。

Here, "bù néng" has the sense of "not permitted to".

因此A类可能补语和"能/不能+动词+结果补语/趋向补语"不是完全等同的。当表达否定意义（主、客观条件不容许实现某种结果）时，一般要用否定形式的可能补语；表达肯定的意义时，一般用"能+动词+结果补语/趋向补语"形式。也就是说，否定形式的可能补语是学习汉语时不能回避的。

For this reason, A-type potential complements are not completely equivalent to "néng/bù néng + V+RC/DC". To express negation (that is, subjective or objective conditions prevent the realization of some result), the negative form of A-type potential complements is generally used; to express the positive, "néng + V+RC/DC" is the usual form. In other words, in learning to speak Chinese, there is no way to avoid using the negative form of A-type potential complements.

肯定形式的可能补语主要用在和疑问有关的句子：

The positive form of A-type potential complements is used mostly in sentences related to questions:

（1）发问时，既可以用可能补语，也可以用"能/不能+动词+结果补语/趋向补语"。

In questions, both the potential form and the pattern "néng/bù néng + V+RC/DC" can be used.

⑪ 我刚才说的话你能不能听懂?

Wǒ gāngcái shuō de huà nǐ néng bu néng tīngdǒng?

Do you understand what I just said?

⑫ 我刚才说的话你能听懂吗?

Wǒ gāngcái shuō de huà nǐ néng tīngdǒng ma?

⑬ 我刚才说的话你听得懂听不懂?

Wǒ gāngcái shuō de huà nǐ tīng de dǒng tīng bu dǒng?

⑭ 我刚才说的话，你听得懂吗?

Wǒ gāngcái shuō de huà , nǐ tīng de dǒng ma?

但用否定句来发问时，只能用可能补语的形式。

However, if the question is asked in the negative, then only the potential form is possible.

⑮ 我刚才说的话你听不懂吗?

Wǒ gāngcái shuō de huà nǐ tīng bu dǒng ma?

Didn't you understand what I just said?

问话人用这个句子发问，包含有觉得奇怪的意味，即他认为对方应该“能听懂/听得懂”。

In this case, the question has a tone of surprise or disbelief; that is, the expectation is that the person addressed *would* understand what was said.

但是不能说：

But one cannot say:

* 我刚才说的话你不能听懂吗?

* Wǒ gāngcái shuō de huà nǐ bù néng tīngdǒng ma?

（2）如果问话用可能补语，回答时“承前”，可以用肯定形式的可能补语肯定。

If there is a potential complement in the question, then the response can take its cue from the question, and answer with the positive potential, as in the following examples.

⑯ A: 你看得懂看不懂法文报?

Nǐ kàn de dǒng kàn bu dǒng Fǎwénbào?

Can you read a French newspaper?

B: 我看得懂。

Wǒ kàn de dǒng.

Yes, I can.

⑰ A: 今天的功课晚饭以前你做得完吗?

Jīntiān de gōngkè wǎnfàn yǐqián nǐ zuò de wán ma?

Can you get today's homework done before dinner?

B: 做得完。

Zuò de wán.

Yes, I can.

肯定形式的可能补语还有含义比较特殊的用法，请参看《实用现代汉语语法》（增订本）第582—589页。

The positive potential complements have some special usages; for discussion, see

A practical Grammar of Modern Chinese (revised edition), pp.582–589.

3. 用A类可能补语时在句子结构上要注意

The following points pertain to the use of A-type potential complements

（1）不能用于“把”字句。

Potential complements cannot appear with pre-posed objects marked with “bǎ”.

不能说：

Instead of the ungrammatical:

⑱ *晚饭前我把功课做不完。

*Wǎnfàn qián wǒ bǎ gōngkè zuò bu wán,

而应该说：

One says:

晚饭前我做不完功课。

Wǎnfàn qián wǒ zuò bu wán gōngkè.

I can't get my homework finished before dinner.

（2）动词前不能有描写性的修饰语。

Potential complements do not permit preverbal modifiers.

不能说：

Instead of:

⑲ *这个故事我很快说不完。

*Zhège gùshi wǒ hěn kuài shuō bu wán.

而应该说：

One says:

这个故事我不能很快说完。

Zhège gùshi wǒ bù néng hěn kuài shuōwán.

I can't finish this story very quickly.

第二节 B类可能补语

B-type potential complements

B类可能补语指由“不/得+了”充任的补语，表示主、客观条件是否容许实现某动作或状态。

B-type potential complements consist of “bu/de+liǎo” and they indicate that subjective or objective conditions make the realization of the verbal action or state possible, or not.

① 他病了，上不了课了。（主观条件）

Tā bìng le，shàng bu liǎo kè le.

He's ill and can't go to class. (subjective condition)

② 老师今天不能来了，我们上不了课了。（客观条件）

Lǎoshī jīntiān bù néng lái le，wǒmen shàng bu liǎo kè le.

The teacher can't make it to class today; we won't have class. (objective condition)

③ 我今天有事，看不了电影。（主观条件）

Wǒ jīntiān yǒu shì，kàn bu liǎo diànyǐng.

I'm busy today; I can't watch a movie. (subjective condition)

④ 今天网络出问题了，我上不了网了。（客观条件）

Jīntiān wǎngluò chū wèntí le，wǒ shàng bu liǎo wǎng le.

There are problems with the web today; I can't get online. (objective condition)

B类可能补语也主要用否定形式。这类可能补语一般都可以用“能/不能”替换。

B-type potential complements also appear mostly in the negative form and can generally be replaced by “néng/bù néng”.

①' 他病了，不能上课了。

Tā bìng le，bù néng shàng kè le.

②' 老师今天不能来了，我们不能上课了。

Lǎoshī jīntiān bù néng lái le，wǒmen bù néng shàng kè le.

③' 我今天有事，不能看电影。

Wǒ jīntiān yǒu shì，bù néng kàn diànyǐng.

④' 今天网络出问题了，我不能上网了。

Jīntiān wǎngluò chū wèntí le，wǒ bù néng shàng wǎng le.

形容词后也可以用“不了”，通常表示说话人的一种看法、估计。

The “bu liǎo” complement can also be used after adjectives; such cases generally indicate an opinion or an appraisal of the speaker.

⑤ 这只小狗病得太重了，好不了了。（意思是：不会好了）

Zhè zhī xiǎogǒu bìng de tài zhòng le，hǎo bu liǎo le.

This little dog is just too seriously ill; it can’t be cured. (i.e., won’t get well)

⑥ 明天是期中考试，难不了。（意思是：不会太难）

Míngtiān shì qīzhōng kǎo shì，nán bu liǎo.

Tomorrow is the midterm exam; it won’t be at all difficult. (i.e., won’t be difficult)

这种句子可以用“会/不会”替换可能补语。

In such sentences, “huì (will be)” or “bú huì (won’t be)” can be substituted for the potential complement.

⑤' 这只小狗病得太重了，不会好了。

Zhè zhī xiǎogǒu bìng de tài zhòng le，bú huì hǎo le.

⑥' 明天是期中考试，不会太难。

Míngtiān shì qīzhōng kǎo shì，bú huì tài nán.

B类可能补语是一种口语现象，因此补语前的动词或形容词以单音节为多。此类补语在正式的语言中较少使用，因此不必作为教学重点。

The B-type is rather colloquial so it tends to appear with monosyllabic verbs. This type of complement is rare in formal language. For this reason, it need not occupy a prominent position in the curriculum.

第三节 C类可能补语

C-type potential complements

C类可能补语由“动词+不得”构成。

C-type potential complements consist of the combination “bude” following a verb.

① 那个地方太危险，去不得。

Nàge dìfang tài wēixiǎn，qù bude.

That place is too dangerous; you shouldn’t go there.

② 这个电影里的故事很可怕，小孩子看不得。

Zhège diànyǐng li de gùshi hěn kěpà，xiǎoháizi kàn bude.

This film has a scary plot; children shouldn’t see it.

③ 这次考试非常重要，马虎不得。

Zhè cì kǎo shì fēicháng zhòngyào，mǎhu bude.

This exam is extremely important; it shouldn’t be messed up.

这类补语也主要用否定形式，意思是“不应该”，也是一种口语现象，学生能理解意思就可以了。

This type of complement is generally used in the negative, with the meaning of “shouldn’t”. It is also colloquial usage. Students probably will not use this pattern much; but they should understand its sense.

第四节 可能补语教学建议

Suggestions for teaching potential complements

要让学生明白什么是可能补语以及可能补语和“能/不能”的语义差别。可能补语用于说明主、客观条件是否容许实现某种结果。它与“能/不能”在语义上虽然有一些重合，但没有“能/不能”的 “准许/不准许”的意思。老师应通过例句在语境中向学生展示二者的不同。

Students should know what potential complements are and the semantic difference between potential complements and “néng/bù néng”. Potential complements are used to state whether or not a particular result is achievable under the subjective or objective conditions stated. Although they overlap with “néng/bù néng” semantically, they do not have the meaning of “allowed/not allowed”, which does “néng/bù néng” have. Our teachers should show the difference between the two through some examples in the context.

学生也很容易混淆可能补语与结果补语。因此老师在可能补语教学中不能只满足于对结构形式的介绍，还要在语境中对可能补语与结果补语进行对比和区分。

Potential and resultative complements are two categories confused easily for students. Therefore, in the teaching of potential complements, teachers should not only be satisfied with the introduction of structural forms, but also contrast and distinguish potential and resultant complements in the context.

	肯定 positive	否定 negative
可能补语 Potential Complements （主、客观条件是否允许实现某种结果） (whether or not a particular result is achievable under the subjective or objective conditions stated)	动词+得+结果补语 V+de+RC A: 你的作业多不多？做得完吗？ B: 我每天都做得完。 A: Nǐ de zuòyè duō bu duō? Zuòde wán ma? B: Wǒ měi tiān dōu zuò de wán.	动词+不+结果补语 V+bu+RC 老师，你给我们的作业太多了，我们做不完。 Lǎoshī, nǐ gěi wǒmen de zuòyè tài duō le, wǒmen zuò bu wán.

补语释析 Understanding Complements

结果补语 Resultative Complements （动作是否产生某种结果） (some result is achieved or not by action)	动词+结果补语+了 V+RC+le A: 你的作业做完了吗? B: 我昨天就做完作业了。 **A:** Nǐ de zuòyè duō bu duō? Zuò de wán ma? **B:** Wǒ zuótiān jiù zuòwán zuòyè le.	没+动词+结果补语 méi+V+RC 我昨天没做完作业。 Wǒ zuótiān méi zuòwán zuòyè.

第五章 Chapter 5

描写性补语
Descriptive complements

描写性补语指动词或形容词后用“得”连接的补语。如：

Descriptive complements are initiated by a “de” that directly follows the verb or adjective. For example:

① 妹妹跳舞跳得很好。

Mèimei tiào wǔ tiào de hěn hǎo.

Little sister dances very well.

② 看见老朋友来了，李明高兴得跳了起来。

Kànjiàn lǎo péngyou lái le，Lǐ Míng gāoxìng de tiàole qilai.

When he saw his old friend, Li Ming was so happy that he started to jump up and down.

第一节 描写性补语与句中其他成分之间的意义关系

Semantic relationships between descriptive complements and other sentence elements

1. 描写性补语说明动词

Descriptive complements evaluate the verbal actions.

补语说明、评价动作，动词和补语一起描写动作者。

These complements evaluate or characterize the verbal actions; the verb and the complement together describe the actor.

① 她中文说得很好。

Tā Zhōngwén shuō de hěn hǎo.

She speaks Chinese very well.

"很好"说明、评价"说"，"中文说得很好"描写"她"。

"Hěn hǎo (very well)" is an evaluation of "shuō (speaking)", while "Zhōngwén shuō de hěn hǎo (speaks Chinese very well)" describes the subject "tā (she)".

② 他每天起得很早，睡得很晚。

Tā měi tiān qǐ de hěn zǎo，shuì de hěn wǎn.

Everyday, he rises early and goes to bed late.

"很早"说明、评价"起"，"很晚"说明、评价"睡"，"每天起得很早，睡得很晚"描写"他"。

"Hěn zǎo (early)" charaterizes "qǐ (rising)", "hěn wǎn (late)" characterizes "shuì (going to bed)", while "měi tiān qǐ de hěn zǎo, shuì de hěn wǎn (everyday rises early and goes to bed late)" describes the subject "tā (he)".

③ 哥哥跑得很快，我追不上他。

Gēge pǎo de hěn kuài，wǒ zhuī bu shàng tā.

Big brother is a fast runner — I can't keep up with him.

"很快"说明、评价"跑"，"跑得很快"描写"哥哥"。

"Hěn kuài (quickly)" conveys the quality of "pǎo (running)", while "pǎo de hěn kuài (runs fast)" describes the subject "gēge (big brother)".

这类补语有否定形式：

This type of complement can be negated:

④ A: 你唱歌唱得好不好？

Nǐ chàng gē chàng de hǎo bu hǎo?

Do you sing well?

B: 我唱歌唱得不太好。

Wǒ chàng gē chàng de bú tài hǎo.

I don't sing very well.

⑤ 我中文说得不好，不能给你当翻译。

Wǒ Zhōngwén shuō de bù hǎo，bù néng gěi nǐ dāng fānyì.

I don't speak Chinese very well so I can't be a translator for you.

⑥ 妹妹跑得很快，姐姐跑得不快。

Mèimei pǎo de hěn kuài，jiějie pǎo de bú kuài.

The little sister runs fast, but the big sister doesn't.

2. "得"前后存在因果关系

The two parts before and after "de" are related as "cause and effect"

描写性补语的谓语部分描写动作的施事者或受事者，"得"前的动词或形容词一般包含有很高的程度的意思，而且是引起"得"后的动作或变化的原因，即其间存在因果关系。

The predicative portion of a descriptive complement (i.e., that part that follows "de") applies to the sentential subject (whether "agent" or "patient" — "doer" or "the one done to"). The verb or adjective before "de" generally suggests a heightened intensity, which leads to the action or change expressed after "de". As a result, the two parts of the sentence (before and after "de") can seem to be related as "cause and effect".

① 我看书看得忘了吃晚饭。

Wǒ kàn shū kàn de wàngle chī wǎnfàn.

I was so into my reading that I forgot about dinner.

这句话的意思是："我看书看得特别专心，所以忘了吃晚饭"。"看书看得忘了吃晚饭"是描写"我"的。

As the fairly free English translation indicates, the sense of the sentence is that the speaker "was reading with such concentration that he or she forgot to eat dinner". The whole sentence is about "I", the subject.

② 看见妈妈买的礼物，小明高兴<u>得跳了起来</u>。

Kànjiàn māma mǎi de lǐwù，Xiǎomíng gāoxìng <u>de tiàole qilai</u>.

When he saw the present his mother had bought, Xiaoming started jumping up and down.

这句话的意思是："小明因为看见妈妈买的礼物，他非常高兴，所以跳了起来。""高兴得跳了起来"描写"小明"。

Here, the sense of the sentence is: "Xiaoming started jumping up and down because he saw the present his mother had bought." "gāoxìng de tiàole qilai (so happy that he started jumping up and down)" refers to Xiaoming.

③ 妹妹叫小狗吓<u>得哭了起来</u>。（妹妹因为非常害怕小狗，所以哭了起来）

Mèimei jiào xiǎogǒu xià <u>de kūle qilai</u>.

Little sister was so scared by the little dog that she burst into tears.

④ 弟弟跑步跑<u>得满头大汗</u>。（弟弟因为跑步很累很热，所以满头大汗）

Dìdi pǎo bù pǎo <u>de mǎntóu dàhàn</u>.

Little brother ran so hard that he got all sweaty.

⑤ 老师讲课讲<u>得很高兴</u>，忘了下课。（老师因为讲课，所以很高兴，［所以］忘了下课）

Lǎoshī jiǎng kè jiǎng <u>de hěn gāoxìng</u>，wàngle xià kè.

The teacher was so happy teaching class that she forgot to dismiss the students.

⑥ 那包饼干被她压<u>得碎成一块一块的</u>了。

Nà bāo bǐnggān bèi tā yā <u>de suìchéng yí kuài yí kuài de</u> le.

The crackers in the packet were crushed by her into little bits.

这类描写性补语前的动词或形容词前一般没有否定副词。如一般不说：

Descriptive complements like these are not usually negatable. Generally, one doesn't say:

⑦ ＊我没看书看得忘了吃饭。

＊Wǒ méi kàn shū kàn de wàngle chī fàn.

⑧ ＊听到这个好消息，小红没高兴得跳起来。

＊Tīngdào zhège hǎo xiāoxi，Xiǎohóng méi gāoxìng de tiào qilai.

除非为了反驳：

Possible exceptions are those cases where something is being refuted or denied:

⑨ A: 听说你看书看得饭都忘了吃了。

Tīngshuō nǐ kàn shū kàn de fàn dōu wàngle chī le.

I heard that you were so into the book that you forgot to eat.

B: ？谁说的，我没看书看得忘了吃饭。

？Shuí shuō de，wǒ méi kàn shū kàn de wàngle chī fàn.

Who said that? It's not true that I was so into the book that I forgot to eat.

补语一般也不以否定形式出现，除非为了反驳：

Normally, then, except in refuting a statement, complements also do not appear in the negative:

⑩ 你看书看得都忘了吃饭了。

Nǐ kàn shū kàn de dōu wàngle chī fàn le.

⑪ ？我看书看得没忘了吃饭。

？Wǒ kàn shū kàn de méi wàngle chī fàn.

⑫ ＊听到这个好消息，小红高兴得没跳起来。

＊Tīngdào zhège hǎo xiāoxi，Xiǎohóng gāoxìng de méi tiào qilai.

可能补语可以出现在"得"后：

Potential complements can appear after "de" (i.e., within descriptive complements):

⑬ 听说考试考得不好，弟弟难过得吃不下饭了。

Tīngshuō kǎo shì kǎo de bù hǎo，dìdi nánguò de chī bu xià fàn le.

这句话的意思是"因为考试考得不好，弟弟非常难过，所以吃不下饭了"。

The meaning of this sentence is "When he heard that he'd done badly on the exam, little brother was so sad that he couldn't eat anymore".

3. 描写性补语描写“把”的宾语（动作的受事者）

Descriptive complements with objects (“patients”) introduced with “bǎ”

① 这个项目把老张忙得吃不好饭，睡不好觉。（因为太忙，所以老张吃不好饭，睡不好觉）

Zhège xiàngmù bǎ Lǎo Zhāng máng de chī bu hǎo fàn，shuì bu hǎo jiào.

Lao Zhang is so busy with this project that he’s not able to eat or sleep well.

② 中文书找不到了，把我急得快要哭了。（因为找不到中文书，我非常着急，所以快要哭了）

Zhōngwénshū zhǎo bu dào le，bǎ wǒ jí de kuài yào kū le.

Not finding the Chinese book has made me so anxious that I want to cry.

③ 弟弟把爸爸气得说不出话来。（爸爸因为非常生气，所以说不出话来）

Dìdi bǎ bàba qì de shuō bu chū huà lai.

Younger brother made Dad so angry that he couldn’t speak.

这类描写性补语前的动词或形容词前一般没有否定副词。

These descriptive complements are not generally negatable.

4. 描写性补语包含主谓短语

“Sentential” descriptive complements (containing subject and predicate)

① 太阳晒得我睁不开眼睛。（因为太阳太晒，我睁不开眼睛）

Tàiyáng shài de wǒ zhēng bu kāi yǎnjing.

The sun’s shining so brightly, I can’t open my eyes.

② 听说小明在学校病了，急得他妈妈马上坐飞机去学校看他。（因为小明病了，妈妈非常着急，所以马上坐飞机去学校看他）

Tīngshuō Xiǎomíng zài xuéxiào bìng le，jí de tā māma mǎshàng zuò fēijī qù xuéxiào kàn tā.

On hearing that Xiaoming had got ill at school, his mother was so worried that she immediately flew to the school to see him.

③ 大风吹得海上游玩的人头昏眼花。（大风把海上游玩的人吹得太厉害了，所以他们头昏眼花）

Dàfēng chuī de hǎishang yóuwán de rén tóuhūn-yǎnhuā.

The wind blew so hard that people playing on the sea got disoriented.

这类描写性补语前的动词或形容词前一般也没有否定副词。

These descriptive complements are also not generally negatable.

第二节 描写性补语的功能

The function of descriptive complements

描写性补语虽然叫“补语”，但是在句子中是表达意义的中心，表示句子的“焦点”信息，也是全句的重音所在。比如：

Even though descriptive complements are called “complements”, they actually contain the main information focus of the sentence and carry the intonational emphasis. For example:

① 我唱歌唱得'很好。

Wǒ chàng gē chàng de hěn hǎo.

I sing well.

这个句子重点不在告诉别人“我唱歌”，而在“（唱歌唱得）很好”上，“很好”要重读。

In this example, the point of the sentence is not the fact that “I sing”; rather, it is the fact that “I sing well”. “Hěn hǎo” gets the intonational emphasis.

② 听到这个好消息，小李高兴得'跳了起来。

Tīngdào zhège hǎo xiāoxi，Xiǎo Lǐ gāoxìng de tiàole qilai.

When he heard the good news, Xiao Li was so happy that he started jumping up and down.

③ 我肚子疼得'站不起来了。

Wǒ dùzi téng de zhàn bu qǐlái le.

My stomach hurt so much that I couldn’t stand up.

正因为如此，描写性补语在汉语语法学习中是很重要的。

It is for this reason that descriptive complements are so important in the study of Chinese grammar.

第三节 包含描写性补语的句子的结构特点

Special constraints on sentences with descriptive complements

1. 描写性补语前面的动词不能用重叠形式

Verbs in front of descriptive complements cannot be reduplicated

① * 她唱唱歌唱得很好。

* Tā chàngchang gē chàng de hěn hǎo.

② * 他开开车开得特别快。

* Tā kāikai chē kāi de tèbié kuài.

2. 句子中不能有描写性的状语

Sentences that contain descriptive complements cannot be modified by manner adverbials

① * 他很快地高兴得跳了起来。

* Tā hěn kuài de gāoxìng de tiàole qilai.

② * 妹妹慢慢地难过得哭了起来。

* Mèimei mànmàn de nánguò de kūle qilai.

③ * 小李难过地哭得眼睛红红的。

* Xiǎo Lǐ nánguò de kū de yǎnjing hónghóng de.

3. "得"后形容词的用法

Usage of the adjective after "de"

和形容词作谓语一样，形容词作描写性补语时，前面要用"很"等表示程度的词语。

As is the case when they serve as predicates, adjectives must be modified by "hěn", or some comparable expressions of degree, before they can function as descriptive complements.

① 王朋写字写得很快，李友写得很慢。

Wáng Péng xiě zì xiě de hěn kuài，Lǐ Yǒu xiě de hěn màn.

Wang Peng writes fast; Li You writes slowly.

② 小白英语说得非常流利。

Xiǎo Bái Yīngyǔ shuō de fēicháng liúlì.

Xiao Bai speaks English very fluently.

4. "得"前动词的用法

Usage of the verb before "de"

"得"前的动词后有宾语时，要重复动词，或不重复动词，把宾语放在动词前。

When the verb before the complement (before "de") has an object, then either the verb needs to be reiterated, or the object needs to be "fronted" and placed before the verb.

① 小白说英语说得很流利。

Xiǎo Bái shuō Yīngyǔ shuō de hěn liúlì.

小白英语说得很流利。

Xiǎo Bái Yīngyǔ shuō de hěn liúlì.

Xiao Bai speaks English fluently.

② 妹妹唱歌唱得很好。

Mèimei chàng gē chàng de hěn hǎo.

妹妹歌唱得很好。

Mèimei gē chàng de hěn hǎo.

Younger sister sings well.

③ 我写汉字写得很慢。

Wǒ xiě Hànzì xiě de hěn màn.

我汉字写得很慢。

Wǒ Hànzì xiě de hěn màn.

I write characters rather slowly.

第四节 描写性补语教学建议

Suggestions for teaching descriptive complements

描写性补语与句中其他成分之间的语义关系，有的简单，有的很复杂。我们建议先学“他今天起得很早”“妹妹唱歌唱得很好”这一类。在教材中稍后的阶段再教“妹妹高兴得跳了起来”“我急得吃不下饭”这类。至于“大风把我吹得晕头转向/大风吹得我晕头转向”“弟弟把爸爸气得说不出话来/弟弟气得爸爸说不出话来”可以在较高阶段再教给学生。

The semantic relationships between descriptive complements and other sentence elements can be simple or complicated. We recommend beginning with constructions such as “Tā jīntiān qǐ de hěn zǎo (He rose early today)” and “Mèimei chàng gē chàng de hěn hǎo (Younger sister sings well)”. At later stages of instruction, one can continue with more complicated options, such as “Mèimei gāoxìng de tiàole qilai (Younger sister was so happy that she started jumping up and down)” and “Wǒ jí de chī bu xià fàn (I was so anxious that I couldn't eat anything)”. Patterns such as “Dàfēng bǎ wǒ chuī de yūntóu-zhuànxiàng/Dàfēng chuī de wǒ yūntóu-zhuànxiàng (The wind blew so hard that I got disoriented)” or “Dìdi bǎ bàba qì de shuō bu chū huà lai/Dìdi qì de bàba shuō bu chū huà lai (Younger brother made Dad so mad that he was speechless)” can be left until students reach higher levels of study.

教描写性补语时，一定要把句中各成分的结构语义关系向学生讲清楚，也要让学生体会出某类句子中所包含的程度意义和因果关系。学生清楚了上述关系，是真正掌握这种补语的第一步，也是最重要的一步。不清楚这些关系，他们就很难自然地输出这类句子，很难真正掌握这个语法点。

When teaching descriptive complements, it is important to explain the semantic relationships between the constituent parts of a sentence clearly to the students. Learners need to have a clear understanding of the semantics of intensification in such sentences as well as the causal relationship between the sentence elements. Otherwise, it will be very difficult for them to have the sort of understanding needed to produce such sentences on their own.

第六章 Chapter 6

动词后其他非名词成分

Other non-nominal post-verbal elements

另外有几种语法现象，一般语法著作作为补语处理。在汉语教学界，一直有人呼吁减少补语，他们的建议是有道理的。补语本来就是外国人学习汉语语法的难点，如果包含的内容太多，会增加他们的负担，引起学习者的畏难情绪。我们认为在对外汉语教材中，有些语法现象可以不归入补语，而是分别处理，分散难点。

There are a number of additional grammatical constructions that are commonly regarded as complements by grammarians. But in Chinese teaching circles, there have always been calls for a reduction in the number of elements labeled as complements, and their recommendations make a certain amount of sense. Verbal complements have always been regarded as one of the more difficult topics for Chinese language learners; if the label is applied too broadly, learners will be unduly burdened and get discouraged. Instead, we recommend dealing with some post-verbal elements separately.

1. 动作持续的时间

Time-duration expressions

表示时间的词语可以分为时间点（如：2001年、三月、二十五日、三点钟、两点五十八分、星期五、昨天）和时间段（一年、两个月、三天、两个小时、十分钟）。时间点一般要放在动词前，作状语，表示动作发生的时间。如：

Time expressions can be divided into two major groups: "time-when" expressions (e.g., èr líng líng yī nián; Sānyuè; èrshíwǔ rì; sān diǎnzhōng; liǎng diǎn wǔshíbā fēn; Xīngqīwǔ; zuótiān); and "time-duration" expressions (yì nián; liǎng ge yuè; sān tiān; liǎng ge xiǎoshí; shí fēnzhōng). In general, a time-when expression is normally placed before the main verb to indicate when the action takes place. Here are some examples:

① 下个星期我们要考中文。

Xià ge xīngqī wǒmen yào kǎo Zhōngwén.

Next week we have a Chinese test.

② 你下午三点有空儿吗？

Nǐ xiàwǔ sān diǎn yǒu kòngr ma?

Are you free at 3:00 this afternoon?

在肯定句里，表示时间段的词语要放在动词后，表示动作持续的时间。如：

In positive sentences, a time-duration expression is placed after the verb to indicate how long the action lasts. For example:

③ 我学中文才学了一个学期。

Wǒ xué Zhōngwén cái xuéle yí ge xuéqī.

I've only studied one semester of Chinese.

④ 你们放寒假放多长时间？

Nǐmen fàng hánjià fàng duō cháng shíjiān?

How long is your winter break?

⑤ 我们上课只听了5分钟录音。

Wǒmen shàng kè zhǐ tīngle wǔ fēnzhōng lùyīn.

During class we only listened to 5 minutes of recordings.

以上句子中的动词都表示可以持续进行的动作。此类动词很多，另如“跑、搬（家）、上（课）、吃、喝、买”等；有些动词表示不能持续的动作，如“来、去、结婚、毕业、退休、死”等，这时后面表示时间段的词语，表示动作发生到说话时的时间：

The verbs in these sentences signify actions that can persist through time. There are numerous verbs that can be followed by time-duration expressions, including: “pǎo (run)” “bān [jiā] (move [house])” “shàng [kè] (attend [class])” “chī (eat)” “hē (drink)” and “mǎi (buy)”. However, time-duration expressions that follow verbs such as “lái (come)” “qù (go)” “jié hūn (get married)” “bì yè (graduate)” “tuì xiū (retire)” and “sǐ (die)” express the time elapsed between an event (e.g., “getting married” “graduating”) and the time of speaking (usually, the present).

⑥ 我来中国三年了。

Wǒ lái Zhōngguó sān nián le.

It's 3 years since I arrived in China.

⑦ 小张结婚刚一年。

Xiǎo Zhāng jié hūn gāng yì nián.

Xiao Zhang's been married exactly 1 year.

⑧ 老李退休很久了。

Lǎo Lǐ tuì xiū hěn jiǔ le.

Lao Li's been retired for ages.

句子里有表示动作持续时间的词语又有宾语时，有两种表达方式，一种是重复动词，一种是把时间词放在宾语前作定语，时间词后可以用“的”。如：

When a sentence contains both a time-duration expression and an object, there are two possible grammatical strategies: one, is to repeat the verb; the other, is to add "de" to the time-duration expression and make it a modifier of the object. The following examples illustrate (with the English also reflecting the two options):

⑨ 我昨天晚上听录音听了三个小时。

Wǒ zuótiān wǎnshang tīng lùyīn tīngle sān ge xiǎoshí.

Yesterday evening I listened to recordings for 3 hours.

我昨天晚上听了三个小时的录音。

Wǒ zuótiān wǎnshang tīngle sān ge xiǎoshí de lùyīn.

Yesterday evening, I listened to 3 hours of recordings.

⑩ 我们刚才滑冰滑了三十分钟。

Wǒmen gāngcái huá bīng huále sānshí fēnzhōng.

Just now we skated for 30 minutes.

我们刚才滑了三十分钟的冰。

Wǒmen gāngcái huále sānshí fēnzhōng de bīng.

Just now, we did 30 minutes of skating.

⑪ 今年圣诞节我们放假要多放两天。

Jīnnián Shèngdàn Jié wǒmen fàng jià yào duō fàng liǎng tiān.

This Christmas we are going to have an extended holiday of two extra days.

今年圣诞节我们要多放两天的假。

Jīnnián Shèngdàn Jié wǒmen yào duō fàng liǎng tiān de jià.

This Christmas we are going to have two extra days of holiday.

要注意，像例⑥“我来中国三年了”这样不表示动作持续时间的句子，不能用上述任何一种方式。

Note that in sentences such as ⑥ above, "Wǒ lái Zhōngguó sān nián le", in which the verb "lái" does not signify an action that persists, neither of the two options ("*lái Zhōngguó lái sān nián le" or "* lái sān nián de Zhōngguó le") is possible.

为什么很多汉语语法书把表示动作持续时间的时间词语看作补语呢？这一方面因为它位于动词后，动词后的词语要么看作宾语，要么看作补语。显然看作补语更合适。另一方面，表示动作持续时间的词语不仅位于动词后，而且有宾语时，一种方式是，可以像其他补语一样要重复动词（见例③、④），所以很多语法著作就把它处理作补语，叫时量补语或时间补语。

Why is it that so many grammars of Chinese regard time-duration expressions such as those illustrated above as complements? The answer is that, on the one hand, many grammarians classify all post-verbal elements as either objects or complements, and since they are not objects, they must be complements. On the other hand, like other complements, time-duration expressions that occur with (proper) objects can also be distributed across repeated verbs (as in examples ③、④ above). As complements, they are usually labeled time-duration complements or time complements.

也有的语法著作把它叫准宾语，因为数量词不是谓词性的，是体词性的。

But there are also grammarians who, because such phrases are more nominal than verbal, label them "para-objects".

在否定句中，表示时间段的词语要放在动词前，如：

In negative sentences, the time-duration expression is placed before the verb. For example:

⑫ 小明两个星期没回家了。

Xiǎomíng liǎng ge xīngqī méi huí jiā le.

Xiaoming hasn't been home for two weeks.

⑬ 他病了，三天没吃东西了。

Tā bìng le, sān tiān méi chī dōngxi le.

He's been ill and hasn't eaten for three days.

在上述句子中，"两个星期""三天"是状语。

In those examples, "liǎng ge xīngqī" and "sān tiān" are adverbials (not time-duration complements).

我们认为在汉语教材中，动词后的时间词作为语言点时，标题可以是“表示动作持续的时间”，不必贴上补语的标签。

We feel that in Chinese materials, time phrases that follow the verb can be treated under the heading of “time-duration expressions ” rather than labeled “complements”.

2. 动作进行的次数

Actions occurring multiple times

动词后可以用动量词，表示动作进行的次数。例如：

Verbs can be followed by verbal measures that indicate that the verbal action occurs more than once. For example:

① 我走到小王的门前，轻轻地敲了两下门。

Wǒ zǒudào Xiǎo Wáng de mén qián, qīngqīng de qiāole liǎng xià mén.

I walked up to Xiao Wang’s door and softly knocked twice.

② 我在老王的楼下喊了他两声，没有人答应。

Wǒ zài Lǎo Wáng de lóuxià hǎnle tā liǎng shēng, méiyǒu rén dāying.

I called out twice to Lao Wang from downstairs but no one answered.

③ 我念课文已经念了三遍了，不想再念了。

Wǒ niàn kèwén yǐjīng niàn le sān biàn le, bù xiǎng zài niàn le.

I’ve already read the lesson aloud three times, I don’t feel like reading it again.

④ 去年我回了两趟老家。

Qùnián wǒ huíle liǎng tàng lǎojiā.

Last year I went back home twice.

有动量词又有宾语时，在句子中动量词和宾语的位置跟宾语的性质有关。

When both an object and a verbal measure phrase are present, the position of the measure phrase depends on the nature of the object.

（1）宾语表示一般事物，包括抽象事物，要位于补语后。如：

When the object is general or involves an abstract entity, it is placed after the complement. For example:

⑤ 这一课我听了三遍录音，念了两遍课文。

Zhè yí kè wǒ tīngle sān biàn lùyīn, niànle liǎng biàn kèwén.

For this lesson, I've listened to recordings 3 times and read the text twice.

⑥ 昨天我们打了两场篮球，很累。

Zuótiān wǒmen dǎle liǎng chǎng lánqiú, hěn lèi.

We played two games of basketball yesterday — we're tired.

⑦ 你上个星期去了几趟超市？

Nǐ shàng ge xīngqī qùle jǐ tàng chāoshì?

How many times did you go to a supermarket last week?

⑧ 我刚才给哥哥打了好几次电话，他都不在。

Wǒ gāngcái gěi gēge dǎle hǎojǐ cì diànhuà, tā dōu bú zài.

I just made a bunch of phone calls to my older brother; he wasn't home.

（2）宾语表示确定的人、动物以及地名时，可以位于补语前，也可以位于补语后。如：

When the object signifies a specific person, animal or place name, the complement can be placed either before or after the object. For example:

⑨ 已经7点多了，你叫一声小李吧。

Yǐjīng qī diǎn duō le, nǐ jiào yì shēng Xiǎo Lǐ ba.

已经7点多了，你叫小李一声吧。

Yǐjīng qī diǎn duō le, nǐ jiào Xiǎo Lǐ yì shēng ba.

It's already past 7 — better give Xiao Li a shout.

⑩ 有人推了一下正在睡觉的老王，他马上醒了。

Yǒu rén tuīle yí xià zhèngzài shuì jiào de Lǎo Wáng, tā mǎshàng xǐng le.

有人推了正在睡觉的老王一下，他马上醒了。

Yǒu rén tuīle zhèngzài shuì jiào de Lǎo Wáng yí xià, tā mǎshàng xǐng le.

Someone gave a shove to the sleeping Lao Wang, who immediately awoke.

⑪ 我看了小黄狗一眼，它就跑过来了。

Wǒ kànle xiǎo huánggǒu yì yǎn, tā jiù pǎo guolai le.

我看了一眼小黄狗，它就跑过来了。

Wǒ kànle yì yǎn xiǎo huánggǒu, tā jiù pǎo guolai le.

I glanced at the little yellow dog and it ran over to me.

⑫ 你去年去了几次北京？

Nǐ qùnián qùle jǐ cì Běijīng?

你去年去了北京几次？

Nǐ qùnián qùle Běijīng jǐ cì?

How many times did you go to Beijing last year?

（3）宾语是代词，或者动量词是“刀、脚、拳、巴掌”等借用量词时，只能位于补语前。如：

When the object is a pronoun, or the complement contains select verbal measures such as “dāo (knife)” “jiǎo (foot)” “quán (fist)” or “bāzhang (palm of the hand)”, the object always precedes. For example:

⑬ 我看见他踢了狗一脚。

Wǒ kànjiàn tā tīle gǒu yì jiǎo.

I saw him give the dog a kick.

＊我看见他踢了一脚狗。

＊Wǒ kànjiàn tā tīle yì jiǎo gǒu.

⑭ 你赶快叫他一声，要晚了。

Nǐ gǎnkuài jiào tā yì shēng，yào wǎn le.

Give him a shout right away — we’ll be late.

＊你赶快叫一声他，要晚了。[①]

＊Nǐ gǎnkuài jiào yì shēng tā，yào wǎn le.

---

① 补语如果是“一下”，似乎可有两个位置：

a. 一会儿你别忘了叫他一下。 b. 一会儿你别忘了叫一下他。

If the complement is “yíxià”, there are apparently two options:

a.Yíhuìr nǐ bié wàngle jiào tā yíxià. b.Yíhuìr nǐ bié wàngle jiào yíxià tā.

Both “Don’t forget to call him in a while”.

⑮ 我看见他打了妹妹一拳就跑了。

Wǒ kànjiàn tā dǎle mèimei yì quán jiù pǎo le.

I saw him strike little sister a blow and then run.

＊我看见他打了一拳妹妹就跑了。

＊Wǒ kànjiàn tā dǎle yì quán mèimei jiù pǎo le.

这类动量词很多语法书也作为补语（动量补语）处理，也主要是因为包含此类动量词语的句子有宾语时也可以重复动词。如："念课文念了三遍""听录音听了三遍""叫他叫了三声""敲门敲了三下""去学校去了三趟""看这个电影看了三场"等等。也有的语法书把它叫作"准宾语"。

Many books on Chinese grammar treat such verbal measures as complements (the complement of frequency) the complement of frequeney primarily because when such phrases occur in a sentence with an object, the verb can be repeated (first with object, then with verbal measure phrase). So, for example: "niàn kèwén niànle sān biàn (read the text three times)" "tīng lùyīn tīngle sān biàn (listen to recordings three times)" "jiào tā jiàole sān shēng (called him three times)" "qiāo mén qiāole sān xià (knocked on the door three times)" "qù xuéxiào qùle sān tàng (visit the school three times)" "kàn zhège diànyǐng kànle sān chǎng (watch this movie three times)" and so on. Some grammars also label such phrases as "para-objects".

我们认为在对外汉语教材中，动词后的动量词也不必贴上补语的标签，作为语言点，标题就直接说：动词后的动量词，表示动作进行的次数。

We feel that, for the teaching of Chinese to foreigners, there is no need to include these post-verbal measure phrases in the category of complements. It is better to just call them what they are: "post-verbal measure phrases that convey the number of times a verbal action occurs".

3. 动词后的介词短语

Post-verbal prepositional phrases

下面几个句子的动词后包含由介词"于""向""自"构成的介词短语：

The following sentences contain post-verbal preposition phases with prepositions "yú (at)" "xiàng (towards)" and "zì (from)":

① 那位作家生于1818年。

Nà wèi zuòjiā shēng yú yī bā yī bā nián.

That author was born in 1818.

② 我们会从胜利走向胜利。

Wǒmen huì cóng shènglì zǒu xiàng shènglì.

We will move from victory to victory.

③ 这个班的学生来自不同的国家。

Zhège bān de xuéshēng lái zì bù tóng de guójiā.

This class of students comes from various countries.

此类介词短语不少语法书叫作"介词短语补语"。我们认为能这样用的介词短语有限，不必单立一类补语，增加学生的负担。而且这些介词短语补语一般出现在书面语中，学生较晚才能学到。当教到这类用法时，只讲清结构、意义就可以了，不必说明是什么句子成分。

A lot of grammar books call these post-verbal prepositional phrases "prepositional phrase complements". However, we feel that prepositional phrases of this type are so restricted that there is no need to add to the burden of students by labeling them a subcategory of complements. Moreover, since many of these post-verbal prepositions are limited to formal or written language, students do not encounter them until rather late in their study of Chinese. When they do encounter them, they can be explained quite easily without saying exactly what sort of a sentence component they are.

"在+名词""给+名词"位于动词后时，很多语法书作为"介词短语补语"处理。但是为了不增加一类补语，我们认为把动词后的"在""给"作为结果补语处理是有道理的，因为"在""给"本来就是动词。

So while a lot of grammar texts regard prepositional phrases such as "zài+noun" or "gěi+noun" as complements when they appear after the verb, we feel that it makes more sense to treat "zài" and "gěi" after the verb as types of resultative complements. After all, both "zài" and "gěi" were, originally, verbs.

④ 小李在家吗？

Xiǎo Lǐ zài jiā ma?

Is Xiao Li at home?

⑤ 我每天都在办公室，你来找我吧。

Wǒ měi tiān dōu zài bàngōngshì，nǐ lái zhǎo wǒ ba.

I'm in my office everyday; feel free to come and find me there.

汉语的很多介词是由动词转化来的，“在”“给”也一样，既可以作动词也可以作介词。

Most words that function as prepositions in modern Chinese — including “zài” and “gěi” — are derived from verbs and in fact can function as verbs or prepositions.

⑥ 我在飞机上写字。（“在”是介词，“飞机”是“写字”的处所）

Wǒ zài fēijī shang xiě zì.

I'm writing on the plane. (“zài” is a preposition; “fēijī” is the location of the writing)

⑦ 我把字写在了飞机上。（“飞机”是“字”写完后所在的处所）

Wǒ bǎ zì xiězàile fēijī shang.

I wrote characters on the plane. (the plane itself is what gets written on)

⑧ 姐姐给妹妹一本书。

Jiějie gěi mèimei yì běn shū.

Older sister gave younger sister a book.

姐姐把那本书送给了妹妹。

Jiějie bǎ nà běn shū sònggěile mèimei.

Older sister gave the book to younger sister.

但是当“在”“给”位于动词后时，其基本意义并未改变，而且，动词与“在”“给”结合得很紧，如果有动态助词，要放在“在”“给”的后边，如果有停顿，也是在动词和“在”“给”的后边，所以我们仍然把“在”“给”看作结果补语，而不把“在+处所词”“给+名词”作为介词短语处理。

But when “zài” or “gěi” follow the verb, they retain their verbal meanings; what is more, they attach closely to the main verb so that if there are aspect particles, they generally follow "zài" or "gěi"; and pauses, if present, also follow "zài" or "gěi". So we regard "zài" and "gěi" as resultative complements rather than prepositional phrases made up of "zài + location" and "gěi + noun".

4. 动词和形容词后用"得很"等

Elements such as "de hěn (very)" that follow verbs and adjectives

动词和形容词后还可以用"得很""得不得了""得多"以及"极了"等等。此类词语一般语法书处理作程度补语。这类词语是有限的，我们主张在教材中，遇到一个，解释一个，不必贴上补语的标签。

Verbs and adjectives can also be followed by elements such as "de hěn (very)" "de bùdéliǎo (extremely)" "de duō (a lot)" or "jí le (extremely)". Generally, these elements are treated as degree complements in grammatical works. However, this type of post-verbal elements are few in number. We propose that for instruction, they simply be explained as they are encountered, one by one. No need to label them complements.

出现在形容词和动词后表示程度意义的词语可以分为两类。一类是用"得"的，如"得很""得不得了""得要死""得要命""得慌""得厉害""得邪乎""得够呛""得不行""得可以""得多"等等。除了"得很"以外，其他表示程度的词语都出现在口语中。

Grammatical elements expressing degree that appear directly after verbs or adjectives can be divided into two groups: those that involve an intervening "de" and those that do not. Those with "de" are: "de hěn (very)" "de bùdéliǎo (awfully)" "de yào sǐ (awfully)" "de yào mìng (awfully)" "de huang (incredibly)" "de lìhai (awfully)" "de xiéhu (incredibly)" "de gòuqiang (unbearably)" "de bùxíng (extremely)" "de kěyǐ (awfully)" "de duō (much more)". Except for "de hěn", all are colloquial in tone.

（1）"得很"作补语，表示程度很高。如：

"De hěn" indicates a high degree. For example:

① 爸爸今天心情好得很，你提什么要求他都会满足你。

Bàba jīntiān xīnqíng hǎo de hěn, nǐ tí shénme yāoqiú tā dōu huì mǎnzú nǐ.

Dad's in a great mood today, he'll agree to whatever you ask.

② 这个地方冬天冷得很，不适合居住。

Zhège dìfang dōngtiān lěng de hěn，bú shìhé jūzhù.

Winter here is really cold, it's not a good place to live.

③ 很久没回家了，我想家想得很。

Hěn jiǔ méi huí jiā le，wǒ xiǎng jiā xiǎng de hěn.

I haven't been home for ages; I'm very homesick.

④ 能上这所大学，我满足得很。

Néng shàng zhè suǒ dàxué，wǒ mǎnzú de hěn.

I'm very glad to be able to attend this university.

（2）“得不得了”作补语，表示很高的程度，正面和负面的情况都可以用。如：

“De bùdéliǎo” indicates a very high degree, with either positive or negative situations. For example:

⑤ 这几天的天气真怪，昨天冷得不得了，今天又热得不得了。

Zhè jǐ tiān de tiānqì zhēn guài，zuótiān lěng de bùdéliǎo，jīntiān yòu rè de bùdéliǎo.

The weather for the last few days has been really weird; yesterday was extremely cold, today is extremely hot.

⑥ 你快给你妈妈打个电话吧，她一个月没接到你的电话了，急得不得了。

Nǐ kuài gěi nǐ māma dǎ ge diànhuà ba，tā yí ge yuè méi jiēdào nǐ de diànhuà le，jí de bùdéliǎo.

Phone your mother right away; she hasn't heard from you for a month and is worried to bits.

⑦ 这个演员现在红得不得了。

Zhège yǎnyuán xiànzài hóng de bùdéliǎo.

Nowadays, this actor is extremely popular.

⑧ 这个饭馆儿的菜好吃得不得了，我每个星期都去。

Zhège fànguǎnr de cài hǎochī de bùdéliǎo，wǒ měi ge xīngqī dōu qù.

The food at this restaurant is really tasty; I go there every week.

（3）“得要死”“得要命”作补语，表示程度高，多用于负面情况。如：

“De yào sǐ” (lit. “want to die”), “de yào mìng” (lit. “want destiny”) both indicate a high degree; they are more used for unpleasant things. For example:

⑨ 别去那儿工作，累得要死/要命，工资也不高。

Bié qù nàr gōngzuò，lèi de yào sǐ /yào mìng，gōngzī yě bù gāo.

Don’t work there, you’ll die from exhaustion, and the salary is low.

⑩ 今天热得要死/要命，我差点儿晕倒。

Jīntiān rè de yào sǐ /yào mìng，wǒ chàdiǎnr yūndǎo.

It’s hotter than hell today, I almost fainted.

⑪ 那个地方远得要死/要命，你别去了。

Nàge dìfang yuǎn de yào sǐ /yào mìng，nǐ bié qù le.

That place is miles from here — don’t go.

“要命”有时也可以用于正面的情况：

“Yào mìng” can sometimes be used in positive situations as well:

⑫ 有了新工作，弟弟高兴得要命，一定要请我吃饭。

Yǒule xīn gōngzuò，dìdi gāoxìng de yào mìng，yídìng yào qǐng wǒ chī fàn.

Having got a new job, younger brother is happy as a clam; he’ll surely invite me out for a meal.

⑬ 他们俩好得要命，一天到晚都在一起。

Tāmen liǎ hǎo de yào mìng，yìtiān-dàowǎn dōu zài yìqǐ.

Those two are close as two pages in a book — they’re together from morn till night.

（4）“得慌”作补语，表示的程度不太高。用于负面的情况，可以用于动词和形容词后。如：

“De huang” indicates a moderate degree; used in negative situations, after both verbs and adjectives. For example:

⑭ 坐在车后面，颠得慌。

Zuò zài chē hòumiàn，diān de huang.

Sitting in the back of the truck is bumpy as hell.

⑮ 这件毛衣穿着不舒服，扎得慌。

Zhè jiàn máoyī chuānzhe bù shūfu，zhā de huang.

This item of clothing isn't comfortable — it's incredibly prickly.

⑯ 听了这个令人难过的消息，我心里堵得慌。

Tīngle zhège lìng rén nánguò de xiāoxi，wǒ xīnli dǔ de huang.

When I heard the sad news, my heart almost stopped.

⑰ 我累得慌，别走了。

Wǒ lèi de huang，bié zǒu le.

I'm on my last legs — don't leave.

（5）“得厉害”“得邪乎”意思一样，后者是北方口语。一般用于负面情况。如：

“De lìhai” and “de xiéhu” have much the same meaning; the latter is colloquial northern speech. These are generally used in negative situations. For example:

⑱ 她感冒了，烧得厉害/邪乎。

Tā gǎnmào le，shāo de lìhai/xiéhu.

She's got a cold; her fever's off the scale.

⑲ 我的手烫伤了，疼得厉害/邪乎。

Wǒ de shǒu tàngshāng le，téng de lìhai/xiéhu.

I burnt my hand — it hurts terribly.

⑳ 他没有得什么大病，就是叫得厉害/邪乎。

Tā méiyǒu dé shénme dàbìng，jiùshì jiào de lìhai/xiéhu.

He hasn't got a serious illness, he's just screaming his head off.

㉑ 孩子一定哪儿不舒服，不然不会哭得这么厉害/邪乎。

Háizi yídìng nǎr bù shūfu，bùrán bú huì kū de zhème lìhai/xiéhu.

The child must have something wrong, otherwise he wouldn't be crying so desperately.

（6）“得够呛”也表示程度高，用于负面的情况，是北方口语。如：

“De gòuqiàng” also signifies an intense degree, usually in reference to something negative; it is northern colloquial usage. For example:

㉒ 帮朋友搬了一天家，他累得够呛。

Bāng péngyou bānle yì tiān jiā，tā lèi de gòuqiàng.

He spent the day helping his friend move house; he's absolutely exhausted.

㉓ 邻居家在院子里烤肉，把他呛得够呛。

Línjū jiā zài yuànzi li kǎo ròu，bǎ tā qiàng de gòuqiàng.

The neighbors barbecuing in their back yard annoyed the hell out of him.

（7）“得不行”表示程度高，常用于表示感觉和心理活动的词语后。如：

“De bùxíng” also signifies a high degree, it is often used in reference to feelings or psychological events. For example:

㉔ 刚才他的员工非常不客气地顶撞他，他气得不行，想开除那个员工。

Gāngcái tā de yuángōng fēicháng bú kèqi de dǐngzhuàng tā，tā qì de bùxíng，xiǎng kāichú nàge yuángōng.

Just now one of his staff was extremely rude to him, arguing and talking back; he got extremely angry and wanted to get rid of him.

㉕ 快扶我一下，我突然晕得不行。

Kuài fú wǒ yí xià，wǒ tūrán yūn de bùxíng.

Quick take my hand, I'm suddenly feeling very dizzy.

㉖ 她想孩子想得不行，一定叫孩子马上坐飞机回来。

Tā xiǎng háizi xiǎng de bùxíng，yídìng jiào háizi mǎshàng zuò fēijī huilai.

She's missing her child terribly; I expect she'll ask the kid to fly back right away.

（8）“可以”有“行”的意思，“得可以”表示程度，常常是说话人的一种评价，有讽刺意味，常用于“坏、滑、笨、淘气、顽皮、懒”等。如：

“Kěyǐ” has the same meaning as “xíng”. “De kěyǐ” signifies a certain extent, often suggesting a judgment by the speaker with a mocking tone. It is often attached to adjectives such as “huài (bad)” “huá (slippery)” “bèn (silly)” “táoqì (mischievous)” “wánpí (naughty)” “lǎn (lazy)”. For example:

㉗ 这个人坏得可以，你千万别跟他打交道。

Zhège rén huài de kěyǐ，nǐ qiānwàn bié gēn tā dǎ jiāodào.

This person's a loser; be sure you don't have any dealings with him.

㉘ 你这个人笨得可以，这么简单的题都做不出来。

Nǐ zhège rén bèn de kěyǐ，zhème jiǎndān de tí dōu zuò bu chūlái.

You're an imbecile not to be able to figure out such simple questions.

㉙ 她的丈夫懒得可以，饭不做，衣服不洗，什么活儿都是她干。

Tā de zhàngfu lǎn de kěyǐ，fàn bú zuò，yīfu bù xǐ，shénme huór dōu shì tā gàn.

Her husband is awfully lazy; he doesn't cook or do the washing; she does all the work.

（9）“得多”也表示程度高，“一点儿”表示程度不高，用于比较。如：

“De duō” signifies “a lot”, while “yìdiǎnr” signifies “a little”; both are used in comparisons. For example:

㉚ 我儿子比你儿子高得多/一点儿。

Wǒ érzi bǐ nǐ érzi gāo de duō/yìdiǎnr.

My son's a lot / a little taller than yours.

㉛ 今年的东西比去年贵得多/一点儿。

Jīnnián de dōngxi bǐ qùnián guì de duō/yìdiǎnr.

Things are much more / a little more expensive this year than last.

㉜ 小张的英文比老王好得多/一点儿。

Xiǎo Zhāng de Yīngwén bǐ Lǎo Wáng hǎo de duō/yìdiǎnr.

Xiao Zhang's English is much better / a little better than Lao Wang's.

㉝ 学生活动中心比图书馆远得多/一点儿。

Xuéshēng huódòng zhōngxīn bǐ túshūguǎn yuǎn de duō/yìdiǎnr.

The student union is a lot / a little farther away than the library.

另一类是不用“得”的，直接用在形容词和动词后，表示程度。

There are also some phrases expressing extent that can follow verbs or adjectives directly (without an intervening "de").

（10）"极了"用在形容词后，表示程度很高。如：

One is "jí le" (to the extreme), which follows adjectives to express a high degree. For example:

㉞ 今天热<u>极了</u>。

Jīntiān rè <u>jí le</u> .

Today is extremely hot.

㉟ 那个电影好看<u>极了</u>。

Nàge diànyǐng hǎokàn <u>jí le</u>.

That film's really great.

㊱ 今天是儿童节，孩子们高兴<u>极了</u>。

Jīntiān shì Értóng Jié，háizimen gāoxìng <u>jí le</u>.

Today's Children's Day; the kids are really happy.

也可以用在表示心理活动的动词，如"喜欢、想、像"等。

"Jí le" can also follow verbs that express mental attitudes or impressions, such as "xǐhuan (like)" "xiǎng (feel like)" and "xiàng (resemble)":

㊲ 这件衣服妹妹喜欢<u>极了</u>。

Zhè jiàn yīfu mèimei xǐhuan <u>jí le</u>.

Younger sister really likes this item of clothing.

㊳ 离开家快一年了，我想家想<u>极了</u>。

Líkāi jiā kuài yì nián le，wǒ xiǎng jiā xiǎng <u>jí le</u>.

I've been away from home for almost a year and am extremely homesick.

㊴ 她跟姐姐长得像<u>极了</u>。

Tā gēn jiějie zhǎng de xiàng <u>jí le</u>.

She's grown to be very like her older sister.

（11）"透"可以用在动词后，表示很高的程度。如：

Another post-verbal element that expresses a high degree is "tòu (seep through)", which can appear after a verb. For example:

㊵ 衣服都叫雨淋透了。

Yīfu dōu jiào yǔ líntòu le.

The clothes got soaked through by the rain.

㊶ 我这双鞋穿了好几年了，鞋底都磨透了。

Wǒ zhè shuāng xié chuānle hǎojǐ nián le，xiédǐ dōu mótòu le.

I've worn these shoes for years; the soles are all worn through.

㊷ 这件事我看透了，他们一定有阴谋。

Zhè jiàn shì wǒ kàntòu le，tāmen yídìng yǒu yīnmóu.

I've checked this thoroughly; there's got to have been a conspiracy.

用在形容词后也可以表示程度高，多用于贬义。如：

After adjectives, "tòu" tends to appear with unfavorable judgements. For example:

㊸ 那个高个子的人坏透了。

Nàge gāo gèzi de rén huàitòu le.

That tall guy is rotten to the core.

㊹ 我今天倒霉透了，把钱包和手机都丢了。

Wǒ jīntiān dǎo méi tòu le，bǎ qiánbāo hé shǒujī dōu diū le.

Today was a total disaster; I lost my wallet and my cellphone.

㊺ 那个人恨透你了，你小心一点儿吧。

Nàge rén hèntòu nǐ le，nǐ xiǎoxīn yìdiǎnr ba.

That person dislikes you intensely; you'd better watch out.

可以跟"透"一起用的形容词和动词有限，学习者不能随意使用，要用自己学过和听到过的。

The number of verbs and adjectives that can combine with "tòu" is limited, so instead of trying to compose novel combinations, students should only use those which they have already seen or heard.

（12）"坏"用本义，可以作结果补语。如：

"Huài" acting as a resultative complement keeps its basic meaning of "bad". For example:

㊻ 我昨天吃了不干净的东西，把肚子吃坏了。

Wǒ zuótiān chīle bù gānjìng de dōngxi，bǎ dùzi chīhuài le.

Yesterday I ate something bad which upset my stomach.

㊼ 食物放了好几天了，放坏了，不能吃了。

Shíwù fàngle hǎojǐ tiān le，fànghuài le，bù néng chī le.

I've kept the food a few days and it's gone bad; it can't be eaten now.

㊽ 你不会修理电脑还一定要修，你看修坏了吧。

Nǐ bú huì xiūlǐ diànnǎo hái yídìng yào xiū，nǐ kàn xiūhuài le ba.

You insisted on repairing the computer even though you didn't know how to do it; look, you've ruined it.

"坏"用在动词和形容词后，也可以表示较高的程度，可以用于不太好的情况。如：

When "huài" follows a verb or adjective, it can also signify a relatively high degree, but it applies to undesirable situations. For example:

㊾ 病了两天，不能吃饭，她饿坏了。

Bìngle liǎng tiān，bù néng chī fàn，tā èhuài le.

She was ill for two days and couldn't eat, she was beside herself with hunger.

㊿ 他听说儿子做的事，气坏了。

Tā tīngshuō érzi zuò de shì，qìhuài le.

When he heard what his son had done, he was furious.

51 一声惊雷，把孩子吓坏了。

Yì shēng jīngléi，bǎ háizi xiàhuài le.

The clap of thunder frightened the child out of its wits.

也可以用于"高兴""乐"等的后边。如：

"Huài" can also appear after words like "gāoxìng (happy)" or "lè (happy)". For example:

52 收到那个大学的录取通知书，妹妹乐坏了。

Shōudào nàge dàxué de lùqǔ tōngzhīshū，mèimei lèhuài le.

When she got the notification of acceptance from the university, younger sister was ecstatic.

53 几年没回家了，马上就到家了，我高兴坏了。

Jǐ nián méi huí jiā le，mǎshàng jiù dào jiā le，wǒ gāoxìng huài le.

I'm almost home after being away for several years, I'm quite ecstatic.

（13）"死"用本义，可以作结果补语。如：

"Sǐ" can act as a resultative complement, keeping its basic meaning of "die". For example:

54 那只狼被猎人打死了。

Nà zhī láng bèi lièrén dǎsǐ le.

That wolf was killed by hunters.

55 这头猪是病死的，肉不能吃。

Zhè tóu zhū shì bìngsǐ de，ròu bù néng chī.

That pig died of an illness, it shouldn't be eaten.

也可以用在形容词后，表示程度。可以用于不好的情况。如：

"Sǐ" can also be used after adjectives to express degree in unfortunate situations. For example:

56 这么晚了，你快走吧，大家等你等得急死了。

Zhème wǎn le，nǐ kuài zǒu ba，dàjiā děng nǐ děng de jísǐ le.

It's so late, you should get going, everyone's getting really impatient waiting for you.

57 她走路慢死了，真叫人着急。

Tā zǒu lù mànsǐ le，zhēn jiào rén zháo jí.

She walks so slowly, it's infuriating!

58 屋里热死了，开空调了吗？

Wū li rèsǐ le，kāi kōngtiáo le ma?

It's boiling in the room; is the airconditioner on?

也可以用在“高兴”“美”后。如：

It can also appear after “gāoxìng (happy)” and “měi (pretty)”. For example:

59 弟弟知道你要回来，高兴死了。

Dìdi zhīdào nǐ yào huílai，gāoxìng sǐ le.

When younger brother found out you were coming back, he was ecstatic.

60 穿这么漂亮的衣服，美死你了。

Chuān zhème piàoliang de yīfu，měisǐ nǐ le.

What a killer outfit you've got on!

（14）用于表示比较的句子，“多了”表示程度高，“一点儿”表示程度不高。

In sentences expressing comparison, “duō le” signifies a high degree, “yìdiǎnr” a low degree (“a bit”).

61 我比妹妹矮多了/一点儿。

Wǒ bǐ mèimei ǎi duō le/yìdiǎnr.

I'm much shorter / a little shorter than younger sister.

62 今天比昨天热多了/一点儿。

Jīntiān bǐ zuótiān rè duō le/yìdiǎnr.

Today's much hotter / a little warmer than yesterday.

63 她的病好多了/一点儿了。

Tā de bìng hǎo duō le/yìdiǎnr le.

Her illness is much better / a bit better.

64 弟弟比哥哥在体育方面棒多了/一点儿。

Dìdi bǐ gēge zài tǐyù fāngmiàn bàng duō le/yìdiǎnr.

Younger brother's way better / a bit better in sports than older brother.

65 李老师比以前和气多了/一点儿了。

Lǐ lǎoshī bǐ yǐqián héqi duō le/yìdiǎnr le.

Teacher Li is much friendlier / a bit friendlier than before.

（15）“远”也可以表示程度高，只用在动词“差”后。如：

“Yuǎn” can also indicate a high degree, it is only used after the verb “chà (less)”. For example:

⑯ 他的中文比小王差远了。

Tā de Zhōngwén bǐ Xiǎo Wáng chà yuǎn le.

His Chinese is far worse than Xiao Wang’s.

⑰ 我的旧手机比新手机差远了。

Wǒ de jiù shǒujī bǐ xīn shǒujī chà yuǎn le.

My old cellphone isn’t nearly as good as the new one.

综合练习
Exercises

一. 结果补语填空题
Fill in the blank with the appropriate resultative complement

好 坏 错 完 住 见 清楚
在 懂 会 走 成 给 掉 倒

1. 如果你想学______汉语，就得每天练习。

2. 你看______王老师了吗？李老师正在找他。

3. 昨天的考试，我做得不太好，有些生词没记______。

4. 零度的时候，水会变______冰。

5. 听说那个饭馆儿的饺子很好吃，可是上周五我们去吃饭的时候，饺子都卖______了。

6. 我们去医院看她的时候，她正躺______床上打游戏。

7. 等我把这封重要的电子邮件写______，就跟你去健身房。

8. 我的行李都准备______了，就等你开车来接我了。

9. 昨天下课以后，发现手机不见了，原来是同学拿______了。

10. 还有半小时就要去机场了，你怎么还没打______电话？

11. 老师，我那天听______了，以为您只让我们做练习一到练习四，所以没有做练习五。

12. 请再说一遍你的号码，刚才没听______。

13. Tom说他18岁的时候，上网看了几次YouTube视频，就学______开车了。

14. 我们商量______了，周末一起到郊外滑雪。

15. 这些剩菜已经放了好几天了，扔______吧。要不，会吃______肚子的。

16. 我可能因为最近工作太紧张了，这几天都没睡______觉。

17. 昨天夜里风真大，今天早上我看到楼前边的一棵树都被刮______了。

18. 她那辆奔驰车才开了两三年，就卖______朋友了。

19. 抓______这根绳子，千万别松手。

20. 我弟弟酷爱跑步，无论什么样的天气，他都出去跑，一年穿______了三双运动鞋。

21. 昨天的考试题太多了，很多同学都没做______。

22. 这个故事发生______古代。

23. 接电话的是个外国人，她说的话我大部分没有听______。

24. 请你记______，本月25号之前一定要把书还给我。

25. 上个星期她在图书馆学习的时候，上了一趟厕所，电脑就被人拿______了。

26. 你为什么要辞______那么好的工作！

27. 最后一场比赛就是因为3号队员没接______球输给了对方。

28. 坐在前边的人太高了，完全挡______了我的视线，什么都看不______。

29. 他的电话我怎么打不通啊？是不是你把他的号码记______了？

30. 她拿着一杯水，送______了门口的老人。

二. 结果补语翻译题

Translate the following Chinese sentences containing resultative complements into English

1. 我昨天把中文功课都做完了。

____

2. 这个电话号码你记错了。

____

3. 老师刚说的话我都听懂了。

____

4. 她昨天跑马拉松累坏了。

____

5．那座大楼被拆掉了。

____

6．妈妈说做完了功课才能看电视。

____

7．他刚一躺下就睡着了。

____

8．我们约好了周末一起去逛街。

____

9．明天的考试你准备好了吗？

____

10．这件毛衣你买大了。

____

11．老师让我们写三页的文章，你只写了两页，写少了。

____

12．今天晚饭我吃多了，现在很不舒服。

____

13．我们来早了，晚会7点半才开始。

____

14．这张照片挂低了，应该再高一点儿。

____

15．他洗碗的时候不小心把一个杯子打破了。

____

16．她因为写错了三个汉字，没得满分。

____

17．昨天我们看了一个Robin Williams的电影，把肚子都笑疼了。

____

18．她已经摔坏两个iPad了。

____

19．我的钥匙找不到了，你看见没有？

____

20．你这两件衬衫没洗干净。

____

21．我朋友上午把我的车开走了，现在还没回来呢。

____

22．很多独生子女都被父母惯坏了。

____

23．秋天还没到，有的树叶就开始变红了。

____

24．你把这个西瓜切成小块吧。

____

25．昨天的剩菜忘记放冰箱了，好像坏了，倒掉吧 。

____

26．我已经吃饱了，不再吃了。

____

三. 可能补语选择题

Select the potential complement that fits the blank best

1．这么贵的房子咱买得______吗？

A.上　　B.完　　C.到　　D.起

2．书架太高了，我够不______。

A.着　　B.上　　C.了　　D.好

3．你的电脑包小王给你看着呢，丢不______。

A.着　　B.到　　C.了　　D.起

4．我奶奶年纪大了，耳朵不好，你声音太小的话，她听______。

A.不懂　　B.不见　　C.不了　　D.不上

5．我去了好几家电器店，就是买______你要的那种插头。

A.不到　　B.不起　　C.不了　　D.不见

6．我刚到日本的时候，吃______生鱼片，现在已经习惯多了。

A.不了　　B.不到　　C.不起　　D.不上

7．张经理真忙，我每次来都碰______她。

A.得到　　B.不起　　C.不了　　D.不到

8．这个地方树多，又没有灯，黑乎乎的，什么也看______。

A.不懂　　B.不上　　C.不起　　D.不见

9．你的老师每天给你这么多作业，你做______吗？

A.得完　　B.不完　　C.得上　　D.得到

10. 这块地毯上不知道洒的是什么？我洗了好几遍都洗______。

A.不干净　　B.得干净　　C.得了　　D.不了

11. 别看我奶奶90岁了，这么长的手机号，她都记______。

A.得上　　B.不下来　　C.得下来　　D.不上

12. 手机上的字太小了，我看______，所以很少用它上网。

A.不清　B.不对　C.得清　D.得对

13. 这次作业不多，一个小时应该写______。

A.得上　B.不完　C.得完　D.不上

14. 他解释得很清楚，连我这个外行都听______。

A.不懂　B.得懂　C.得对　D.不对

15. 这段台阶太陡，我担心你爬______。

A.不上去　B.得上去　C.得了　D.不能下去

16. 他说我的车发动机坏了，要修的话，得两三千块钱，我现在可修______。

A.不好　B.得起　C.不起　D.得好

17. 这件衣服不是那么脏，怎么洗______呢?

A.不干净　B.得了　C.不了　D.得干净

18. 汉语是不容易学，但只要你愿意努力，能坚持，最终一定学______。

A.得了　B.得会　C.得起　D.得到

19. 我的汉语水平不高，心里虽然有很多东西想表达，但是说______。

A.得了　B.不得　C.不出来　D.得出来

20. 今天老师生病了，上______课了。

A.不了　B.不起　C.得了　D.得起

21. 我昨晚感冒了，今天说______话。

A.不了　B.得了　C.出来　D.得出来

22. 师傅，能开快点儿吗？我20分钟内到不了机场就赶______飞机了！真急死人了！

A.得上　B.不上　C.不成　D.得成

23. 老师说话很快，但发音很清楚，我都听______。

A.不明白　　B.得明白　　C.得了　　D.不了

24. 我的汉语水平还很低，让我说这篇文章的内容，我可能说______。

A.不懂　　B.不下　　C.不出来　　D.不出去

25. 五年前第一次见到她，我就对她印象很深，直到今天还忘______。

A.不起　　B.不了　　C.得了　　D.得起

26. 我进门的时候还在打电话，但进门以后手机放在什么地方了就完全记______了。

A.不清　　B.不好　　C.得好　　D.不下

27. 这么多东西我一个人可拿______。

A.得动　　B.不得　　C.不得了　　D.不动

28. 没有洗的水果千万吃______。

A.不得　　B、不了　　C.不好　　D.不下

29. 如果你总是说话不算话，将来谁还信______你?

A.得过　　B.得了　　C.不过　　D.不了

30. 刚到那个地方时，吃______那里的饭，一个月瘦了快10斤。

A.不好　　B.不完　　C.不到　　D.不惯

31. 你点的菜太多了，我们仨人肯定吃______。

A.得过　　B.不过　　C.得完　　D.不完

32. 这么多年没见面了，你要是不先叫我，我还真认______你了!

A.得出　　B.得了　　C.不了　　D.不出

33. 帮帮忙，这个瓶子盖得太紧了，我打______。

A.不开　　B.得开　　C.不起　　D.得起

34. 这个公寓这么新，位置也好，我们薪水不高，应该租______吧。

A.得起　　B.不起　　C.不得　　D.得了

35. 这个箱子看起来很大但是不重，她一个人就拿______。

A.不完　　B.不动　　C.得完　　D.得动

36. 你买书买得太多，看______吗？

A.不完　　B.得下　　C.得完　　D.不下

37. 她妈妈说，女儿刚开始工作，让她马上出去自己租房住，怕她拿______这么多钱。

A.不出　　B.得出　　C.得了　　D.不得

38. 总的来说，他的听力和阅读还不错，就是有的音发______。

A.不到　　B.不得　　C.不好　　D.不完

四. 可能补语改正题

Correct the underlined part of each sentence with the correct potential complement

1. 对我来说，考试的听力部分比较难，每次都有一些问题我不能答得出来。

2. 工作不太多，我一个人做得了完。

3. 她这个人就是好聊天儿，一聊起来就不停下。

4. 我住的宿舍特别吵，尤其是周末，吵得我都不能睡着觉。

5. 这个春假我不打算回家了，因为不能买到便宜的机票，而且我还有一篇20页的论文没写完。

6. 坐在后边的同学请往前坐一点儿，不然我讲话你们不能听清楚。

7．A：就剩这两个饺子了，你都吃了吧！
   B：我可<u>不能吃下</u>了，太饱了！

8．A：你怎么搬到那么远的地方去了？原来住的公寓不是挺好吗？
   B：房东一下子把房租涨了五百块，我<u>不能租起</u>了。

9.看见我的手机了吗？我刚才接了一个电话，现在就<u>不能找到</u>了。

10.我发现我的记性越来越差了，刚学的生词一下就<u>不能想起来</u>了。

11.我现在在等一个重要的电话，<u>不能走成</u>。

12.天气不好，你这么晚了才开车走，恐怕半夜以前都<u>不可以到家</u>。

13.我昨天晚上刚在电脑上写好的期末报告，现在怎么<u>不打开</u>了？真急死人了！

14.这个车库太小了，<u>不能停下</u>两辆车。

15.你的签证10号前可<u>不能办成</u>，因为大使馆国庆节要放七天假。

五. 趋向补语选择题

Select the directional complement that fits the blank best

1．开快一点儿吧，后边的车已经跟______了。
   A.回来　　B.上来　　C.下来　　D.起来

2．我们办培训班剩______的钱，买些水果分给大家吃吧！
   A.起来　　B.上来　　C.下来　　D.过来

3．椅子可能不够，你把隔壁教室的椅子搬______几把！
   A.回来　　B.上来　　C.出来　　D.过来

4．很多人退休以后没事做，又不注意饮食和运动，于是很快就胖______了。

A.下来　　B.上来　　C.起来　　D.过来

5．老师一进来，教室里马上就安静______了。

A.下来　　B.起来　　C.下去　　D.过来

6．大家一直在机场门口等着，一看到他从机场里走______，就赶紧跑______帮他拿行李。

A.过来/出去　　B.出来/过去　　C.进来/出去　　D.过去/出来

7．最近我母亲身体不好，我想过完年暂时不回公司上班了，留______照顾母亲。

A.下来　　B.起来　　C.下去　　D.过来

8．很多农民工到了大城市都拼命工作，把钱省______寄回家。

A.下去　　B.上去　　C.下来　　D.上来

9．老王对谁都特别热情，只要有人找他帮忙，他都会答应______。

A.下去　　B.上去　　C.下来　　D.上来

10. 时间过得真快！算______我已经在中国住了7年了！

A.上来　　B.起来　　C.下去　　D.过来

11. 最近西方媒体报道说中国的一些军事技术已经赶______了。

A.下去　　B.上去　　C.下来　　D.上来

12. 那个小女孩儿很可爱，笑的时候露______一排好看的牙齿。

A.起来　　B.出来　　C.进来　　D.回来

13．她在这里教了一年英文以后竟爱______了这里，便决定在这里长期住______。

A.下/上来　　B.上/起来　　C.上/下来　　D.下/过来

14. 很多严重的健康问题都是由一些不良的生活习惯引______的。

A.下　　B.起　　C.上　　D.来

15. 我打算回家时先把一些不用的书和衣服带______，免得毕业搬家时东西太多。

A.回来　　B.回去　　C.过来　　D.过去

16. 昨天老师说的考试内容，你都记______了吗？

A.下去　　B.上去　　C.下来　　D.起来

17. 你这个问题很有意思，但我现在回答不______，需要查一下资料。

A.过来　　B.得来　　C.起来　　D.上来

18. 自从母亲去世以后，她就一直没有从抑郁的状态中解脱______。

A.过来　　B.出来　　C.起来　　D.回来

19. 我把球给你扔______，你接______。

A.过来/到　　B.出来/过　　C.回去/住　　D.过去/来

20. 这件事我已经答应______了，就一定得做。

A.过来　　B.出来　　C.下来　　D.起来

21. 这次考试看着容易，可是一做______就不那么容易了。

A.过来　　B.出来　　C.上来　　D.起来

22. 这件大衣你穿着真漂亮。虽然贵了一点儿，我劝你还是买______吧。

A.过来　　B.出来　　C.下来　　D.起来

23. 经过医生的努力，他终于从昏迷中醒______了。

A.过来　　B.出来　　C.下来　　D.起来

24. 你们下次再出去旅游，把我也算______。

A.来　　B.进　　C.下　　D.上

25. 她做了整容手术以后，我们都认不______她了。

A.出　　B.起　　C.来　　D.上

26. 这个标签粘得太结实了，撕不______。

A.去　　B.下去　　C.来　　D.上来

27. 外边下大雨了，别走了。今天就在这儿住______吧！

A.起来　　B.下　　C.来　　D.上

28. 如果他自己不说，这件事怎么能传______呢？

A.起去　　B.过来　　C.出去　　D.下来

六. 趋向补语填空题

Fill in the blank with the appropriate directional complement

1．请你把脚抬______，我要擦地板。

2．你在这儿等着，我去把车开______。

3．她话还没说完，大家都笑______了。

4．电梯门关______了，我们走______吧。

5．我的脚自从那次受伤以后，一走______路______就疼。

6．经过一段时间的努力，他的学习成绩终于赶______了。

7．我昨天坐地铁的时候睡着了，坐______了好几站。

8．最近天气有点儿冷，出门时别忘了穿______大衣。

9．就凭我一个实习生挣的钱，哪儿能买得______苹果手机？

10．这两年房价都涨疯了！据说几年内也降不______。

11．这个日期写错了，你把它改______。

12．喂，前台服务员吗？我房间的马桶堵了，水流不______了。

13．你别不好意思了，把你想跟她说的话说______吧。

14．孩子十一二岁正是叛逆的时候，父母说什么都听不______。

15．按照这个方法锻炼______，过不了半年，你就能瘦______。

16．才下午三点钟，天忽然变黑了，看______是要下暴雨。

17．别挤了，挤不______了，咱们还是等下一趟车吧！

18．你屋子里的东西太多了，不用的东西可以先收______。

19．他的车撞得挺厉害的，前边的车门都瘪______了。

20．上次跑马拉松的时候，他脚受伤了，但还是坚持跑了______。

21．昨天老师说的考试范围，你都记______了吗？

22．连很多专家都不明白为什么中国有些城市的房价涨得停不______。

23．房东说他下个月要装修房子，让我们都搬______，所以我得赶快找房子。

24．他妈妈让他过春节的时候把女朋友带______家______让她看看。

25．在这次奥运会上，很多运动员看到自己国家的国旗升______的时候，都激动得流______了眼泪。

26．上大学以后，我跟高中同学再没见过面。上个周末同学聚会，有几个人我完全认不______了。

27．她离婚这件事只有我知道，她让我千万别说______。

28．从字典里我查______这个字的发音和意思了，可是还不知道怎么用。

29．那个人是谁，你打听______了吗？

30．直到这件事的严重后果出现了，我才明白______，我错了。

七. 趋向补语翻译题

Translate the following sentences into Chinese sentences containing directional complements

1. Can you say what you really feel?

____

2. He has already come up with a pretty name for his unborn baby girl.

____

3. I have rented out my apartment.

____

4. Upon hearing the good news, everyone started screaming.

____

5. When the speaker came in, all the audience stood up.

____

6. I stuck my hand into my backpack to search for my cellphone.

____

7. You can park your car inside.

____

8. Can you tell (see) who wrote these characters?

____

9. I couldn't figure out the riddle.

____

10. Look, they are coming to you.

____

11. The teacher has not graded all the tests from yesterday.

____

12. He feels that his current dorm room is too small; it won't even fit a sofa. So he wants to move out next semester.

____

13. I'm on the phone with my insurance company. Can I call you back in 20 minutes?

____

14. Could you please help me put my suitcase up there?

____

15. As soon as she gets nervous, she starts speaking faster.

____

16. When some high tech companies moved here a few years ago, house prices quickly started to rise.

____

17. It has started raining. Go upstairs and close the windows!

____

18. There may be an accident up ahead, so the cars on the road have all stopped.

____

19. How come you suddenly got so skinny?

____

20. He played computer games all day except when he was sleeping, and quickly squandered the entire summer.

____

21. Although it's an old car, it runs pretty smoothly.

____

22. Can you help me hang this picture on the wall?

____

23. I wonder if I can get the money back.

____

24. She received a letter of acceptance from Harvard University and was so excited that she started jumping up and down.

____

八. 程度补语选择题

Select the degree complement that fits the blank best

1. 今天我出门时忘带钱包了，现在又把车钥匙锁在车里了。真是______！
   A.倒霉坏了　B.倒霉得多　C.倒霉得慌　D.倒霉死了

2. 他刚才说的那句话把我们笑得______。
   A.肚子疼　B.肚子不得了　C.肚子疼得多　D.肚子疼厉害

3. 这几天热得______。
   A.极了　B.不得了　C.死了　D.透了

4. 图书馆的空调开得太低了，我在那儿看了一会儿书都快冻______。
   A.极了　B.不得了　C.死了　D.透了

5. 这个商店的东西贵______，我们还是去旁边那家店看看吧。
A.很多　B.得很　C.不得了　D.得极了

6. 给女儿买了一条围巾，她喜欢______，每天上下班都戴着。
A.得多　B.得不行　C.得慌　D.得极了

7. 这次期末考试，我居然考了满分，心里美得______。
A.透了　B.要命　C.死了　D.极了

8. 前边那辆车开着开着突然冒烟了，把她吓______。
A.不行　B.要命　C.极了　D.死了

9. 在飞机上坐的时间太长了，下飞机的时候我的脚麻得______。
A.死了　B.极了　C.透了　D.走不了

九. 用描写性补语完成句子

Complete the following sentences with descriptive complements

1. 昨天我赶写了一个15页的报告，一夜没睡觉。今天上课的时候，我困得
______________________________。

2. 我第一次面试的时候，心跳得______________________________。

3. 周五晚上，他们开晚会开到夜里1点，吵得我______________________________
______________________________。

4. 这几天我在准备面试，忙得______________________________。

5. 最近天气有点儿不正常，昨天温度达到华氏97度，很多人都热得______
______________________________。

6. 你开车开得______________________________，小心出事。

7. 安娜酷爱中文，每天学中文学得____________________。

8. 听到女儿考上北京大学的消息，妈妈高兴得____________________。

9. 你来尝尝，这个菜做得____________________。

10. 昨天我帮朋友搬家搬得____________________。

11. 他打电脑游戏打得____________________。

12. 我每到期末写学期论文都写得____________________。

13. 我每次回北京的时候，都非常惊讶北京的变化，有些地方变得______________________________。

14. 那年冬天特别冷，再加上下了几场大雪，她病了好几次。有一次，她咳嗽得____________________。

15. 我奶奶都90岁了，但是记性好得____________________。

16. 那次我去西雅图开会，到了机场才发现没带钱包，连护照也没带，真把我急____________________。

17. 她第一次去应聘的时候，紧张得____________________。

18. 那天她跟朋友出去爬山，不小心崴了脚，把她疼____________________。

19. 那个饭馆儿的生煎包做得____________________。

20. 他过生日那天请我们去他家吃饭，他做了三个菜和一个汤。真没想到他做中餐做得____________________。

21. 他特别爱惜他父母送给他的那辆奥迪车，每天都擦得______________。

22. 今天是她第一天上班，她把自己打扮得______________。

23. 我的同学都说昨天的考试很难，但是我觉得我考得______________。

24. 我爸爸特别喜欢运动，打网球打得______________。

25. 我发现他从中国回来以后汉语水平大大提高了，汉语说得______________

______________________________。

十. 综合补语选择题

Fill in the blank with the appropriate verb plus complement

1. 主任昨天开会的时候心脏病犯了，所以会没有______。
   A. 开好　　B. 开成　　C. 开了　　D. 开完

2. 因为台风的原因，学校通知这个星期所有的活动都取消，所以迎接新生的大会没有______。
   A. 开好　　B. 开成　　C. 开了　　D. 开完

3. 我一夜没睡，把这本书______了，故事情节真是太精彩了！
   A. 看全　　B. 看成　　C. 看完　　D. 看好

4. 今天的作业太多了，一个小时绝对______。
   A. 不做完　　B. 做不完　　C. 做得完　　D. 做完了

5. 你听，他们正在上听力课呢，你现在______会打扰他们的。
   A. 进教室去　　B. 进去教室　　C. 进教室来　　D. 进来教室

6. 现在人们的生活水平越来越高了，很多家庭都______汽车了。
   A. 买得起　　B. 买过来　　C. 买回来　　D. 买上来

7. 我在图书馆门口等小王等了20分钟，才见他气喘吁吁地向我______。
A.跑回来 B.跑起来 C.跑过来 D.跑上来

8. 现在已经十点多了，你说她今天晚上______？
A.回得来不来 B.回来得不来
C.回来得不得 D.回得来回不来

9. 她每个圣诞节都能______很多礼物，有时候她会把一些礼物______。
A.拿到/送过去 B.得到/送出去
C.收到/送下去 D.买到/送上去

10. 今天的雾真大，连马路两边的树都快______了。
A.不能看见 B.看不见 C.不看见 D.看得见

11. 我们点的菜太多了，两个人恐怕______。
A.吃得完 B.吃不完 C.吃得了 D.不吃完

12. 他把最后一杯酒______以后，就开始讲他当兵打仗的故事。
A.喝下来 B.喝上来 C.喝下去 D.喝上去

13. 你在楼下等着，我把钥匙从窗户给你______。
A.扔上来 B.扔下来 C.扔上去 D.扔下去

14. 那个箱子很重，你一个人______吗？
A.拿得成 B.拿不得 C.拿得了 D.拿不了

15. 这双鞋有点儿小了，我______了。
A.穿不上来 B.穿不下来 C.穿不上 D.穿不出来

16. 你______玛丽了吗？王老师在找她。
A.看了 B.看见 C.看过 D.看成

17. 她穿着一身绿色的短裤背心，______十分凉爽。
A.看过来 B.看上来 C.看起来 D.看下来

18. 我从来没______外国人说汉语能跟中国人一样。
    A.想过来　　B.想上来　　C.想起来　　D.想到

十一. 综合补语填空题

Fill in the blank with the appropriate complement

1. 他打______信封，从里边掉______一张照片。
2. 小丽初中还没读______就跟父母去城里打工了。
3. 你让我寄的那份资料我昨天就寄______了。
4. 有些学生总是习惯于把三声读______二声。
5. 她是一个特别认真的人，有时候会为一些小事想不______。
6. 他去深圳开会的时候，遇______了十年前的恋人，心情一下子无法平静______了。
7. 他不甘心这样平淡地过______。终于有一天，他辞______了工作，办______了一个自闭症儿童艺术学校。
8. 我实在太困了，坚持不______了，先去睡了。
9. 经过一年的艰苦努力，他终于如愿考______了一所有名的大学。
10. 他把儿女孝顺他的钱都捐______了。
11. 这条项链是从我妈妈的奶奶那里传______的。
12. 你提的这个问题比较复杂，我没有准备，现在回答不______。
13. 那个教室不大，恐怕坐______20个人。
14. 搬家的日子还没定______呢！她说得等到放暑假时再说。

15. 我昨天夜里12点还没睡______觉，因为隔壁房间一直响着音乐，直到半夜以后，音乐声才低______，我才睡______。

16. 我现在觉得特别累，想睡一会儿，帮我把窗帘拉______，好吗？

17. 哎，好奇怪！我的电脑怎么打不______了？密码没输______呀！

18. 先生，您个子高，麻烦您帮我把上面那个电脑包拿______，可以吗？我够不______。

19. 他一打______游戏______，你说什么他都听______。

20. 她上大一的时候，人很内向。后来去中国读书，性格一下就开朗______了，就像变了一个人似的。

21. 每个月的房租水电加______，他大概要付差不多1000美元。

23. A：打印机坏了吗？我的申请信怎么没打______？

B：你的电脑跟打印机没连______！

24. 面试的时候，即使你心里很紧张，但脸上也不能表现______。

25. 我下午踢足球时把脚崴了，你看，脚踝都肿______了。

26. 前些时候一些炼油厂被关闭，很多地方的油价都涨______了，最多的涨了50美分。不过，最近油价又降______了。

27. 听说2017年北加州那场山火把近七千栋房屋都烧______了。

28. 我刚到中国的时候，吃不______带头的鱼，现在不但能吃带头的鱼，而且还特别爱吃鱼头。

29. 我从来都记不______别人的手机号，所有的号码都存______手机里。

30. 上周一他去机场的时候遇______堵车，没赶______飞机。

十二. 综合补语语序题

Order the components so that the Chinese sentences containing complements match the sense of the English ones

1. 林小姐　楼　上……去　了

   Miss Lin went upstairs.

   ____

2. 从　来　图书馆　他　一本书　了　借

   He borrowed a book from the library.

   ____

3. 从　买　我　黑色星期五　商店　回来　一台　液晶电视　给妈妈

   On Black Friday, I went to the store and bought back a HDTV for my mom.

   ____

4. 他　什么时候　中国　是　的　到……去

   When did he go to China?

   ____

5. 上课的　请　时候　手机　书包里　放　进　把

   Please put your cellphone in your backpack during class.

   ____

6. 昨天的　冰箱里　你　拿　剩饭　把　从　出来

   Please take yesterday's left-overs out of the refrigerator.

   ____

7. 你　她　把　停　车　过来　让

   Ask her to park over here.

   ____

8. 这本书 帮 你 我 把 上去 放 麻烦

Please do me a favor by putting this book up there.

____

9. 我 就 欧洲 去 听说 房子 把 他们 出去 租 一 了

I heard that they rented out their house and went to Europe.

____

10. 东西 你的 起来 把 收 都 吧

Please put your stuff away.

____

11. 马上 你 我 给 打 过去 等 一下

Hold on a second and I'll call you right back.

____

12. 图书馆 去 回去 你 的时候 帮 这两本书 还 我 把 吧

When you go to the library, please return these two books for me.

____

13. 上楼 你 的时候 搬 把 这把 椅子 上去

When you go upstairs, take this chair up.

____

14. 外边 拿 箱子 吗 进来 了 你 还有 一个

There was still a suitcase outside. Did you bring it in?

____

15. 她爸爸 接 去世 美国 了 她妈妈 把 以后 她 到……来

After her dad passed away, she brought her mom to the US.

____

十三. 综合补语翻译题

Translate the following sentences into Chinese. One of the following items should be used in each sentence

起来 过去 开 会 过来 成 出来
错 完 见 好 走 着 到 上 清楚

1. Have you found your cellphone yet?

____

2. Have you finished remodeling your house?

____

3. Sorry, I grabbed the wrong book. This is your book.

____

4. In general, people tend to gain weight after 40.

____

5. You probably didn't remember it clearly.

____

6. He worked in the lab for 24 hours without eating anything. That's why he passed out.

____

7. Throw the ball over to me!

____

8. He didn't test well for the entrance exam, so he didn't get into his ideal university.

____

9. He fell in love with her when he first spotted her on campus.

____

10. Can you translate this article into English?

____

11. People always take me for my older sister.

____

12.Could you turn the light off?

____

13. Open your suitcase and take out your laptop for a security-check.

____

14. The large-screen TV sets sold out quickly.

____

15. I did listen, but I didn't hear what they said.

____

16. Sorry, I cannot take you to the airport, because my daughter drove my car away.

____

17. Guess whom I ran into at Starbucks? My former boyfriend!

____

18. It took her a month to learn how to drive.

____

19. I hate math class not because it is hard, but because the professor cannot explain things clearly.

____

20. Last night I went to bed at 10 p.m., but didn't fall asleep until about midnight.

____

综合练习答案

Answer keys to exercises

一. 结果补语填空题

Fill in the blank with the appropriate resultative complement

好 坏 错 完 住 见 清楚

在 懂 会 走 成 给 掉 倒

1. 如果你想学_好_汉语，就得每天练习。

2. 你看_见_王老师了吗？李老师正在找他。

3. 昨天的考试，我做得不太好，有些生词没记_住/清楚_。

4. 零度的时候，水会变_成_冰。

5. 听说那个饭馆儿的饺子很好吃，可是上周五我们去吃饭的时候，饺子都卖_完_了。

6. 我们去医院看她的时候，她正躺_在_床上打游戏。

7. 等我把这封重要的电子邮件写_完_，就跟你去健身房。

8. 我的行李都准备_好_了，就等你开车来接我了。

9. 昨天下课以后，发现手机不见了，原来是同学拿_走/错_了。

10. 还有半小时就要去机场了，你怎么还没打__完__电话？

11. 老师，我那天听__错__了，以为您只让我们做练习一到练习四，所以没有做练习五。

12. 请再说一遍你的号码，刚才没听__清楚/见__。

13. Tom说他18岁的时候，上网看了几次YouTube视频，就学__会__开车了。

14. 我们商量__好__了，周末一起到郊外滑雪。

15. 这些剩菜已经放了好几天了，扔__掉__吧。要不，会吃__坏__肚子的。

16. 我可能因为最近工作太紧张了，这几天都没睡__好__觉。

17. 昨天夜里风真大，今天早上我看到楼前边的一棵树都被刮__倒__了。

18. 她那辆奔驰车才开了两三年，就卖__给__朋友了。

19. 抓__住__这根绳子，千万别松手。

20. 我弟弟酷爱跑步，无论什么样的天气，他都出去跑，一年穿__坏__了三双运动鞋。

21. 昨天的考试题太多了，很多同学都没做__完__。

22. 这个故事发生__在__古代。

23. 接电话的是个外国人，她说的话我大部分没有听__懂__。

24. 请你记 住/清楚 ，本月25号之前一定要把书还给我。

25. 上个星期她在图书馆学习的时候，上了一趟厕所，电脑就被人拿 走 了。

26. 你为什么要辞 掉 那么好的工作！

27. 最后一场比赛就是因为3号队员没接 住 球输给了对方。

28. 坐在前边的人太高了，完全挡 住 了我的视线，什么都看不 见 。

29. 他的电话我怎么打不通啊？是不是你把他的号码记 错 了？

30. 她拿着一杯水，送 给 了门口的老人。

二. 结果补语翻译题

Translate the following Chinese sentences containing resultative complements into English

1. 我昨天把中文功课都做完了。

   Yesterday I finished all my Chinese homework.

2. 这个电话号码你记错了。

   You got the phone number wrong.

3. 老师刚说的话我都听懂了。

   I understood what the teacher just said.

4. 她昨天跑马拉松累坏了。

   She was completely drained from running the marathon yesterday.

5．那座大楼被拆掉了。

The building was demolished.

6．妈妈说做完了功课才能看电视。

Mom says that I can't watch TV until I finish my homework.

7．他刚一躺下就睡着了。

He fell asleep as soon as he lay down.

8．我们约好了周末一起去逛街。

We made an appointment to go shopping together this weekend.

9．明天的考试你准备好了吗？

Are you prepared for tomorrow's test?

10. 这件毛衣你买大了。

The sweater you bought is too big.

11. 老师让我们写三页的文章，你只写了两页，写少了。

The teacher asked us to write a three-page article, you only wrote two pages, you wrote too little.

12. 今天晚饭我吃多了，现在很不舒服。

I ate too much for dinner today. Now I feel uncomfortable.

13. 我们来早了，晚会7点半才开始。

We came early. The party won't start until 7:30.

14. 这张照片挂低了，应该再高一点儿。

This photo is hung too low, it should be a little higher.

15. 他洗碗的时候不小心把一个杯子打破了。

He accidently broke a cup while washing the dishes.

16. 她因为写错了三个汉字，没得满分。

She didn't get a perfect score because she wrote three Chinese characters wrong.

17. 昨天我们看了一个Robin Williams的电影，把肚子都笑疼了。

Yesterday we saw a Robin Williams movie and we split our sides laughing.

18. 她已经摔坏两个iPad了。

She has broken two iPads.

19. 我的钥匙找不到了，你看见没有？

I can't find my key, have you seen it?

20. 你这两件衬衫没洗干净。

You didn't wash these two shirts clean.

21. 我朋友上午把我的车开走了，现在还没回来呢。

My friend drove my car away this morning, and he hasn't returned yet.

22. 很多独生子女都被父母惯坏了。

A lot of only children get spoiled by their parents.

23. 秋天还没到，有的树叶就开始变红了。

Autumn has not arrived yet, and some of the leaves are turning red.

24. 你把这个西瓜切成小块吧。

Please cut the watermelon into small pieces.

25. 昨天的剩菜忘记放冰箱了，好像坏了，倒掉吧 。

We forgot to put yesterday's left-over dish in the refrigerator. Looks like it's gone bad; just dump it.

26. 我已经吃饱了，不再吃了。

I'm already full, I can't eat anymore.

三. 可能补语选择题

Select the potential complement that fits the blank best

1．这么贵的房子咱买得__D__吗？

A.上　　B.完　　C.到　　D.起

2．书架太高了，我够不__A__。

A.着　　B.上　　C.了　　D.好

3．你的电脑包小王给你看着呢，丢不__C__。

A.着　　B.到　　C.了　　D.起

4．我奶奶年纪大了，耳朵不好，你声音太小的话，她听__B__。

A.不懂　　B.不见　　C.不了　　D.不上

5．我去了好几家电器店，就是买__A__你要的那种插头。

A.不到　　B.不起　　C.不了　　D.不见

6. 我刚到日本的时候，吃__A__生鱼片，现在已经习惯多了。

A.不了　　B.不到　　C.不起　　D.不上

7. 张经理真忙，我每次来都碰__D__她。

A.得到　　B.不起　　C.不了　　D.不到

8. 这个地方树多，又没有灯，黑乎乎的，什么也看__D__。

A.不懂　　B.不上　　C.不起　　D.不见

9. 你的老师每天给你这么多作业，你做__A__吗？

A.得完　　B.不完　　C.得上　　D.得到

10. 这块地毯上不知道洒的是什么？我洗了好几遍都洗__A__。

A.不干净　　B.得干净　　C.得了　　D.不了

11. 别看我奶奶90岁了，这么长的手机号，她都记__C__。

A.得上　　B.不下来　　C.得下来　　D.不上

12. 手机上的字太小了，我看__A__，所以很少用它上网。

A.不清　　B.不对　　C.得清　　D.得对

13. 这次作业不多，一个小时应该写__C__。

A.得上　　B.不完　　C.得完　　D.不上

14. 他解释得很清楚，连我这个外行都听__B__。

A.不懂　　B.得懂　　C.得对　　D.不对

15. 这段台阶太陡，我担心你爬__A__。

A.不上去　　B.得上去　　C.得了　　D.不能下去

16. 他说我的车发动机坏了，要修的话，得两三千块钱，我现在可修__C__。

A.不好　　B.得起　　C.不起　　D.得好

17. 这件衣服不是那么脏，怎么洗 __A__ 呢？
A. 不干净　　B. 得了　　C. 不了　　D. 得干净

18. 汉语是不容易学，但只要你愿意努力，能坚持，最终一定学 __B__ 。
A. 得了　　B. 得会　　C. 得起　　D. 得到

19. 我的汉语水平不高，心里虽然有很多东西想表达，但是说 __C__ 。
A. 得了　　B. 不得　　C. 不出来　　D. 得出来

20. 今天老师生病了，上 __A__ 课了。
A. 不了　　B. 不起　　C. 得了　　D. 得起

21. 我昨晚感冒了，今天说 __A__ 话。
A. 不了　　B. 得了　　C. 出来　　D. 得出来

22. 师傅，能开快点儿吗？我20分钟内到不了机场就赶 __B__ 飞机了！真急死人了！
A. 得上　　B. 不上　　C. 不成　　D. 得成

23. 老师说话很快，但发音很清楚，我都听 __B__ 。
A. 不明白　　B. 得明白　　C. 得了　　D. 不了

24. 我的汉语水平还很低，让我说这篇文章的内容，我可能说 __C__ 。
A. 不懂　　B. 不下　　C. 不出来　　D. 不出去

25. 五年前第一次见到她，我就对她印象很深，直到今天还忘 __B__ 。
A. 不起　　B. 不了　　C. 得了　　D. 得起

26. 我进门的时候还在打电话，但进门以后手机放在什么地方了就完全记 __A__ 了。
A. 不清　　B. 不好　　C. 得好　　D. 不下

27. 这么多东西我一个人可拿 __D__ 。
A. 得动　　B. 不得　　C. 不得了　　D. 不动

28. 没有洗的水果千万吃___A___。
    A. 不得　　B、不了　　C. 不好　　D. 不下

29. 如果你总是说话不算话，将来谁还信___A___你？
    A. 得过　　B. 得了　　C. 不过　　D. 不了

30. 刚到那个地方时，吃___D___那里的饭，一个月瘦了快10斤。
    A. 不好　　B. 不完　　C. 不到　　D. 不惯

31. 你点的菜太多了，我们仨人肯定吃___D___。
    A. 得过　　B. 不过　　C. 得完　　D. 不完

32. 这么多年没见面了，你要是不先叫我，我还真认___D___你了！
    A. 得出　　B. 得了　　C. 不了　　D. 不出

33. 帮帮忙，这个瓶子盖得太紧了，我打___A___。
    A. 不开　　B. 得开　　C. 不起　　D. 得起

34. 这个公寓这么新，位置也好，我们薪水不高，应该租___B___吧。
    A. 得起　　B. 不起　　C. 不得　　D. 得了

35. 这个箱子看起来很大但是不重，她一个人就拿___D___。
    A. 不完　　B. 不动　　C. 得完　　D. 得动

36. 你买书买得太多，看___C___吗？
    A. 不完　　B. 得下　　C. 得完　　D. 不下

37. 她妈妈说，女儿刚开始工作，让她马上出去自己租房住，怕她拿___A___这么多钱。
    A. 不出　　B. 得出　　C. 得了　　D. 不得

38. 总的来说，他的听力和阅读还不错，就是有的音发___C___。
    A. 不到　　B. 不得　　C. 不好　　D. 不完

四. 可能补语改正题

Correct the underlined part of each sentence with the correct potential complement

1. 对我来说，考试的听力部分比较难，每次都有一些问题我<u>不能答得出来</u>。
答不出来

2. 工作不太多，我一个人<u>做得了完</u>。
做得完

3. 她这个人就是好聊天儿，一聊起来就<u>不停下</u>。
停不下

4. 我住的宿舍特别吵，尤其是周末，吵得我都<u>不能睡着觉</u>。
睡不着觉

5. 这个春假我不打算回家了，因为<u>不能买到</u>便宜的机票，而且我还有一篇20页的论文没写完。
买不到

6. 坐在后边的同学请往前坐一点儿，不然我讲话你们<u>不能听清楚</u>。
听不清楚

7. A：就剩这两个饺子了，你都吃了吧！
B：我可<u>不能吃下</u>了，太饱了！
吃不下

8. A：你怎么搬到那么远的地方去了？原来住的公寓不是挺好吗？
B：房东一下子把房租涨了五百块，我<u>不能租起</u>了。
租不起

9. 看见我的手机了吗？我刚才接了一个电话，现在就<u>不能找到</u>了。
找不到

10. 我发现我的记性越来越差了，刚学的生词一下就<u>不能想起来</u>了。
想不起来

11. 我现在在等一个重要的电话，<u>不能走成</u>。
走不成

12. 天气不好，你这么晚了才开车走，恐怕半夜以前都不可以到家。

到不了家

13. 我昨天晚上刚在电脑上写好的期末报告，现在怎么不打开了？真急死人了！

打不开

14. 这个车库太小了，不能停下两辆车。

停不下

15. 你的签证10号前可不能办成，因为大使馆国庆节要放七天假。

办不成

五. 趋向补语选择题

Select the directional complement that fits the blank best

1. 开快一点儿吧，后边的车已经跟__B__了。

   A. 回来　B. 上来　C. 下来　D. 起来

2. 我们办培训班剩__C__的钱，买些水果分给大家吃吧！

   A. 起来　B. 上来　C. 下来　D. 过来

3. 椅子可能不够，你把隔壁教室的椅子搬__D__几把！

   A. 回来　B. 上来　C. 出来　D. 过来

4. 很多人退休以后没事做，又不注意饮食和运动，于是很快就胖__C__了。

   A. 下来　B. 上来　C. 起来　D. 过来

5. 老师一进来，教室里马上就安静__A__了。

   A. 下来　B. 起来　C. 下去　D. 过来

6. 大家一直在机场门口等着，一看到他从机场里走__B__，就赶紧跑__B__帮他拿行李。

   A. 过来/出去　B. 出来/过去　C. 进来/出去　D. 过去/出来

7. 最近我母亲身体不好，我想过完年暂时不回公司上班了，留___A___照顾母亲。

A.下来　　B.起来　　C.下去　　D.过来

8. 很多农民工到了大城市都拼命工作，把钱省___C___寄回家。

A.下去　　B.上去　　C.下来　　D.上来

9. 老王对谁都特别热情，只要有人找他帮忙，他都会答应___C___。

A.下去　　B.上去　　C.下来　　D.上来

10. 时间过得真快！算___B___我已经在中国住了7年了！

A.上来　　B.起来　　C.下去　　D.过来

11. 最近西方媒体报道说中国的一些军事技术已经赶___D___了。

A.下去　　B.上去　　C.下来　　D.上来

12. 那个小女孩儿很可爱，笑的时候露___B___一排好看的牙齿。

A.起来　　B.出来　　C.进来　　D.回来

13. 她在这里教了一年英文以后竟爱___C___了这里，便决定在这里长期住___C___。

A.下/上来　　B.上/起来　　C.上/下来　　D.下/过来

14. 很多严重的健康问题都是由一些不良的生活习惯引___B___的。

A.下　　B.起　　C.上　　D.来

15. 我打算回家时先把一些不用的书和衣服带___B___，免得毕业搬家时东西太多。

A.回来　　B.回去　　C.过来　　D.过去

16. 昨天老师说的考试内容，你都记___C___了吗？

A.下去　　B.上去　　C.下来　　D.起来

17. 你这个问题很有意思，但我现在回答不___D___，需要查一下资料。

A.过来　　B.得来　　C.起来　　D.上来

18. 自从母亲去世以后，她就一直没有从抑郁的状态中解脱__B__。
A.过来　　B.出来　　C.起来　　D.回来

19. 我把球给你扔__C__，你接__C__。
A.过来/到　　B.出来/过　　C.回去/住　　D.过去/来

20. 这件事我已经答应__C__了，就一定得做。
A.过来　　B.出来　　C.下来　　D.起来

21. 这次考试看着容易，可是一做__D__就不那么容易了。
A.过来　　B.出来　　C.上来　　D.起来

22. 这件大衣你穿着真漂亮。虽然贵了一点儿，我劝你还是买__C__吧。
A.过来　　B.出来　　C.下来　　D.起来

23. 经过医生的努力，他终于从昏迷中醒__A__了。
A.过来　　B.出来　　C.下来　　D.起来

24. 你们下次再出去旅游，把我也算__D__。
A.来　　B.进　　C.下　　D.上

25. 她做了整容手术以后，我们都认不__A__她了。
A.出　　B.起　　C.来　　D.上

26. 这个标签粘得太结实了，撕不__B__。
A.去　　B.下去　　C.来　　D.上来

27. 外边下大雨了，别走了。今天就在这儿住__B__吧！
A.起来　　B.下　　C.来　　D.上

28. 如果他自己不说，这件事怎么能传__C__呢？
A.起去　　B.过来　　C.出去　　D.下来

六. 趋向补语填空题

Fill in the blank with the appropriate directional complement

1．请你把脚抬__起来__，我要擦地板。

2．你在这儿等着，我去把车开__过来__。

3．她话还没说完，大家都笑__起来__了。

4．电梯门关__上__了，我们走__上去/下去__吧。

5．我的脚自从那次受伤以后，一走__起__路__来__就疼。

6．经过一段时间的努力，他的学习成绩终于赶__上来__了。

7．我昨天坐地铁的时候睡着了，坐__过__了好几站。

8．最近天气有点儿冷，出门时别忘了穿__上__大衣。

9．就凭我一个实习生挣的钱，哪儿能买得__起__苹果手机?

10．这两年房价都涨疯了！据说几年内也降不__下来__。

11．这个日期写错了，你把它改__过来__。

12．喂，前台服务员吗？我房间的马桶堵了，水流不__下去__了。

13．你别不好意思了，把你想跟她说的话说__出来__吧。

14．孩子十一二岁正是叛逆的时候，父母说什么都听不__进去__。

15．按照这个方法锻炼__下去__，过不了半年，你就能瘦__下来/下去__。

16．才下午三点钟，天忽然变黑了，看__起来__是要下暴雨。

17．别挤了，挤不__上去__了，咱们还是等下一趟车吧!

18．你屋子里的东西太多了，不用的东西可以先收__起来__。

19．他的车撞得挺厉害的，前边的车门都瘪__进去__了。

20. 上次跑马拉松的时候，他脚受伤了，但还是坚持跑了＿下来＿。

21. 昨天老师说的考试范围，你都记＿下来＿了吗？

22. 连很多专家都不明白为什么中国有些城市的房价涨得停不＿下来＿。

23. 房东说他下个月要装修房子，让我们都搬＿出去/出来＿，所以我得赶快找房子。

24. 他妈妈让他过春节的时候把女朋友带＿回＿家＿来＿让她看看。

25. 在这次奥运会上，很多运动员看到自己国家的国旗升＿起来＿的时候，都激动得流＿下/出＿了眼泪。

26. 上大学以后，我跟高中同学再没见过面。上个周末同学聚会，有几个人我完全认不＿出/出来＿了。

27. 她离婚这件事只有我知道，她让我千万别说＿出去＿。

28. 从字典里我查＿到＿这个字的发音和意思了，可是还不知道怎么用。

29. 那个人是谁，你打听＿出来/到＿了吗？

30. 直到这件事的严重后果出现了，我才明白＿过来＿，我错了。

七. 趋向补语翻译题

Translate the following sentences into Chinese sentences containing directional complements

1. Can you say what you really feel?

你能把你的真实感受说出来吗？

2. He has already come up with a pretty name for his unborn baby girl.

他已经给他未出生的女儿想出来一个好听的名字了。

3. I have rented out my apartment.

我把公寓租出去了。

4. Upon hearing the good news, everyone started screaming.

听到这个好消息，大家都叫了起来。

5. When the speaker came in, all the audience stood up.

报告人进来的时候，听众都站起来了/站了起来。

6. I stuck my hand into my backpack to search for my cellphone.

我把手伸进背包里找手机。

7. You can park your car inside.

你可以把车停到里边。

8. Can you tell (see) who wrote these characters?

你能看出这些字是谁写的吗?

9. I couldn't figure out the riddle.

这个谜语我猜不出来。

10. Look, they are coming to you.

看，他们朝你走过来了。

11. The teacher has not graded all the tests from yesterday.

昨天的考试老师还没改出来。

12. He feels that his current dorm room is too small; it won't even fit a sofa. So he wants to move out next semester.

他觉得现在的宿舍太小，连一个沙发都放不下，所以下个学期他想搬出去。

13. I'm on the phone with my insurance company. Can I call you back in 20 minutes?

我正跟我的保险公司打电话，20分钟以后给你打回去/过去，可以吗？

14. Could you please help me put my suitcase up there?

你可以帮我把箱子放上去吗？

15. As soon as she gets nervous, she starts speaking faster.

她一紧张，说话就快起来了。

16. When some high tech companies moved here a few years ago, house prices quickly started to rise.

这几年一些高科技公司搬到这里，房价很快就涨上来/起来了。

17. It has started raining. Go upstairs and close the windows!

下起雨来了，你上楼把窗户关上吧！

18. There may be an accident up ahead, so the cars on the road have all stopped.

前边可能出事了，路上的车都停下来了。

19. How come you suddenly got so skinny?

你怎么突然瘦下来了？

20. He played computer games all day except when he was sleeping, and quickly squandered the entire summer.

他每天除了睡觉就是打电脑游戏，很快就把整个夏天混过去了。

21. Although it's an old car, it runs pretty smoothly.

这辆车虽然很旧了，但开起来还很顺畅。

22. Can you help me hang this picture on the wall?

你能帮我把这幅画儿挂到墙上吗？

23. I wonder if I can get the money back.

我不知道我能不能把钱要回来。

24. She received a letter of acceptance from Harvard University and was so excited that she started jumping up and down.

她收到哈佛大学录取通知书的时候，高兴得跳了起来。

八. 程度补语选择题

Select the degree complement that fits the blank best

1. 今天我出门时忘带钱包了，现在又把车钥匙锁在车里了。真是___D___！
   A. 倒霉坏了　B. 倒霉得多　C. 倒霉得慌　D. 倒霉死了

2. 他刚才说的那句话把我们笑得___A___。
   A. 肚子疼　B. 肚子不得了　C. 肚子疼得多　D. 肚子疼厉害

3. 这几天热得___B___。
   A. 极了　B. 不得了　C. 死了　D. 透了

4. 图书馆的空调开得太低了，我在那儿看了一会儿书都快冻___C___。
   A. 极了　B. 不得了　C. 死了　D. 透了

5. 这个商店的东西贵___B___，我们还是去旁边那家店看看吧。
   A. 很多　B. 得很　C. 不得了　D. 得极了

6. 给女儿买了一条围巾，她喜欢___B___，每天上下班都戴着。
   A. 得多　B. 得不行　C. 得慌　D. 得极了

7. 这次期末考试，我居然考了满分，心里美得___B___。
   A. 透了　B. 要命　C. 死了　D. 极了

8. 前边那辆车开着开着突然冒烟了，把她吓___D___。
A.不行　　B.要命　　C.极了　　D.死了

9. 在飞机上坐的时间太长了，下飞机的时候我的脚麻得___D___。
A.死了　　B.极了　　C.透了　　D.走不了

九. 用描写性补语完成句子

Complete the following sentences with descriptive complements

略。

十. 综合补语选择题

Fill in the blank with the appropriate verb plus complement

1. 主任昨天开会的时候心脏病犯了，所以会没有___D___。
A.开好　　B.开成　　C.开了　　D.开完

2. 因为台风的原因，学校通知这个星期所有的活动都取消，所以迎接新生的大会没有___B___。
A.开好　　B.开成　　C.开了　　D.开完

3. 我一夜没睡，把这本书___C___了，故事情节真是太精彩了！
A.看全　　B.看成　　C.看完　　D.看好

4. 今天的作业太多了，一个小时绝对___B___。
A.不做完　　B.做不完　　C.做得完　　D.做完了

5. 你听，他们正在上听力课呢，你现在___A___会打扰他们的。
A.进教室去　　B.进去教室　　C.进教室来　　D.进来教室

6. 现在人们的生活水平越来越高了，很多家庭都___A___汽车了。
A.买得起　　B.买过来　　C.买回来　　D.买上来

7. 我在图书馆门口等小王等了20分钟，才见他气喘吁吁地向我___C___。
A.跑回来　B.跑起来　C.跑过来　D.跑上来

8. 现在已经十点多了，你说她今天晚上___D___?
A.回得来不来　B.回来得不来
C.回来得不得　D.回得来回不来

9. 她每个圣诞节都能___B___很多礼物，有时候她会把一些礼物___B___。
A.拿到/送过去　B.得到/送出去
C.收到/送下去　D.买到/送上去

10. 今天的雾真大，连马路两边的树都快___B___了。
A.不能看见　B.看不见　C.不看见　D.看得见

11. 我们点的菜太多了，两个人恐怕___B___。
A.吃得完　B.吃不完　C.吃得了　D.不吃完

12. 他把最后一杯酒___C___以后，就开始讲他当兵打仗的故事。
A.喝下来　B.喝上来　C.喝下去　D.喝上去

13. 你在楼下等着，我把钥匙从窗户给你___D___。
A.扔上来　B.扔下来　C.扔上去　D.扔下去

14. 那个箱子很重，你一个人___C___吗?
A.拿得成　B.拿不得　C.拿得了　D.拿不了

15. 这双鞋有点儿小了，我___C___了。
A.穿不上来　B.穿不下来　C.穿不上　D.穿不出来

16. 你___B___玛丽了吗?王老师在找她。
A.看了　B.看见　C.看过　D.看成

17. 她穿着一身绿色的短裤背心，___C___十分凉爽。
A.看过来　B.看上来　C.看起来　D.看下来

18. 我从来没___D___外国人说汉语能跟中国人一样。

A.想过来　　B.想上来　　C.想起来　　D.想到

十一. 综合补语填空题

Fill in the blank with the appropriate complement

1. 他打___开___信封，从里边掉___出/出来___一张照片。
2. 小丽初中还没读___完___就跟父母去城里打工了。
3. 你让我寄的那份资料我昨天就寄___出去___了。
4. 有些学生总是习惯于把三声读___成___二声。
5. 她是一个特别认真的人，有时候会为一些小事想不___开___。
6. 他去深圳开会的时候，遇___到___了十年前的恋人，心情一下子无法平静___下来___了。
7. 他不甘心这样平淡地过___下去___。终于有一天，他辞___掉___了工作，办___起___了一个自闭症儿童艺术学校。
8. 我实在太困了，坚持不___下去___了，先去睡了。
9. 经过一年的艰苦努力，他终于如愿考___上___了一所有名的大学。
10. 他把儿女孝顺他的钱都捐___出去___了。
11. 这条项链是从我妈妈的奶奶那里传___下来___的。
12. 你提的这个问题比较复杂，我没有准备，现在回答不___上来___。
13. 那个教室不大，恐怕坐___不下___20个人。
14. 搬家的日子还没定___下来___呢！她说得等到放暑假时再说。
15. 我昨天夜里12点还没睡___着___觉，因为隔壁房间一直响着音乐，直到半夜以后，音乐声才低___下来___，我才睡___着___。

16. 我现在觉得特别累，想睡一会儿，帮我把窗帘拉__上/起来__，好吗？

17. 哎，好奇怪！我的电脑怎么打不__开__了？密码没输__错__呀！

18. 先生，您个子高，麻烦您帮我把上面那个电脑包拿__下来__，可以吗？我够不__到/着__。

19. 他一打__起__游戏__来__，你说什么他都听__不见/不进去__。

20. 她上大一的时候，人很内向。后来去中国读书，性格一下就开朗__起来__了，就像变了一个人似的。

21. 每个月的房租水电加__起来__，他大概要付差不多1000美元。

23. A：打印机坏了吗？我的申请信怎么没打__出来__？

B：你的电脑跟打印机没连__上__！

24. 面试的时候，即使你心里很紧张，但脸上也不能表现__出来__。

25. 我下午踢足球时把脚崴了，你看，脚踝都肿__起来__了。

26. 前些时候一些炼油厂被关闭，很多地方的油价都涨__起来/上来__了，最多的涨了50美分。不过，最近油价又降__下去__了。

27. 听说2017年北加州那场山火把近七千栋房屋都烧__掉__了。

28. 我刚到中国的时候，吃不__了/下__带头的鱼，现在不但能吃带头的鱼，而且还特别爱吃鱼头。

29. 我从来都记不__住__别人的手机号，所有的号码都存__在/到__手机里。

30. 上周一他去机场的时候遇__到/上__堵车，没赶__上__飞机。

十二. 综合补语语序题

Order the components so that the Chinese sentences containing complements match the sense of the English ones

1. 林小姐　楼　上……去　了
   Miss Lin went upstairs.
   林小姐上楼去了。

2. 从　来　图书馆　他　一本书　了　借
   He borrowed a book from the library.
   他从图书馆借来了一本书。

3. 从　买　我　黑色星期五　商店　回来　一台　液晶电视　给妈妈
   On Black Friday, I went to the store and bought back a HDTV for my mom.
   黑色星期五我从商店给妈妈买回来一台液晶电视。

4. 他　什么时候　中国　是　的　到……去
   When did he go to China?
   他是什么时候到中国去的?

5. 上课的　请　时候　手机　书包里　放　进　把
   Please put your cellphone in your backpack during class.
   上课的时候请把手机放进书包里。

6. 昨天的　冰箱里　你　拿　剩饭　把　从　出来
   Please take yesterday's left-overs out of the refrigerator.
   你把昨天的剩饭从冰箱里拿出来。

7. 你　她　把　停　车　过来　让
   Ask her to park over here.
   你让她把车停过来。

8. 这本书　帮　你　我　把　上去　放　麻烦

Please do me a favor by putting this book up there.

麻烦你帮我把这本书放上去。

9. 我　就　欧洲　去　听说　房子　把　他们　出去　租　一　了

I heard that they rented out their house and went to Europe.

我听说他们一把房子租出去就去欧洲了。

10. 东西　你的　起来　把　收　都　吧

Please put your stuff away.

把你的东西都收起来吧。

11. 马上　你　我　给　打　过去　等　一下

Hold on a second and I'll call you right back.

等一下，我马上给你打过去。

12. 图书馆　去　回去　你　的时候　帮　这两本书　还　我　把　吧

When you go to the library, please return these two books for me.

你去图书馆的时候，帮我把这两本书还回去吧。

13. 上楼　你　的时候　搬　把　这把　椅子　上去

When you go upstairs, take this chair up.

你上楼的时候，把这把椅子搬上去。

14. 外边　拿　箱子　吗　进来　了　你　还有　一个

There was still a suitcase outside. Did you bring it in?

外边还有一个箱子，你拿进来了吗？

15. 她爸爸　接　去世　美国　了　她妈妈　把　以后　她　到……来

After her dad passed away, she brought her mom to the US.

她爸爸去世以后，她把她妈妈接到美国来了。

十三. 综合补语翻译题

Translate the following sentences into Chinese. One of the following items should be used in each sentence

起来 过去 开 会 过来 成 出来
错 完 见 好 走 着 到 上 清楚

1. Have you found your cellphone yet?

你找到手机了吗?

2. Have you finished remodeling your house?

你的房子装修完了吗?

3. Sorry, I grabbed the wrong book. This is your book.

对不起，我拿错书了，这是你的。

4. In general, people tend to gain weight after 40.

一般来说，人到四十以后就会胖起来。

5. You probably didn't remember it clearly.

可能你记错了。

6. He worked in the lab for 24 hours without eating anything. That's why he passed out.

他在实验室工作了24小时，什么也没吃，所以就晕过去了。

7. Throw the ball over to me!

把球给我扔过来。

8. He didn't test well for the entrance exam, so he didn't get into his ideal university.

他高考没有考好，所以没有考上他理想的大学。

9. He fell in love with her when he first spotted her on campus.

他在校园第一次看到她就爱上她了。

10. Can you translate this article into English?

你能把这篇文章翻译成英文吗？

11. People always take me for my older sister.

大家总是把我当成我姐姐。

12.Could you turn the light off?

可以把灯关上吗？

13. Open your suitcase and take out your laptop for a security-check.

打开你的箱子，把电脑拿出来过安检。

14. The large-screen TV sets sold out quickly.

大屏幕电视很快就卖完了。

15. I did listen, but I didn't hear what they said.

我确实听了，可是没有听见他们说什么。

16. Sorry, I cannot take you to the airport, because my daughter drove my car away.

对不起，我送不了你去机场，因为我女儿把我的车开走了。

17. Guess whom I ran into at Starbucks? My former boyfriend!

你猜我在星巴克碰见/遇见谁了？我的前男友！

18.It took her a month to learn how to drive.

她学了一个月才学会开车。

19. I hate math class not because it is hard, but because the professor cannot explain things clearly.

    我不喜欢数学不是因为难，而是因为这个数学老师讲得不清楚。

20. Last night I went to bed at 10 p.m., but didn't fall asleep until about midnight.

    昨天晚上十点我就去睡觉了，但直到半夜还没睡着呢。